WE DON'T TALK ABOUT THAT

ABOUT THAT

Giselle Roeder

AN AMAZING STORY OF SURVIVAL

To Herb, —
I read & love your
poems.
Enjoy my trip
through life!

Giselle Roeder
oct. 2015

Produced by:

FriesenPress

Suite 300 – 852 Fort Street
Victoria, BC, Canada V8W 1H8

www.friesenpress.com

Distributed to the trade by The Ingram Book Company

Also by Giselle Roeder:

"Healing with Water – Kneipp-Therapy at Home" – 2000

"Sauna – The Hottest Way to Good Health" – 2001

Table of Contents

Dedication

To Trevor Cradduck, my Englishman, the one with whom I choose to spend my twilight years. Trevor's encouragement, his help with the formatting, the computer glitches, his patience when I was depressed because I could not sleep when re-living the horrors that a whole generation "did not talk about" or waking me in the middle of a nightmare, kept me going. Although I was motivated by being the last of my clan who remembers, as well as by my son trying to get me to keep busy during long winter days when my garden was asleep, and even by people who wanted to know more of my memories after hearing me speak at their clubs, without Trevor this book might never have been written.

To Eric, my son, who, after reading an early draft of my manuscript, confided, "Mom, I now know and understand you a whole lot better."

And to my friends: Geri, who is responsible for the subtitle and pointing out the sentences where I had put "the cart before the horse"; Colleen who did the first copy-reading; Peter and Bob who read the first draft manuscript and encouraged me to go on writing because "I can't wait to read the next chapter...."

Last, but not least, a BIG THANK YOU to all of you who encouraged me to write my story in the first place.

Preface

When he was a young boy, my son Eric never wanted to hear stories of my earlier life, but he has since been pushing me to write *My Book* for the last twenty-five years. I even started writing it during a writer's workshop twenty years ago. I had set up the chapters and written one of them and the two teachers told me, "If you keep writing, in five years you'll have a bestseller on your hands."

For some reason I never wrote another line. I wrote poems and short stories but I put this topic on the backburner. Perhaps it was too close to my heart or perhaps I was afraid to open up. I just did not want to talk about it or maybe I did not trust myself to "just do it," I do not know.

I asked my son, "Who would want to read it?"

His answer, "I will. My generation will. We are interested in what went on during and after WW II. One day, when your generation is gone, we will never know for sure. Speeches on Remembrance Day will be just that: Speeches! We should know. We want to know. If we have a personal connection to it we will not forget."

In 2012, I lost my aunts, the younger sisters of both Mother and Father. Shortly before they passed on they opened up a little and very carefully shared some of their own memories. I have included those as well. Previously, whenever I had asked them (or any older German women) guarded questions about their experiences or about any direct confrontations they experienced with the victorious soldiers, the common answer of every single one was, and is to this day **"We don't talk about that."**

How is it possible that the women of a whole country silently and unconsciously agreed not to talk about it?

I am the last of my family who still remembers. My strongest motivation to write my memoir was the expression of shock and disbelief I saw on peoples' faces during several speeches I delivered at different clubs about my experiences. It drove home the fact that EVERYONE NEEDS TO KNOW how war affects every family.

Exclamations like, "My God, we didn't know that! It's horrible how much women and children had to suffer during and after the war. We always just heard about the Nazis and the Jews. We did not even appreciate how lucky we were to live in Canada."

Many of them asked, "Do you have a book?"

"No," was my reply.

"Then you must write one...."

Giselle Roeder

January, 2014

1: A Condensed Background of my Story

"Lest we forget"

Germany was a country consisting of many small kingdoms and only became united under an Emperor in the latter part of the nineteenth century. After WW I, the Emperor was forced to abdicate in 1921 and a Republic was established, named the Weimar Republic. The Treaty of Versailles following WW I stipulated that Germany pay more than a hundred billion marks worth of land and money to England, France and the USA. England and the USA were willing to reduce it after the German representatives declared they would not be able to meet the obligation and suggested it would be counter-productive, but France remained obdurate.

Unrest started after WW I in all the larger German cities. It continued to grow into brawls, fights and killings over a period of about a dozen years. Socialists and communists tried to get the upper hand but a new movement sprouted like a weed. Men joined the German Workers Party in droves; even a large number of generals and many former soldiers signed up. They held meetings in beer halls where they raved and ranted about the loss of the war, claiming it had all been fixed with the enemy by socialist and communist political powers in Berlin. A young, decorated, Austrian-born WW I Corporal, Adolf Hitler, heard about these meetings, attended one and knew immediately that this would be the perfect platform for him to spread his ideas and gain power. When he spoke up the first time, the other members did not like his aggressive approach, but then realized, "This guy has the gift of gab – he could be what we need."

The others surely did not expect him to stab them in the back. Hitler joined the party and within a year renamed it to NSDAP, (National Sozialistische Demokratische Arbeiter Partei) the National Socialistic Democratic Workers' Party.

The name appealed to the nationalists, the socialists, the democrats, and the workers. Hitler designed a new flag: Red with a white circle adorned with an ancient mythical symbol, the swastika. He became the leader and insisted that they call him "Führer".

Hitler demanded that the country stop paying the requested billions in reparation to the allies. There was no money; the German mark became known as the Papiermark (paper money) due to its drop in value. It was not backed by gold and inflation had hit hard. The German mark was worth four to one to the dollar in early 1923 but by the end of November 1923, people needed more than four billion marks to buy one dollar. Salaries were worthless. Half a loaf of bread cost billions. My father reminisced that people were paid every hour and would often take a wheelbarrow full of money to buy food. Hunger riots started in all of the big cities.

Hitler knew his time had come. In his many speeches he talked about rebuilding Germany, promising work and bread for all; his party grew exponentially. A number of men who made history were individuals such as:

- WW I General Erich Ludendorff, promoter of *Total War* – who was demanding, "The whole nation should be mobilized. Peace is just an interlude between Wars."

- Ernst Röhm (later executed by the Nazis) the co-founder of the Sturm Abteilung (SA) or Storm troopers (which grew to multiple millions of members) also known as the Brown Shirts.

- Hermann Göring, close advisor and protector of Hitler.

- Rudolf Hess, Hitler's most loyal follower and the militant deputy leader of the NSDAP.

- Heinrich Himmler, who founded the SS and became the second most powerful man in Nazi Germany.

A plot to kidnap Bavarian government officials in the spring of 1924 failed and Hitler was arrested. Unfortunately, they allowed him a public trial where he declined a lawyer and chose to defend himself. Never denying what he had done, he simply explained (with great passion in his charismatic way) what he wanted to achieve, the re-building of Germany.

His self-defence speeches made him famous across Germany. Journalists had a field day. Aristocrats, politicians, business people, workers and farmers read about him. They discussed him in pubs and homes where they laughed about his outspokenness and said he must be *nuts* or *crazy*, but, despite everything, everyone was discussing his ideas because of their own economic misery.

They sentenced Hitler to five years in prison with the possibility of early parole. Even some of the judges fell for his ability to convince everybody of his great plans for the country. They gave him a comfortable cell in the prison in Landsberg, a small city in Bavaria, and allowed him visitors, including Rudolf Hess as his private secretary. To Hess he dictated his ideas and these writings later became his infamous book, *Mein Kampf (My Fight or My Struggle)*. When he was in power, every young couple received a copy of this book as a wedding gift! They released him at Christmas in 1924 after just a few months in jail. He settled in Berchtesgaden in the Bavarian Alps to finish his book. By chance, he met Joseph Goebbels, a failed writer with a Ph.D. in literature, who added a lot of fuel to the fire, so to speak, and many new ideas for Hitler's book. Later Goebbels became his Propaganda Minister and wrote his rousing speeches.

The government of the young German Republic under Chancellor Gustav Stresemann brought the run-away inflation under control by borrowing millions from the U.S. government in 1923 and introduced a new currency, the Rentenmark, backed by mortgaging land and investment in industrial development, since there was no gold available. One trillion Papiermarks equaled one Rentenmark, and now 4.2 RM were worth one U.S. dollar.

Twenty years later, I found a large carton full of billions of the old Papiermarks in our attic. Thinking that we were very rich, I asked my father about it. Smiling, he explained the billions,

"My dear girl, one day we will paper our outhouse with it!"

In August 1924, the new Reichsmark replaced the Rentenmark and remained Germany's legal tender until 1948.

The country saw an incredible development and improvement during what became known as the *roaring twenties*. The women cut their hair short, danced the Charleston and knew again, what it was like to be young, pretty and happy, and the men had work. Innovations like the radio, automobiles, aviation, the telephone and the power grid made life exciting and comfortable.

The Wall Street crash in October 1929 caused what we know as the Great Depression. Anybody who had anything lost everything. Paul von Hindenburg, the President of Germany and the then-Chancellor Bruening decided to hold elections. The year was 1930 and the NSDAP, Hitler's party, won 107 seats in the Reichstag and became the second largest party in the country next to the SDP (Social Democratic Party). The Storm troopers, already consisting of hundreds of thousands of men, started a big celebration in the streets and smashed Jewish-owned shop windows – although what became known as the *Kristallnacht* (crystal night) did not take place until November 1938.

The following years saw much upheaval in the political arena. Germany had four million unemployed by 1931. The NSDAP grew. Paul von Hindenburg, who had been re-elected in 1932, realized what Hitler was up to and, despite his age of over eighty, tried desperately to save the fragile Republic.

Adolf Hitler continued his rise to power and became Chancellor in 1933. Through thousands of speeches across the country promising bread, work and peace he instilled hope and won the approval of the German people; all they had to lose was misery, starvation and unemployment. They needed hope – he gave it to them. The Germans needed work – he provided it. The Germans needed encouragement – Hitler, who may have been one of the greatest demagogues and persuasive orators who ever lived, knew how to motivate, to excite them.

The years after 1933 saw an incredible development in all facets of life in the downtrodden country. Most people did not know, and some chose not to see what began to happen to the Jewish people. These were folks who had lived in Germany for hundreds of years, who had inter-married, who considered themselves and were considered to be, Germans like everyone else. Jewish people started disappearing – either they were warned and had a chance to flee or they were picked up by the Brown Shirts on false accusations. Socialists, communists and anyone who spoke out against Hitler were put into concentration camps or worse – tortured and killed.

"If you are not for me, you are against me," (Matthew 12:30). It seems that some of today's politicians follow the same line of thinking.

People overlooked the growing war machinery because it provided jobs. The army attracted thousands of young men to sign up and become professional soldiers. Industry and commerce prospered.

The Berlin Olympics in 1936 became a big showcase to the world of a recovering proud Germany. Hitler promised that every German could afford an automobile. His conception of such a car was the first Volkswagen Beetle; it cost only 600 Reichsmark. Hitler needed thousands of workers to build his *Autobahns*, the highways crossing the country from one end to the other. Nobody appreciated the future importance of these highways to move war machinery to where it was needed and fast because nobody thought of or wanted another war. Everything was about jobs for desperate people. Hitler used his artistic talents to design buildings and had many grand architectural edifices constructed. He made Berlin into a world-class city again.

Such is the (condensed) background of how and why the German people voted for this Austrian man, a man who annexed his native country to his *German Reich*. Here was a man who promised bread, and kept his promise, a man who started with nothing but his crazy righteous ideas, who was laughed at and put in prison, but used his *gift of gab* to sway the masses, seemingly hypnotising them. He talked of building a *Thousand-year Reich*. He talked about "Volk ohne Raum" (people without land) and then the day came when his Propaganda Minister Goebbels screamed at the end of a rousing speech in a packed Olympic Stadium in Berlin, "I ask you – do you want total war?"

Thousands screamed back, "YES!"

God forgive them, for they knew not what they were doing. Screaming back "NO," would not have made any difference. The Führer was a dictator and nobody would dare to stand in his way. Dozens of assassination attempts on Hitler's life occurred over the years. These attempts were made not by socialist or communist factions but by some of his high officers and they failed. It seemed that he was indestructible or even untouchable. This man started a war that became the war of all wars: a war that cost millions of people their homeland and their lives, a war so horrible that the people who lived through it had nightmares for the rest of their lives.

2: Meet the Players

My father's family

Friedrich Wilhelm and Martha

My paternal grandfather, Friedrich Wilhelm, a blacksmith by trade, was married to a beautiful woman, my paternal grandmother, Martha. They had leased a smithy with a small farm consisting of twenty-two acres of land in the village of Stresow in Pomerania, Germany (now Strzeszów, Poland).

Their home was situated on two acres of land: the smithy close to the village road, the house about fifty metres up a slight incline, barn, stables and a laborer's house were part of it. Behind the stables was the rest of the land, which was used to grow household staples and feed (potatoes, turnips, clover) for a cow, some pigs and other small farm animals. He sublet most of the land to a big farmer who provided grain, straw and hay. Two large gardens, one with lots of fruit bushes and trees, the other to grow vegetables and flowers, were Martha's domain.

They originally had nine children but only five survived.

Erich (referred to as Erich, Dad, Daddy or Father)

My father was the oldest son and trained with my grandfather to become a blacksmith. He had a lot of drive and in order to complete his training, had to go away as a journeyman for several years to get his Blacksmith Master degree in order to be able to train apprentices himself. After he finished the required years and passed the examinations, he returned home to work with my grandfather.

Gertrud (referred to as "Aunt Tutti" or Trudi)

Aunt Tutti was my father's oldest sister. She was married to Fritz Z., a railway man who was often transferred to different locations. They lived on the Baltic Sea Island of Rügen (still part of Germany today). Aunt Tutti and her sons, my cousins Siegfried and Manfred, spent almost all of their summer holidays with her parents in Stresow.

Irene

Aunt Irene, another sister, apprenticed in a grocery shop and later ran one herself close to the old German-Polish border, in Prechlau, Germany (now Przechlewo, Poland). Her shop closed in 1944 and Irene was absorbed into the German army and trained as a Red Cross nurse.

Curt

Uncle Curt, my dad's younger and only brother, also apprenticed with my grandfather and became a blacksmith, working with my dad and his father.

Lisa

Aunt Lisa was my dad's youngest sister. She was born when my dad, Erich, was already twenty-six years old.

There was also Fritze My great-grandmother, Martha's mother Johanna, had, like Martha, a baby later in life and became a widow shortly after her boy, named Fritze, was born. Although Fritze was technically an uncle to Erich, Gertrud, Irene, Curt, and Lisa, he was actually a year younger than his nephew, Erich was. Being so close in age, the two of them grew up like brothers. Fritze lived two kilometers away in the town of Bad Schönfliess, Germany (now Trzcińsko-Zdrój, Poland), but they spent a lot of time together.

My mother's family

Karl L. and Emma

My maternal grandfather, Karl L., was a well-to-do farmer with lots of land and his own house located within and adjacent to the ancient city wall in Bad Schönfliess, next to one of the city gates. In Germany, use of the term "Bad" before a city name always indicates that the city itself is a government-approved health resort, usually featuring baths of some sort. In the case of Bad Schönfliess, it was because of the landscape: bogs with endless deposits of mud containing special beneficial minerals. This mud was used for treating rheumatic and arthritic conditions. The small city was a very pleasant place with nice homes, parks, entertainment and boulevard shopping. Karl L. married my maternal grandmother, Emma, who brought an illegitimate son named Willy into the marriage, together with a sizable amount of money meant for Willy's upkeep and to make up for the fact that she was not a virgin. The marriage produced four daughters:

Emmi

Aunt Emmi married a plumber, Erich L., who had his own business and a couple of apprentices. He had inherited his parents' house. Aunt Emmi and Uncle Erich L. lived on the second floor; his sister occupied the ground floor and part of it was a small grocery shop.

Elsbeth (referred to as Else, Mother, Mom, Mommy)

My mother, Else, for some reason was always singled out by her father to do heavier farm work. She had to help him to work the farm as if she were a boy. Her father did not like Willy much and with each new baby he fathered, he hoped that it would be a boy. For my mother, Else, he had picked out a gentleman's son to become her future husband. This proposed husband was slightly older than she was, but very wealthy with a beautiful villa in a large park. My grandfather Karl L. and the gentleman had cooked up the plot between friends over a beer when Else was about twenty and sealed the arrangement with a handshake.

Johanna (referred to as Hanni)

Aunt Hanni also had to work on the farm. One day she introduced a well-to-do chicken farmer named Robert S. from Stresow to her family.

My grandfather Karl L. did not believe in idleness. Before they married, all the girls were expected to work in the barn, the gardens, the fields, help with threshing, bring in the hay, muck out the stables, feed and look after the five or six horses, milk the cows and look after all the other farm animals.

Elisabeth

It was different for the fourth girl, my Aunt Elisabeth. She could wrap her father around her proverbial little finger; she was the "princess." She was prettier than the others were, got away with almost everything and grew up a young lady with beautiful skin and soft hands.

After finishing primary school, all four sisters had to complete a year at the *Household School,* an institution where young women learned to run a household, cook, bake, entertain, wash, do fancy needlework, sew simple dresses and fix torn sheets or workmen's clothing, handle babies and grow a garden, harvest vegetables and fruit and preserve everything that was not consumed when fresh.

My parents and sisters

My dad, Erich, had gone to a dance in the city with his young uncle Fritze. Fritze knew my future mother, Else, because he lived with his mother in a small suite on the same street where my maternal grandparents' large house was located. Uncle Fritze was dancing with Else when my future dad, Erich noticed a big red spot on her white dress. In order to save her an incredible amount of embarrassment, he dared to walk up to the two, and after his polite, "May I break in?" she stepped away from Fritze and into Erich's arms. He put his hand on her back, turned and walking close behind to shield her, steered her towards the exit and the outside restrooms, quietly telling her to check the backside of her dress. Then he offered to walk her home. My dad was a very handsome and charming man, so you can't blame her for falling in love with him.

Consequently, my dad lost Fritze. From that moment, Fritze never spoke to him again, a few years later he married a girl named Kate and they immigrated to the USA.

After a two-year courtship, followed by a short engagement during which Else had to suffer much family disapproval, my future parents, Erich and Else were married in 1932. He was twenty-nine and she was twenty-three years old.

As was customary, their wedding was held at her parents' house in the city. During the wedding dinner, relatives teased Erich relentlessly about his inability to give his bride the kind of presents that Hanni received from her rich chicken farmer, Robert S. The more the guests drank the worse it got and the teasing was finally topped off with, "If Robert wanted to, he could buy Hanni a horse, but Erich could only afford to give Else the whip...."

The comment caused raucous laughter and it got to the point that Erich took his new wife by the hand and got up. Together they left the party.

Else was disinherited because she did not want to marry the wealthy gentleman's son her father had picked out for her and had instead stubbornly insisted on marrying Erich, the blacksmith from a small village two kilometers away. To her parents he was an unsuitable man and her father never forgave her.

Erich had only recently lost his own father and became the guardian of his younger sister, Lisa, who, by then, was only eight years old.

Since he was now a married man, and became the head of the household, his mother and the remaining siblings, Irene, Curt and Lisa moved into the dowager part of the house. It faced the front garden while the young couple took over the more convenient work part of the house facing the yard where the barn, the stables and the workers' house formed a square with the manure pile almost, but not quite, in the middle. There were stables for pigs, a couple of cows, a horse and Else's favorites: the chickens, geese and ducks. There was a special room for milling grains for feed, a tack room and next door was a sleeping room for one or two workmen. The garage next to that housed a carriage and a sleigh, both of which were later replaced by a motor car. From the garage, a ladder went up to the hayloft.

Attached to the garage was the workers' house. It was rented to Mrs. Richter and her adult son Paul. A small stable for them was in front of it. They had chickens, rabbits and a smelly white goat with horns. Sometimes Mrs. Richter would offer us a cup of milk but it tasted just like the way the goat smelled. Not even the cats wanted to lick the milk.

Erich loved his pigeons. They lived in a gable above the chickens. They loved him too, sat on his hand or shoulder and did not fly away when he climbed up the ladder to clean their quarters. Occasionally a pair of them would become a Sunday meal for us. They had very small, thin bones and not much flesh but tasted somewhat like a young tender chicken.

Else was used to hard farm work. Having married a country man, she was glad to have the know-how and was able to do her part in house, garden, fields and stables. Her mother-in-law felt pushed aside and, at first, made her life quite miserable. Erich explained to his mother, "I am twenty-nine and married. I want my wife to be in charge of my household but I would appreciate any help you could give her. You have been running this place for so many years and I am sure Else will appreciate your friendly advice. But let her make some of her own mistakes, it will help her to learn."

Else missed her own mother, but there was no contact for two years after the wedding until the first grandchild was born, and that was me.

They expected their first baby at the end of January 1934. I was to be named Friedrich Wilhelm after Erich's father and grandfather. It was too big a name for me and I decided, instead, to be a girl! They named me "Gisela" because there was no other Gisela in the village. I was the first, and they just added both my grandmothers' names, Martha and Emma, in that order. It would lead to some jealousy between the grandmothers. The maternal grandmother felt that her name, Emma, should be first since she was the older one. Had my parents done that my first initials would be G.E.M., and they would have had a real gem. Funny but we kids always called Martha, my younger paternal grandmother who lived with us, the *old* granny, and Emma, my older maternal grandmother, the *new* grandma, probably because we met her later and everything in her city house was so much fancier and more formal.

My birth was a home birth with a midwife; there was no doctor in the village. The village folks were used to the midwife; giving birth was a natural thing. Erich was disappointed his first-born was a girl but there was hope for a future son. They wanted a large family.

Erich's youngest sister, Lisa, was now ten years old and she became my big sister babysitter instead of the aunt that she really was. Erich's mother became my dear Granny. She loved me, and looking after me gave her life purpose. Little me, I was nicknamed "Gila." I slept during the days but I was not a happy camper at night. I did not like the cold world and cried my little heart out. I wanted to sleep next to my mommy, feeling warm and safe like I did when she fed me, but Daddy did not allow it.

"She could be squished," he warned.

Granny would come running and carry me around for hours and hum and sing to me. My mom did not like it but had to go along with it for the sake of peace and quiet; besides, she was out of commission for a week after giving birth to me, a nine-pound baby. She nursed me for well over a year. I started walking at nine months. When I was one year old, my parents were advised to shave off all my hair. There was lots of superstition in the country and folks insisted that, if shaved, then a child would regrow a really healthy and beautiful head of hair.

Mother told me that I stopped holding still once half of my head was bald and I was kicking and screaming and would not let them do the other half for several days. Interestingly, I was born with very dark hair like my mother's and after having it all shaved off, it grew in quite blond.

Almost three years later, in December 1936, my sister, Christel Irene Elisabeth joined our young family. My first or earliest memory is of a day when Mom got mad at me. I was standing on the table after a bath in the baby bathtub, dressed only in a little undershirt. I was not quite three years old, and I was singing and dancing on the spot while lifting my little shirt up and down as if it were a skirt.

"Don't do that," she said very sternly, in a tone I had never heard before.

She pulled my shirt down and slapped me. I was shocked and startled and just stood there and watched her wrapping up my new baby sister. My exuberance was gone, I felt very sad and I did not know what I had done that caused her to be so cross with me. Tears rolled down my cheeks but I did not cry out.

This memory came back to me unexpectedly and with great force in adulthood forty years later. An elderly English lady occupied the main floor in a large house we had bought. It had been duplexed and she had lived on the main floor for several years. We did not have the heart to turn her out. I knew she was not well and one night I heard some disturbing noise. I went down the servant's stairway to check on her. She was sitting on the edge of her bed, rocking back and forth and lifting her very thin nighty up and down … just as I did all those years before.

"Don't do that," I admonished her, and I heard my mother's voice. It troubled me for days.

My baby sister Christel became Granny's favorite girl. "She looks just like my late husband," Granny happily exclaimed.

I couldn't see it because he had a moustache with curled ends. He was in heaven but I often looked at his very large, framed photograph over Granny's bed and tried to find my little sister's resemblance to him.

Christel was a sneaky little girl. She did not want to play with her own things but instead always played with my toys, throwing and often breaking them. When I tried to protect my precious possessions or push her away, she would cry with those false tears that small children manage so well and scream as loud as she could. My mom, Granny or even Father would come running to inquire, "What's going on here?"

She would always sob, "Gila hit me…."

On one of those occasions, my father put me over his knee and I got my first real spanking. I felt totally innocent and I never forgot or forgave him during my childhood. It surely was not a fair case of innocent until proven guilty. I was not given a chance to tell him what happened.

I did finally tell him when he was over seventy years old. He remembered and was amazed that I did too.

One day Christel had the whole family worried about her safety. It was summer and Aunt Tutti's boys, my cousins Siegfried and Manfred, were visiting. We played hide-and-seek but could not find her and finally called my mom. We all looked everywhere and then my mom noticed the cows being somewhat restless. Christel had crawled way under the feeding trough and had fallen asleep, enveloped in the animal warmth. Mother was not able to get in between the cows but she was able to wake Christel up. Not surprisingly, she started sobbing and was afraid to come out. The young bull on her one side was very upset and the young heifer on her other side was also moving around as far as the chain allowed.

My oldest cousin, Siegfried, went to get my father. He came running and got straight in there, but was hit in the arm by one of the bull's horns and started bleeding. He told Christel to stay put and admonished her not to move. When he and my mother managed to get the bull's chain loosened and finally got the beast to move out backwards, my mom grabbed Christel and pulled her out before the bull came back in. Mother had to tear her apron into strips and wind them tightly around Father's arm. I was glad when I did not see all that blood running down my father's arm anymore. It made me feel sick to my tummy. He had to drive his motorbike to the city where the doctor sewed up the deep flesh wound. When he returned, it looked like he had a zipper.

In August 1940 Erich and Else had another girl, Ingrid Doris. She was my favorite sister. She had eyes like our mother's and mine. She was an easy baby, just fitting in, never demanding much attention and somehow self-contained. Neighbours would look into her pram, nod their heads and wisely proclaim, "Yes, later children are much easier."

Can one only have "later" children? That is what I would want when I grew up, to have only later children. I often put Ingrid in my doll-carriage and pushed her around our yard as if she were a doll. Naturally, Aunt Lisa would be supervising this exercise.

My parents and the parents of the boys were always joking about the fact that each of the first three girls was born a year after each of the boys. Aunt Gertrud, dubbed "Aunt Tutti" by me when I was a toddler, and could not say Aunt Trudi, had given birth to another son, Dietrich (Dieter) in 1939, a year earlier. Ingrid was the result of my father's renewed hope for a boy. They always joked about trading the children and I heard them say, "Life is not fair, the sister has three boys and the brother has three girls…."

Since the boys spent most of the summer holidays each year in Stresow, we kids got to know each other quite well, and enjoyed playing together. Acting out a fairy tale or playing wedding and house, dressed in Mom's old dresses and high-heeled shoes (there was a pair of bright red ones I could not even imagine my mother wearing) were our favorite pastimes.

Family inter-relationships

It must have been around this time that my Aunt Irene, still single, went to the village of Prechlau close to the Polish border to run a small grocery shop. She was quite proud to get this job. Granny was sad that she went so far away.

My Uncle Curt, Dad's only brother, had left home as well. He had learned the blacksmith trade apprenticing with my grandfather. Both brothers, Erich and Curt, worked with him. After my grandfather died, Curt did not like working with or under his brother who now was in charge, so he simply signed up with the army in November 1934 to become a professional soldier. The army trained him in Stettin, Germany (now Szczecin, Poland) for several years; he could use his blacksmith training and shoe horses. Before the war broke out, they transferred him to an Infantry Regiment in Schleswig Holstein. There he met his future wife, Frieda. She was a real city girl, with very short, pale blond hair, with white skin, light blue eyes and soft hands. She wore silk dresses with large flower designs and chic shoes. I overheard Granny mention to Mrs. Richter, "I don't know what Curt sees in her. Will she ever do any housework? She is a fancy girl and such a cold fish. With his looks, he could have had a gold fish."

When Aunt Frieda visited, I admired her but always felt shy around her. She was very different from all our other aunts, and did not speak High German as we did but the Hamburg-Holstein dialect where the "s-t" is very distinctly pronounced, "...s-tolpert ueber'n s-pitzen s-tein" – get it?

She and Uncle Curt had two daughters, my cousins, Irmgard and Ingeborg. We did not see much of them and I only began to know them years later.

My Aunt Hanni had married Robert, the rich chicken farmer, in 1933. They had a son, Joachim in May 1934. Her in-laws took the baby away from her; she was just allowed to nurse him, but otherwise, his paternal grandparents raised him as their heir. Aunt Hanni was relegated to a maid's room behind the kitchen and her husband would only come to her when he wanted his conjugal rights. After Joachim, she had two little girls, Marianne and Anneliese, and the same thing happened. She kept her husband's treatment of her a secret from her own parents and her sisters, as she felt very ashamed and just suffered quietly. Until one day when she came running along the back path to our house and, breaking down completely, told my mother that she got the whip.

We had a whip hanging on a stable wall. It consisted of a handle about a foot long with seven long strings of cut up leather fastened onto one end of it. I was playing in the next room at the time, and the door was open. I was a serious child and thought she meant she had received a whip as a gift. She was sobbing hard and divulging her terrible story about her babies to my mother. Evidently, Aunt Hanni did not get the promised horse after all, but instead the whip and that, not as a gift, but in the cruelest way.

"I am not allowed to eat in the dining room with the family. I have to eat in the kitchen with the maids and workers. I am not allowed to be in the living room or play with my children. I feel like a slave, my in-laws are much nicer to their employees than to me. Oh, Else, what can I do?"

After this first visit, Aunt Hanni came more often. She never walked along the village road but sneaked along the back pathway, sometimes hiding in the bushes, to avoid other people. She was very afraid and knew she would be severely punished if she were caught. She was always hungry and my mother would bake waffles, her favorite treat. She was not allowed to make them in her own home and had not been able to enjoy them for years. Her little boy, Joachim, copied his grandparents and treated her the way they did. Growing up he became, "the nicest son you could have," she told my mother after about fifteen years. When her husband was drafted, she became the servant for her in-laws but at least that way she could see her children more often. Still, she was not allowed to eat with the family. She had to do everything for her in-laws: clean their quarters, make their beds, empty their night potties and practically replaced a maid.

My Aunt Emmi had also married a tradesman but he must have been good enough for her parents since she did not have my mother's problems. I surmise Aunt Emmi must have already been pregnant when they married because she wasn't wearing a white dress but instead wore a very dark dress in her wedding picture. That was customary for a pregnant bride.

She and Uncle Erich L. had two daughters, my cousins Erika and Renate. Renate was born in May 1934 and she and I became soul mates until the war tore us apart. Erika was five years older. She was a very beautiful girl with a face like Grace Kelly.

My mother's youngest sister, my Aunt Elisabeth, had fallen madly in love with a good- looking Hauptmann (major) when she was fairly young. She was hardly out of school and got permission to marry him after a few years when she was just nineteen in 1939. They had a little girl, Marianne. He was sent to the frontlines and never came back. She was a very young widow. Little Marianne died of pneumonia when she was four years old.

The stepbrother, Willy, had run away and nobody knows what has become of him.

3: Life in Stresow

Memories such as those re-lived in this book started at an early age when life was easy. We enjoyed great times during mostly sunny summers on the beach at the lake, when our cousins visited from the Island of Rügen. Then, during snow-packed winters in between, we had sleigh rides and our horse, Lotte, had jingle bells attached to her harness. During the twilight hours, we would sit in Granny's living room on the bench against the warm ceramic tile oven. She would tell us of her childhood or of *Little Red Riding Hood, Snow White and the Seven Dwarfs* and all the other wonderful fairy tales. Peter, my father's old cat, would sit between us and purr. After a while, stroking him the right way I would start stroking against the hair growth and little sparks would fly and crackle. Oh, he did not like it at all, but I did! It was exciting. He would hit my arm with his paw but he never scratched me. His reaction was always funny and now I hope it did not hurt him. We were a normal, happy family and so were all the other families living in Stresow/Pomerania, Germany.

Imagine a small village with 1000 inhabitants, including children. Except for the pub owner, the blacksmith, a tailor, a fisherman, two teachers, the owners of the two grocery shops (one of them had a bakery too), a cobbler, and the pastor, all the men were farmers. Every farmer had a workers' house attached to the barn with either one or two families living there. There was also an Almshouse. This provided a place where people could go when the spouse died and the bereaved had nothing to live on, or if they were incapacitated or too old to work. Naturally, everyone knew one another. Even the mayor was one of the farmers. He was the only one who had a telephone. I don't remember anyone having running water or an indoor toilet. Water was brought in from the pump in the yard and dirty water would be brought out and chucked onto the road or the manure pile. Every child knew, "The bigger the manure pile the richer the farmer."

Wood for cooking and heating was chopped, and was usually piled high against the wall of a building or cleverly placed in a circle and built up higher and higher, getting the circle tighter until it had a point on the top. That way a tarp could be placed over it to protect the wood against rain and snow. Every evening the fires were doused, every morning the ashes had to be scraped out of the ovens or stoves and a new fire started with newspaper and kindling. Sometimes smoke would be blowing in your face, depending on the wind direction as it hit the chimney.

Washday was a big undertaking. The laundry was boiled in huge pots. We had a tilt pot – meaning the huge pot could be tilted to pour the water out. This pot was also used to boil potatoes for feed for the animals. The boiled laundry was taken out with narrow wooden paddles and put into shallow, oval, wooden tubs. On a washboard (you may know this only from looking at one in an antique shop), the women would scrub every piece of laundry until their hands were raw. Wringing the water out of the bigger bed sheets required two people. Everything was pegged on a clothesline running across the yard. A long, sturdy forked pole held up the weight on the line.

Sometimes pigeons would alight on the clothesline and their droppings on the clean laundry could drive the women to tears.

When dry, the large pieces of laundry were put through a "roller" located in a smaller part of the barn. It consisted of a base with a lined platform about four by eight feet. On this were two thick wooden rollers and a long box filled with huge rocks was set on those. This box was pushed back and forth and, as small children, we loved to sit on the rocks and enjoy the motion with either Granny or Mother doing the pulling and pushing. The sheets were placed on the platform, the motion would pull them through and they would come out at the other end. After the roller did its prep work, everything was ironed. Granny still had an old iron into which she put glowing coals. She always spat on the bottom to see if it was hot enough. She insisted, "It does a much better job than the new electric iron."

She had grown up when there was no other, and now was happy when she could use it during power outages. I was intrigued by the fact that it did not burn what she was ironing, even though you could see the glowing coals within.

None of the farmers lived on their land as many do in North America. Everyone lived in the village with the church surrounded by the cemetery, in the centre. The wealthy families had family plots where generations were buried. The poor or farm workers had a corner of the cemetery to themselves. It was said that in another very small corner, shaded by a huge chestnut tree, were the overgrown graves of three people who had committed suicide by hanging themselves a long time ago. Maybe they did not know of other ways to do it. In the fourth corner, a number of very old gravestones were piled up, taken from graves of families who had died out.

Someone from each family, mostly a woman of the older generation, would come to the cemetery to plant, tidy or rake their family's gravesite every week. Because it was raked all around, people always knew by the footprints if someone had visited a grave. I felt sad for a dog who visited his dead master every day. He would stay by his grave and only go home when it got dark. His footprints talked about his love, his loss and the way he grieved. The cemetery looked more like a garden with many different flower beds, except for the headstones in granite, marble or rock with the names and dates of the dearly departed inscribed. These would read like a family history. We had two graves: one of my grandfather Friedrich Wilhelm and a small one next to him with little baby Dorothea, Aunt Tutti's firstborn.

Keeping the gravesites tidy gave the women a chance to get together and chat, since they could not go to the pub like the men.

Rolling hills hugged the village of Stresow on one side, with the mill hill being the highest. On the other side were three lakes, bordered by extensive forests. The village was shaped like the letter Y. The road into the village from the next town, Bad Schönfliess (two kilometers away and simply called the city) connected about two thirds down the right arm of the Y. The grocer with the bakery, the two schools, the cemetery, the church, the other grocer, and the pub were in the middle between the two arms. A memorial for WW I was at the central tip. We lived on the left side of the single leg. We could see the road to the city from our living room because our house was on higher ground than the rest of the village. At the bottom of our land was a ditch, along which my father had planted acacia trees. The pathway that went all around the village was the divide between the mill hill and us. Just as my grandfather had done, Dad planted household staples on these two acres, but added alfalfa and several rows of apple trees. I remember the trees blooming with soft pink blossoms. I thought it looked very pretty.

People, who did not want to be seen meeting with their sweethearts (or going to the city or coming home), would use the narrow pathway. Originally, there had been a windmill on top of the mill hill but it had been hit by lightning and had burned down. During the summer, wheat or rye would grow on the hill, along with dark blue cornflowers, bright red poppies and white daisies around the edges and several metres into the field. I loved picking nice bouquets of blue, red, and white flowers, along with some horsetail to bring to my mother. Granny warned us, "Don't step into the grain field, stay carefully at the edges if you don't want to be grabbed by the Grain Fairy. She will carry you away and you'll never be seen again."

I can admit it now that I tried to get to know or at least see her once. I carefully stepped about five meters into the field, held my breath and waited but nothing happened. I thought I was probably not far enough into the field but did not dare to go further.

In the wintertime, the mill hill was a paradise for all the village kids. We would pull our sleighs up the hill, then race screaming down into the ditch or go flying over it and end up between the apple trees, competing to go the farthest. I still remember how cold and red the exposed skin of my thighs between my stockings and my panties would get after sleighing for several hours. Skirt and coat would fly up and expose us to the cold in that area. To avoid it we started to lie down on the sleigh instead of sitting on it. Girls did not wear long pants like the boys in winter. We did not even possess any.

My dad, the business man

Father had purchased the smithy and small farm and extended the business to sell and repair farm machinery. He purchased modern machines to be able to add fancy ironwork to the usual day to day smithy labour. He had two apprentices, and employed two journeymen who would occupy the room along the row of stables. I loved watching the men at the two fires in the forge, especially when they hammered the red-hot iron into shapes, like horseshoes or parts for fancy wrought iron garden gates. The sparks would fly! Big, heavy leather aprons protected them but still, I could not understand that the sparks did not hurt their bare arms. They did wear caps to protect their hair, though. I was fascinated when my dad worked the drill machines and shaved very fine, silvery metal hair curls off larger pieces of iron. Suddenly he had created something that you would not think he could have made. I just did not like the noise and always covered my ears with my cupped hands. Usually I had to stand in the door anyway and was not allowed to come in. He would wave me in only when he was alone and wanted to show or explain something to me.

Most of our land was still leased to the farmer who supplied us with grains and straw for the stables. He stored his thresher and the bundled straw in our barn. We had a lot of fun climbing way up into the rafters and jumping down into the straw – until the day when I slipped too far into it. I could not extract myself and would have suffocated if help had not arrived in time.

An owl lived in the barn too. When we heard it hoot at night, Granny would say, "Ooohhh my, somebody is going to die…" and sometimes that even happened.

The new car

It was a very exciting day when Dad came home with a new car, a reddish-brown DKW (a trademark that became part of Audi). It was the very first automobile in our village. It did not replace his BMW motorbike with the sidecar of which my mother was very fond. On Sunday afternoons, we would take little outings in the car to visit surrounding villages. I loved the bright sunny Sunday when we visited a fair in the city.

"Mom, I want to ride the white horse! Please...."

We were allowed three rounds on the small carousel but I was very disappointed not to be allowed to ride any one of the colorful horses, not my favorite white one, not the red one, and not even the brown ones. It was not fun to sit in a golden coach and be a good girl, just because Christel was too small to ride a horse, and I had to hold her.

"The horses are for boys," my mother stated.

Oh, yeah? The horses moved up and down and around ... why are the best things always just for boys?

In Wildenbruch (now Swobnica, Poland), another small village just six kilometres away from Stresow was an old, poorly maintained castle. It got me fantasizing about being a princess and living in this old stone castle in medieval times. It belonged to the last Emperor of Germany, the Old Fritz, as the German people lovingly called him. He used it as a summer retreat. The villagers were incredulous about him and said, "He is just like us."

He talked about farming, pulled weeds in his garden, drank beer in the pub and shared stories with them. He told them, "Beer is healthy. I grew up on beer soup...."

One day Dad surprised us with his announcement that we were to drive to the Island of Rügen and visit his sister Gertrud, who, by now, everyone called Tutti. She remained Aunt Tutti for the rest of her life, not just for me after I gave her that name but also for all the other children of her siblings. She was my Godmother. I loved her a lot and I was very excited to see her and my boy cousins in their house at the Baltic Sea.

I was in the back of the car standing between (and looking over) my parents' shoulders while Christel, who was wrapped up in a quilted blanket, slept on my mother's lap. It must have been the summer of 1938 or maybe 1939. It was a dark night and we were driving on a cobblestone road beside a lake. Rain was pelting down onto the car roof. The road was glistening and the raindrops as they hit it, were bouncing back up like little pebbles. The streetlights and the lit windows of the houses across the small lake were reflected in the water. It made quite an impression on me. I had never seen anything so pretty. It was a fairy tale setting. A motorbike was passing us and Dad hardly finished saying, "Crazy to drive that fast on this wet slippery road...."

With screeching brakes, he almost drove into the lake. Mother and I screamed because we saw the motorbike crash into an on-coming coach right between two horses.

It was a most horrible sight. There was blood all over the place. The horses, with their legs now in the air, were neighing in pain and shock. They were obviously very badly injured. The passengers of the coach had been thrown clear and lay scattered across the road with one person right in front of our car. It was a scene frozen in time for a few long seconds. An ambulance and a police car came with screaming tires and stopped next to us. The motorcyclist was dead. A policeman had to shoot the horses. We were told to stay and wait until the police came to help get our car back onto the road. Then they directed us to the Police Station where my parents were interviewed and had to sign a statement. After that, we just sat in the car. They were very quiet for a long time. Then Dad turned, looked at Mom and, without any words spoken, she just nodded to him.

He started the car and we drove back home. We never did finish the trip to Aunt Tutti's place. My father was very badly shaken up and he whispered, "My God, I could have drowned all of us driving into the lake. I am so glad the brakes worked and the car stopped at the water's edge."

Lotte conscripted

One day, two men in brown uniforms came to our village. They inspected, listed and marked all the horses that were not field work-horses. They were to be brought to the village square. Father explained to me that we must also bring our horse, Lotte. We were at war and the Führer needed Lotte to defend the country. I asked Dad, "Why our Lotte? Can't he use another horse?"

I was allowed to ride her into the village. After my dad lifted me off Lotte at the village square, I cried and was despondent for weeks.

There had been a lot of talk on the radio about why the war was necessary. Everybody talked about it. I can still see myself standing with my dad, holding his hand and looking up into his face while he talked to his friend Fritz K., the pub owner, about the possibility of both of them being drafted.

"Oh, Daddy," I thought, "don't go, I love you so much. I want to marry you when I grow up. You are more handsome than Fritz."

This Fritz was younger and he liked both of my aunts, Irene and Lisa, and I always expected him to become my uncle when he married one of them. I was just five years old but always listened to the grown-ups.

I had a gut feeling that I would never see Lotte again and that she would probably be shot dead by the enemy. It seemed to me that Lotte knew, too. When I reached up to her, she bent her head way down to me and looked at me with sad eyes when I tried to put my head against her cheek. Tears are stinging my eyes even now, so many years later just writing about it.

There must have been about twenty or thirty other horses taken that day, all loaded into trucks by the uniformed men. I hated them. Lotte walked up the ramp with her head hanging low. Some of the horses kicked and reared up but in the end, they lost the fight.

That was in September 1939. It was my first taste of war. It was not even long after that day that they came and took the battery out of our DKW car. It now just sat in the garage with an old gramophone with a big horn and a box of records on the back seat. Dad allowed us to sit in the car, wind up the gramophone and listen to music. There was a picture of a little white dog on the gramophone and a caption read, "His Master's Voice."

Granny's hands

Many children had the measles and I got them too. My eyes hurt and I was very sick. I felt lousy, alone and sad, forgotten by everyone. The room was dark with the shutters closed. As the sunlight came through the slanted openings, I imagined it as long, silent fingers playing with the bits of silver and specks of brown in the dark blue wallpaper. I could even imagine faces in the shadows caused by the lilac trees outside

– here and there a ship, and there was the good Lord himself on a cloud with some angels around Him. He had friendly, old eyes but He wiggled a finger at me attached to a long, sinewy hand. I was not afraid but just kept on looking at the imagery. The hand was white with a touch of pink and I could almost see through it. It was a beautiful hand.

The hand was cool and soft. I felt it on my forehead. It helped my eyes not to hurt so much but I did not want to open them, I wanted to feel those cool fingers. Was I an angel now, like those behind Him? It did not matter. I felt suspended between being and not being, I was floating. Please God, just a little longer….

Was it this plea or was it the voice coming from a distance, "She has quite a high temperature and she is delirious…."

All of a sudden, I was back in my bed, the perspiration trickling into my ears, which hurt, too. The long fingers and the streaks of sunlight were gone. There were no faces, no ships, no God, no angels on the wall, just that dark blue wallpaper with bits of silver and specks of brown. This used to be my father's room. My bed was a black ebony sleigh bed. My father had told me proudly that it was his before he got married.

I opened my eyes just a bit and looked right into Granny's wrinkled face. Her one hand was on my forehead and she took my hand in her other one.

"Did you have a nice dream, my girl? You smiled and you looked so happy."

I just nodded – thinking she would laugh at me if I told her of the things I had seen. I felt that she belonged to Christel. She always hugged her, cuddled her, held her on her lap, stroked her wavy hair, and comforted her when she was crying. I was only allowed to just sit beside her, close enough, but never on her lap. She never stroked my hair.

Tears were stinging my eyes. I closed them again. Granny's hand felt so good on my forehead and I wished she would not take it away. I thought of how beautiful her hands were, even though they were wrinkly or maybe because they were wrinkly. Her face was beautiful and wrinkly too. Often I had looked at her, wanting her to hug me so badly that it hurt. My mother did not hug me either, nor did my father. There was just a handshake and a light formal, "Good Night" kiss – nothing else. But I could not let anybody know or show how much I wanted to hug or be hugged – only babies did that. I was a big kid now, a kid ready to go to school. Maybe it was good to be sick. I could feel the hand on my head and it felt so good. I did not want it to stop.

"I want to look like Granny when I am a grandmother," I decided.

My ears got worse and Dad had to go to pick up the doctor from the city. It was a good thing that he still had the motorbike. Granny had to put special drops into my ears at frequent intervals. The drops felt cool and tickled as they ran down into my ear canals. I asked where Mom was. Granny explained that she was not allowed to come close to me because I was contagious. Mom had never had the measles and when grownups get them, they could die. She also explained that the measles were dangerous for a new baby. Which new baby I thought but was too tired to ask.

"Don't worry," she said, "your mother often stands at the door and looks at you. She hopes you will get well soon."

During my whole childhood, I had recurring ear infections and my ears are still very sensitive. Noise hurts, even drives me to tears, and I cannot stand windy days without a cover.

4: School and Other Excitement

First day of school

The last year that children started school in spring rather than in fall was 1940. I could hardly wait to get ready. I wanted to learn to read. That way I would not have to depend on Granny, who had less and less time.

A set of twin girls lived in the workers' house of the mayor, just across from the WW I memorial. They were some months younger than me and therefore not able to start school that year. For some unknown reason they turned up in our house. I was just drinking my baby bottle of milk. My mother had unsuccessfully tried to wean me off it. The girls laughed their heads off. They just could not believe that I, ready to go to school in a few weeks, was still getting the bottle. I told them that the milk tasted much better that way and I did not like it in a cup. Unfortunately, other kids heard about it and it took weeks until they forgot it. Yes, I stopped having a bottle right then and there and my mom was happy. I later suspected that she had arranged the whole scenario. Why would these girls turn up right at that particular time when we were never allowed to bring village kids home to play with us?

I was also looking forward to the big "Schultüte" or "School cone" similar to a cornucopia, or "Horn of plenty." This was a cone-shaped cardboard bag traditionally given to children on their first day of school. It was almost as big as I was and normally filled to the brim with goodies. This tradition was probably developed to make kids look forward to, rather than be afraid of, having to go to school. Well, I must admit that I was disappointed because my cone was filled almost to the top with green Easter-basket grass and only one (yes, only ONE!) orange and two shrivelled apples harvested last fall from our own garden. There were also some candies and a bar of chocolate and that was all. But the "Horn of plenty" was gold with a nice picture and printed on it was "My first day of School." The size of the cone had my hopes up but such was life. Even I, a very grown-up six-year-old, knew there was a war on.

We had two schools: the "little school" for the first two grades and the "School" up to grade eight. I started in the little school but it closed later that same year. The teacher cried when he told us that he had been conscripted into the army. All the children from grade one to grade eight were now crammed into one room in the "School" with only one teacher who was older and not fit for the war. A number of parents decided to send their children to the city school and my cousin Joachim, Aunt Hanni's son, was one of them.

The seat of honor

Mr. König, our teacher, had devised a system to keep the grades together. He placed the youngest ones in the front rows, with girls on one side and boys on the other side of the room, with a narrow aisle in the middle. There he would walk up and down and keep an eye on us working and trying to catch cheaters. He always carried his willow stick with him sometimes pointing at someone's paper, sometimes tickling someone behind the ears with it or smacking someone on the shoulder if he caught them dreaming or looking out the open window. It was hard not to look out because it was sunny outside, the lilac was blooming, and the wonderful scent wafted into our room. Sometimes a whole row of birds would be sitting on the outside windowsill singing happily.

Being seated in the first seat of the row of your class at centre aisle was an honor. For instance, the last rows were the grade eights, then the grade seven and so on down to the grade one kids. In second, third, fourth and the beginning of fifth grade, I was proudly occupying the first seat on the girl's side. I loved school. My schoolwork was good and I always did my homework. Other children bullied me on the way to and from school, pulled me by my braids and pelted me with hard snowballs in winter. Often the other girls ridiculed me during recess because I was too timid to join in the hardball throwing or any of the other rough games they played. I was always afraid they would hurt me on purpose, as they had before. When they chose teams, I was called as one of the last. I always felt like an ugly duckling in a flock of white swans as in that particular fairy tale. But in my imagination, I was the white swan between all the ugly ducklings....

"I do not really belong here," I always thought and felt sad.

One day in grade three, the girl next to me wanted to copy my math homework. She promised to "protect" me and walk me home. I pushed my scribbler a little bit over to her side and pretended I did not notice. But Mr. König saw it! You know what he did? We both had to lay our hands on the desk and he hit each of us three times across the fingers with his stick. It really hurt. The tears shot into my eyes and dripped onto my papers. It was not only the pain but my surprise that he could do that to me! I had considered myself one of his special pupils; he had always been somehow respectful of me. My fingers and my feelings were hurt. Up to that time, I had not openly cried in school and from now on, they called me "crybaby, crybaby, crybaby...."

Every morning when our teacher entered the schoolroom, we had to stand, raise our right arm and wait until he was in front of the class. Before he got there, he passed a spittoon next to a bookcase. He would clear his throat and spit into it with an awful sound, and to my surprise, he never missed. I hated it. It made me feel nauseated. When he finally was in front of us he would stand there, look at us for a few seconds and with a slight wave of his right hand mumble, "Hitler." We would answer in unison, "Heil Hitler." Then he would just say, "Sit down."

His favorite subject must have been geography. He would become very animated as he showed us where countries were located on large maps rolled down in front of the wall and he talked about them. He had visited several, possibly during WW I. Once a week he took us on walks, teaching us about plant biology. We picked healing herbs in the forest, along field paths or in green pastures. He called this "war effort" and it was done for the Red Cross. They prepared teas, salves and tinctures for the wounded soldiers of the army.

Twice a week, young boys from the "HJ," the Hitler Jugend (Hitler Youth) and young girls from the "BDM," the Bund Deutscher Mädel

(League of German Girls) came from the city and we had to stay after school. The HJ was the organization for young boys and the BDM was the equivalent for young girls. You were expected to join as soon as you were ten years old. They had smart-looking outfits with dark blue pants or skirts, white shirts or blouses. When I was old enough, the color of the shirts and blouses had changed and were now a light gray. A dark scarf rolled in a certain way, was worn under the collar so that it showed a small triangular corner in the back and tied with a brown, woven leather knot in the front. We all longed to be old enough to get these uniforms. Aunt Lisa had one and I loved the feel of the leather knot, the way it smelled and the noise it made when you squeezed it.

The Führer knew how to excite the youth. He demanded that they be healthy and fit to become Germany's future soldiers and fight for the "Führer, Folk and Fatherland." His slogan for the Hitler Youth was, "A young German must be as swift as a greyhound, as tough as leather, and as hard as Krupp steel."

These young people talked to us about the Führer and the war and the victories of the ever-advancing German army. One day all of us received a postcard photo of the Führer. I brought mine home and put it on top of a family photo in a frame on my night table. I went out and picked wild violets. I put them in a small vase and placed it next to the picture. I saw my father's face when he came to say good night and I knew he did not like it. I asked if it was all right and he said "yes." What else could he have said? When the violets wilted, I never replaced them and the original family photograph was back in the frame. Hitler's photo was in the drawer underneath my poetry book (autograph book) and I told no one. The poetry book was a book with a fancy cover and empty pages and you would ask all your relatives and friends to write a poem in it for you. "Roses are red, violets are blue..." was the most common.

Grandfather died

My maternal grandfather, Karl, passed on in 1941. He had been unwell for years but now he could not even sit in his beloved pergola anymore. Mother explained that it all went very quickly in the end. I was seven years old and it was the first time that a family member had died. I was very concerned that I did not have any black clothing for the funeral but I was not even allowed to go. Since he was my mother's father, my dad accompanied her to pay his respects. It was the very first time that he agreed to go to one of her family functions since the wedding. They attended the church service and burial in the cemetery (no cremation in those days), and were home earlier than I had anticipated. They did not go to the house for coffee and cake afterwards. I thought that would have been the best part to see all the aunts, uncles and cousins. My father did not have any desire to make friends with his mother-in-law.

My first train trip

During the summer holidays of 1941, I was rewarded for my good report card with a trip to Sydowsaue (now Żydowce, Poland), a place not too far from the big harbour city of Stettin at the Baltic Sea. It was a huge surprise. It was my first train trip and Granny took me to visit her brother Paul and his wife Martha, who had invited me. They lived in a villa in a wonderful park-like garden. They had no children and wanted to get to know me. I was given my own very pretty room and a maid served me breakfast in bed the first morning. Aunt Martha warned me that it would be just this one time. I was glad because I wanted to sit and eat with them and listen to them talking.

They were old like Granny but everything here was very different. They were dressed in "Sunday" clothing every day. Aunt Martha did not even wear an apron like Mother and Granny always did. The table was covered with a white tablecloth and the cups were on saucers as if they had visitors coming for a birthday celebration. They had a bathroom with a big bathtub, hot and cold running water and an indoor toilet. You just had to pull a fancy chain and water came rushing down from a box close to the ceiling, which flushed everything away. There were no torn pieces of newspaper stuck on a nail but a roll of soft white paper on the wall. I was in awe! I wanted to get to know them better and talk to them, listen to them and do things with them. I was there for a whole week. Uncle Paul had a car and drove us to the harbour in Stettin. I saw many big white ships. The grey ones were naval ships. I heard him whisper to Granny, "A lot of Jews have escaped from here and I'm afraid there won't be enough ships."

During my stay, they had visitors. A Professor from the Stettin University, his beautifully dressed wife and a son, who was a few years older than I, came. His name was Gerhard and I liked him. They invited us back and I thought I was in a castle. They had very fancy furniture, carpets with intricate designs on the floors and beautiful paintings on the walls. Gerhard had many books in his room and he showed them to me. I was fascinated by a whole row of blue ones, which were all about the Native Indians in North America. Gerhard told me about the stories in these books. I remember some titles: *Old Shatterhand, The Treasure in Silver Lake, Sons of the Bear Hunter and Winnetou.* The name *Winnetou* really intrigued me by the way it rolled off the tongue, *Winnetou.*

It conjured up so many images of lands unknown with Indians riding wild horses and feathers in their hair. Gerhard was very excited and confided, "I like the books by Karl May. I have read all of them. When there is a new one, Pa buys it for me. When I grow up I will go to America to see all these places."

I just looked at him and envied him for being a boy. That he could plan this and probably even do it one day! It truly was not fair to be a girl.

It was the first time that I sincerely wished I was a boy.

The sad day came when his parents brought Gerhard to Uncle Paul and Aunt Martha. His parents had to escape with the last ship and could not take him. We did not know they were Jewish and who cared? My relatives hid Gerhard until the war was over and then just gave him their name. Since nobody had passports or other papers anymore, it was easy. The ship with his parents on it was torpedoed and had sunk.

Dad becomes a soldier

I am not sure of the year when they drafted my father into the army. They sent him to Italy to be stationed in Sicily. After the war, he told me he had been very lucky not to have been involved in serious fighting.

"My God, Gila," he said, "I couldn't have shot at real people."

He always mentioned Sicily with longing in his eyes and told me how much he liked the countryside, how he would just love to visit it again. In the early nineteen-fifties, I gave him a set of eight books about Italy and Sicily. I visited Sicily with him in my mind approximately thirty years after he had gone to the "pearly gates." During his short time in Sicily, he regularly sent us twenty-pound crates of "Arancia Rossa di Sicilia" – very juicy blood-red oranges. Out of the neat crates, we kids built "furniture" for our playhouse in the empty horse barn. Because of the oranges, I always felt Daddy was safe. Mother liked the crates because the thin wood strips made for very good kindling.

Made out of horses blood?

During recess at school, I first became acquainted with liquorice because some children traded it. I wanted more after the first taste of it. Granny and my mother were in cahoots to prevent that. Both warned me, "Oh, no. That is terrible stuff. It's made from horses' blood. You wouldn't want to eat anything coming from a horse, would you?"

I thought about this long and hard and decided if I traded some of my own treats for it, I would be helping another child to get something better. If it was made from horses' blood, I could not help the horses anymore anyway. So occasionally, I did make trades but I always felt guilty.

One day I needed a little hammer and a nail to fix something in the playhouse. Father kept some small tools in a kitchen drawer, so that's where I looked. Rifling through the drawer, there were all kinds of things. In search of a suitable nail, I opened several small boxes. Surprise! There was one with liquorice! Forbidden to us – but not to my dad? That's not fair I thought and took a little piece. But, oh my dear God, this was truly terrible stuff. Maybe this is the horse blood type? I spat it into the dirt pail and rinsed my mouth several times. I still could not get rid of the taste. I went to find Granny; knowing she would not punish me but help me if she could. I told her and she laughed until tears rolled down her cheeks, "Gila, Gila, you just had a taste of chewing tobacco."

Father wounded

Father surprised us when he suddenly came home for a few days from Italy, only to leave again and go to France. It must have been September 1943 because he left a "gift" with my mother and another little sister was born in May 1944. When he left, my mother was very upset and we children cried and held onto his legs while he hugged Mom.

Now the war felt dangerous. Many families had already received those dreaded telegrams advising them that their father or son had been killed in action for "Führer, Folk and Fatherland." Sure enough, Dad was wounded in France. I am not aware of how it happened because he never talked about it. A kind French woman nursed him. Had she not found him he would have bled to death. Through her, he sent us wonderful sweaters. I sensed that my mother was worried that maybe he might love the French woman more than us. I felt the stabs of jealousy for the first time in my young life. I loved my dad very much but for once, I was totally on Mom's side.

The forge was closed. My mother had tried to keep it open with just the last apprentice, Helmut, who was not yet eighteen. He had apprenticed with my father for almost three years and knew the work. One after another, the other three workers were drafted and went away. Helmut was the last.

It was not very long before Father was released from the army. He had been shot in his right upper arm. Now he could not hold a gun or lift his arm very high. Therefore, he also had trouble performing the correct "Heil Hitler" greeting. To be honest, I do not remember him ever doing so. He opened the smithy again. Strange how his war wound did not hinder his work. His "war effort" was to keep the villagers' farm machinery and tractors going for the women, who now had to plant and harvest the fields because there were hardly any grown men left.

Uncle Robert, Aunt Hanni's husband, also came home from the front after his parents had successfully applied for his release. Without him, their chicken farm could not deliver the required quota of four-thousand eggs a day to the army. Therefore, the chicken farm became "high war priority".

Young boys could not wait to become soldiers but for now had to help their mothers. The old men also tried to do as much as they could. All remaining men, including my father, had to be in the "Volkssturm," a militia organization for men not able or too old to be soldiers. They had to keep an eye on everybody to ensure their blackout paper was in place inside their windows; to make sure the siren worked for the air raid alarm; to insist that people said "Heil Hitler" instead of "Good Morning" and to report any negative comments made about the Führer. They were allowed to enter your house without knocking in order to check if you listened to the enemy's radio broadcasts. They were the "home front." In turn, the Hitler Youth kept an eye on the Volkssturm. The young people felt that the old guys did not take their jobs seriously enough. Parents were afraid their own children would report them. People stopped talking to each other.

Father applied for help to fix farm machinery and shoeing horses. He was advised he could pick up a young Polish man, taken prisoner by the German army. Dad was responsible to ensure that this young man did not escape. Peter Kaczmarek was only nineteen. He had not been a soldier. He spoke a bit of German and almost felt like part of our family. He occupied the room in the stable. My parents had fixed it up very nicely. It had no lock or key. There was a small entrance hall with a makeshift toilet in a curtained corner consisting of a chair with a hole closed by a lid and a pail under it. Peter had to empty and clean it every day. It was more than we had in our house.

The floor was red brick throughout. From the hall, a door opened into the bed/sitting room. Some nice pictures hung on the wall, which hailed from Dad's bachelor room. Dad furnished it with a wardrobe, a chest of drawers and my grandfather's "secretaire" – a stand-up desk with green felt on the slanted writing top, and lots of little drawers and shelves in the back under the lid. There was one comfortable chair with a reading lamp next to it and two wooden chairs – one beside the bed and one beside a small table in front of the window. The single bed had blue chequered covers and the side curtains and valance at the large new window were made of the same material.

A roll-up, blackout window covering gave Peter complete privacy but was also very important for all our safety. Peter promised never to forget to roll it down in the evening. In one corner of the room was an iron stove for heat. He kept a kettle on top so that he had warm water to wash himself. He had the same kind of washstand with a bowl and a pitcher that we had in our kitchen. He would bring Mother his laundry on washday. Light white sheers and two small throw rugs gave the room a cozy feel. The view out of the window was of our playground and over the apple orchard to the mill hill. I told my parents that I wanted the room when I was grown up and the war was over. The chance to read late into the night without anybody switching off my light was very enticing!

Peter ate with us in the big country kitchen but at a small separate table. It disturbed me. I liked Peter and asked my parents, "Why does Peter not sit with us at the big table?"

My father explained we were not allowed to let him sit with us because he was Polish and a prisoner. Dad explained, "If one of the Volkssturm men comes and sees that he sits with us and reports it, I would be taken away and you would never see me again."

That for sure shut me up for good. I asked Peter if he felt bad about it but he laughed and answered, "No, kiddo, I understand."

I also asked him if he would try to run away since his room had no lock and he could even easily climb out of the window.

"I am not crazy, Gila. I would either be shot or I would starve trying to hide. And where would I go? Either the German army would kill me or, if I made it far enough, the Russians would do it. No thanks, I feel much safer here with your family."

My father would listen to the BBC in the late evenings. Sometimes we heard Churchill speak with a translator. Dad was very careful about it. He had his ear close to the radio so nobody could hear anything outside. Instinctively, even as a child, I understood that he could be taken away or shot if caught or reported. After the news, they always played the song *Lily Marlene* and then the radio would go silent. To this day, I still know the melody and all the words of this sad longing soldier's song.

The "Tommies"

Blackout paper would carefully cover all the windows before we switched any lights on, or even lit a kerosene lamp or candle during power outages. The English and the American bombers would fly over our village on their way to unload their deadly cargo over one of the chosen cities. The closest place targeted for bombing because of a military airport was Königsberg (now Chojna, Poland), just fourteen kilometers away. However, this was not the Königsberg in East Prussia which was so vehemently defended by the Germans and fought for by the Russians. That Königsberg is now divided between Russia and Poland because of the access to the Baltic Sea and renamed Kaliningrad. The Germans held it long after the enemy was already deep into Germany and fighting in our area. In the end, they were surrounded and were massacred.

We could see and hear when Berlin was bombed because it was only about fifty kilometers away "as the crow flies." When the sirens screamed at night, we had to get out of bed fast, grab the clothing we had prepared and run in the dark to the far end of our apple orchard. Dad and Peter had built a bunker there over the ditch by placing beams across and covering them with straw and earth.

I remember vividly how the church spire with the weathervane rooster on top stood out against the night sky like a pointed finger. It was very eerie on nights when the moon was full and the loaded bombers flying over us sounded like angry hornets as they came closer. Once, a stray bomb fell into the duck pond not far from us. It exploded and there was hardly any water in the pond the next day. Even people from the far end of the village came to look at it. Dozens of dead frogs and some rats were scattered around it.

Another night a bigger bomb fell close to our village and our bunker almost became our grave. The simple structure was shaking and we just made it out before it collapsed. I remember the earth in my hair and in my collar. Subsequently we just sheltered there in the ditch.

We listened to the noise of the planes flying over and the big bombs exploding in Berlin. We would see the night sky over the mill hill turn blood red. We watched the phosphorus (incendiary) bombs dance and float in the sky like burning Christmas trees, even lighting up our area. We tried to count them but there were too many.

Fifteen years later, I worked with a woman from Berlin who saw her parents run, burning like candles, screaming until they fell down and were consumed by the flames.

"I could not help them," she said with tears in her eyes, "people even jumped into the Spree River or the canals but the phosphorus just kept on burning. That fire could not be doused by any means."

Many women and children were evacuated from Berlin to the country. A very nice lady and her daughter were the first to stay with us. Actually, they were billeted in the house next to the mayor's but I had met the girl at school and liked her so much I got my father to talk to the authorities. They were transferred to us. In time the woman became Aunt Erika and since her daughter, Ingrid, was my age and in my class, we became best friends.

The mayor's secretary would send you a number of people because she knew how many rooms you had. You could not turn anyone away. Hundreds of thousands were on the roads fleeing their homes with the retreating German army and the advancing Russians on their heels. An old man from East Prussia who had lost his wife on the way came to stay with us. He just had to leave his dead wife covered with snow beside the road. With him were his two granddaughters, Betty and Helen, both in their twenties.

They told horror stories. Many people had left with horses and covered wagons from their homes in East Prussia. Often their horse would be confiscated by the army to feed their men, stolen or taken by deserters with pistols or else the creatures would just collapse from lack of food or water or freeze to death at night. People would abandon their wagons and just go on by foot and carry what they could. Old, weak or sick people were left behind, small children would die and they had to leave them where it happened. Some of these refugees would only stay a day or two in our village and then move on going west. We felt so very lucky to have a roof over our heads, food and water and gladly helped them.

The population of our village of one thousand souls more than tripled or even quadrupled in a short time.

5: Life Lessons

You are the oldest

My parents owned a large, beige and brown, fine rug and kept it rolled up stored in a corner of the dining room behind the door. This room was next to the kitchen and not connected to any of the other rooms. It was used only for birthday parties or when many visitors were expected. Only then, would they move the big heavy table and the twelve chairs aside and roll the carpet out before the table was put back in place on top of it. A sideboard and a heavy chest of drawers held all the linens, fine china, silver cutlery and crystal glasses reserved for these occasions. After the party, all crumbs were carefully brushed off the rug and it was rolled up again and stored in its usual place. In the spring, it would be taken outside for cleaning and hung over a bar especially built for the purpose of hitting the carpets with a wicker carpet beater. The carpet beater also came in handy to punish us. Actually, my mother had a quick hand and we knew how that carpet beater felt on our behinds.

Mother loved to tease me by showing off how easily she could make me cry. Every time we had casual or Sunday afternoon visitors (for example, her sisters with my cousins from the city) she would do it. She would look at me and say, "Cry, Gila, come on, cry, it's okay, just cry, why don't you cry? Come on, Gila, cry..."

She would keep on saying it until I cried. I was not allowed to leave the room. If only I could have run away! At the beach, she would splash me with the cold lake water before I was wet and I would cry. Often I just cried because she was so mean to me and I even hated her. Was I a stepdaughter like *Cinderella*? I had an active imagination like *Anne of Green Gables* and concocted all kinds of scenarios in my head, feeling sorry for myself. If she called "Gila, come here…" I had to drop everything, come and help peel peas or get parsley from the garden or other things easy enough for a kid.

I asked, "Why always me, why not Christel?"

Her standard answer was, "You are the oldest."

Once, I guess, she was really scared for me. We were at the lake, sitting in an old wooden boat that someone had left at the beach. The boy cousins and their mother, Aunt Tutti, were there as well. Granny was watching us, staying on dry land. Siegfried, the oldest boy started to rock the boat. We all joined in the fun, screaming with joy and the boat finally tipped over. With lots of laughter, they all scrambled about until Granny called, "Where is Gila?"

Nobody but Granny had missed me. The boat was on top of me, upside down, and I could not get out. I had swallowed a lot of water and I remember sinking twice and touching the ground. That was a funny feeling. Actually it was not very deep – maybe about four feet. Coming up a third time I hit my head on the side of the boat before it was pulled away. My mother grabbed me, carried me to the beach where they held me upside down by the legs, slapped my back and then put me down on the grass sideways, until no more water came out of me and the coughing stopped. During the walk home I heard Granny say to Aunt Tutti, "If she had gone down a third time she would have drowned…."

My mother was very quiet that day.

Learn to ride Mother's bike

Late summer of 1943, my knees always had bandages on them. I learned to ride my mother's bike. I was standing on the pedals because I was too short to sit on the saddle. Father, back from the army, would run along behind me, holding onto the seat. When he thought I did not notice he would let go and, promptly, I would crash. Once I had mastered getting up on the bike on my own, I could ride along the straight street but still had to learn how to stop. One day one of the bullies rolled a ball towards me and I fell. This time, not only did I scrape my knees and my elbows but as I was lying in the gutter, I found a ten-penny coin. It was enough to get five candies! Hurray! We never did get any allowance.

One sunny afternoon I decided to ride the bike to visit Grandma in the city. Close to the first houses of the city was a walkway for pedestrians next to the slightly rounded cobblestone street. It was covered with crushed black coal and it went a bit downhill. Three ladies were walking in front of me as I was rolling along faster and faster but I was afraid to reach for the bell. I could not reach the brake on the handlebar with my small hand either and so just steered right through between two of them before landing on the black stuff, sliding along and tearing my dress. The handlebar of the bike was badly bent. The ladies were really mad at me and wanted to keep the bike. I had to give them my name and two of them happened to be old classmates of my mother.

"Oh no," one stated, "you poor thing, I wouldn't want to be in your shoes tonight!"

They let me go with the warning not to come to the city again before I could really ride a bike and know how to brake. They even tried unsuccessfully to get the handlebars straight and I had a lot of trouble pushing it while limping home the two kilometers.

The intestines will come out

Dad had bought a new special apple tree. It was a "Dwarf Tree" but it would have huge apples in August. He planted it right in the middle of my personal garden spot in the front yard. It surely had some big apples the second year. He warned us, "I know how many there are. Don't you dare pick one. If one has a worm and falls down, then you can have it."

When pulling weeds in my garden I would "bump" against the trunk or softly shake the tree, but not one would have a worm or fall down. So I helped one along. That year I had no front teeth but I did not think of that when I tried to bite into it. Sideways did not work either, it simply was too big. It was as big as and looked like, the fake apples in a bowl in my great grandmother's living room. I was about three-and-a-half years old when, to her delight, I had asked her, if I could eat one of those....

I went to the kitchen, took a cutting board and a knife and proceeded to cut my apple. I held it with my left hand. The apple rolled; the knife slipped and I cut a piece of my left little finger off, right beside the nail on the inside. (Oh yes, I still have the scar!) I slapped the tiny piece of flesh back on, held it tight but it was bleeding like crazy. I was afraid my "intestines" would come out. We were warned this is what would happen if we cut ourselves with the large sharp knife we were not to touch.

I started to cry loudly, the way Christel always did so successfully. Granny was the first to arrive. She grabbed the first aid kit from a drawer, bandaged my finger tightly with the piece of flesh I had cut off in place, then put a black leather "fingerling" over it, which tied with strings to my wrist. By that time, my dad had arrived as well. He looked at the apple, at all the blood on my dress and on the floor, then at me, "Did you pick that apple?"

I kept on crying and uttered – "no-o-o-o". He put me over his knee and I got my second real spanking from him. Granny was trying to stop him saying "she is punished enough…." but he did not listen. When he put me down, he said, sounding and looking sad, "Gila, that was not for picking the apple. It was for lying to me. I would not have punished you if you had told me the truth."

Parents have different ways to teach their children a life lesson. Many years later, I inquired of my mother, "Why did you make me cry and always in front of other people?"

Her answer was, "I wanted to make you tougher."

I had learned my father's lesson and to this day, I do not lie. Either I would tell the truth or I would not say anything. Mother's lesson, on the other hand, did not work. I still cry easily – most of the time against my will.

Wild berries and mushrooms

Granny liked to go to the forest and pick wild berries and mushrooms. I loved to go with her and occasionally Christel came as well. She would always eat the berries instead of picking them into her pail. I was happy when she was not with us and I had Granny to myself. She would show me edible and herbal plants and tell me how they could be used. She knew where the different berries grew: very small but wonderfully sweet strawberries, and raspberries as thick as Granny's thumbnail, very juicy. Blueberries grew on very low bushes, were quite small but very aromatic. Blackberries were growing closer to the next lake, a lake totally overgrown with water lilies. I knew that water lilies had very long stems reaching all the way to the bottom. If you would try to pick one, it would pull you into the water, strangle you and carry you to the fairy living in a castle at the bottom of the very dark lake. I did not like the thorns on the bushes and I was always nervous picking blackberries there. I kept my eye on the lake, just in case....

The worst thing that ever happened in the forest was a tick that had found its way to my vagina. It hurt a lot and we cut our berry picking short and went home. My mother had me lie on the kitchen table, took my panties down and spread my legs. I felt very embarrassed because we were raised with the admonition, "privates are privates and you don't show them to anybody." She proceeded to get that tick out. It was not the only one she found. Berry picking was not as much fun after that.

The mushrooms were a different story. They would grow on dry spots, different ones either on or around different trees. I liked seeing the red one that I recognized from fairy-tale books. It was truly poisonous but what a beauty with a white stem and a bright red cap with white dots! I remember the pretty little song about it:

> "EinMännlein steht im Walde, ganz still und stumm,
> es hat von lauter Purpur ein Mäntlein um,
> sagt wer kann das Männlein sein,
> das da steht auf einem Bein,
> mit dem purpur rotem Mäntelein...."

Translated:

> *"A little man is standing in the forest still and quiet*
> *he's dressed in a crimson coat.*
> *Can you tell me who that little man is,*
> *standing on one leg*
> *and dressed in the crimson coat... ?"*

Many different types of mushrooms grew in the Stresow forests and Granny knew them all. She carried a little silver knife in her pocket and when she was not absolutely sure, she would cut the stem with it. If the knife turned blue, the mushroom was poisonous.

"Gila, poisonous mushrooms will kill you in a few minutes."

I never felt sure of most of them because often the bad ones looked just like the good ones. I did not trust that little silver knife and was apprehensive to eat whenever she made a meal of mixed mushrooms. One type of mushroom I really knew by sight and by the way they smelled were Chanterelles. If you have never eaten fresh Chanterelles, lightly fried in butter with a bit of finely chopped fresh parsley sprinkled on top, then you don't know how heavenly that meal is. To this day, I will drive miles to get Chanterelles for the scent, the taste and the texture of them. The only chance to get some is to know of a shop selling them. No picker would ever tell you where they are and not even your best friend would take you along or pass on the holy secret.

Cats, chickens and pigs

My cousin Renate's cat had several young ones and Christel and I each got our very own little kitten. Christel's cat was all black with yellow eyes; mine had a white underbelly, white boots on its hind legs and white shoes on its front legs. She otherwise had a mottled grey coat, but also had one white ear and a white nose. I called her Mooshie. I loved her more than my dolls and I often dressed her in my doll clothing and let her sleep in my doll carriage. Once, she was scared and jumped out and tried to run away. She repeatedly stepped on that dress she wore and tumbled about. It looked very funny and we laughed heartily. My father happened to see the cat and gave me a good lesson. "If you love Mooshie, you won't do that again. If she has to defend herself she will not be able to do it and if she climbs up a tree she will not be able to come back down."

It happened in the same year when my mother's cat Molly had a very bad eye infection and my father had to shoot her. It disturbed me greatly but he explained that he was being kind to the cat. He cried when he shot his own old cat, Peter, a year later, when it was full of arthritis and could not walk anymore. Peter looked my dad straight into the eyes as if he knew what was coming. It was a very emotional moment for me. I will remember the expression in Peter's eyes forever. I always wanted to have a cat like him.

For our Sunday meal, we very often had a fresh chicken. My mother killed them herself. You witness and accept these things when you are young because it is part of life on even a small farm. It was shocking when one chicken ran away without its head when she put it down on the ground. It was as if my brain was not able to process what my eyes were seeing. Mom said it was "nerves" and the chicken would not even know what it was doing. I learned about killing geese and ducks, rabbits and pigs. Different ways but I would rather not eat meat than have to do the killing myself.

Trading goods

Every family had a "Reichs Ration Card." The simplest thing had a big name, Reich this and Reich that. My mother would pick up everything listed on the ration card, not that she needed it, but because it could be used for trading. Best for trading were cigarettes. They were also on the ration card. Father did not smoke cigarettes but a pipe or cigars. We had a constant stream of people coming from the cities to get something to eat. They would trade jewellery, fine tableware, fancy bed linens, anything they did not need, for potatoes, carrots, turnips or even occasionally for a piece of meat or sausage. My mother did not need any of the things on offer but my dad had told her to help and to take what they offered in order not to make them feel like beggars.

Great Aunt Anna, one of my Granny's sisters, lived in Berlin. She and her husband had a bike shop and they sold any type of rubber wares. It was a big surprise when she turned up at our house. She brought gifts for everyone from her shop. We children received raincoats. Mine was a lovely cornflower blue, my sister Christel's was a bright yellow and little Ingrid loved her pink one. It was the middle of summer but it felt like Christmas. Oh, did we ever pray for rain! We wanted to show off our raincoats but it just did not rain. Mother had received a nice umbrella and she could not use it either.

Aunt Anna went home happy with many gifts from us in her bags, including sausages, meat, potatoes, fresh vegetables and even a glass jar filled with liver sausage. From then on, she came quite regularly. We laughed when she brought a pail and asked for some cow manure. She explained she needed it to fertilize the tomato plants on her balcony. Father filled the pail and covered it with sawdust. On her way home, she encountered an inspection in the train and the officer asked what she had hidden in the pail.

"Cow shit", she said without hesitation in typical Berliner fashion.

He did not believe her. As he was about to stick his hand in it, she added, "I would not do that if I were you."

He did anyway and she told us it was hard for her not to laugh because of his expression, the way he looked at his hand and then at her. However, she had the last laugh.

Not long after this day, I unpacked Mother's shopping bag and saw a small cone shaped blue bag. I recognised it from before the war. All the shops used that shape for candies. Curious because she had not bought candies for ages, I opened the bag and looked. Wow! Rock sugar! I loved to hear it crackle when it was melting in my tea.

I called out, "Mom! You bought rock sugar! Can I have a piece?"

"Yes. But give Christel one as well."

I took two and put one right into my mouth and gave Christel one. I started coughing and spitting and tearing up right away. Christel still had hers in her hand and she stared at me with her big blue eyes. Mother entered the kitchen and laughed, "Serves you right", she said, "It's not rock sugar, its washing soda."

6: The Summer of 1944

It was May of 1944 and we three sisters, Gisela, Christel and Ingrid, were expecting the arrival of a promised little brother. One day after school, we were not allowed into the house.

"The stork is here to bring the baby and you would just be in the way," Granny told us.

We could not believe she lied because we had seen the stork in his nest on our way home. We had even discussed the fact that, when you see the stork the first time sitting on his nest in spring, you will be very lazy. When you see him standing, you will do better and when you see him flying, you will be working hard.

Finally after several hours we were allowed to see Mom and she showed us a little baby sister. Dad always joked with his friends and told them, "The wish to have a son is the father of four girls."

A girl's name was not on our agenda, so focussed had we all been on a boy. Mother cried because Dad had not said a single word to her and she felt it was somehow her fault she still did not give him a boy. Without even discussing it with Mom, our father had gone to the Registry Office and when he came back, we asked him, "Daddy, Daddy, what's her name?" He told us her name was Edith.

"Edith!" I exclaimed, "What an old fashioned name is that! Couldn't we call her Reingard or Krimhild, Brunhilde or something fancy?"

Little did we know that several months later baby Edith would save our mother from a terrible fate.

Playing "doctor"

My big sister (actually aunt) babysitter Lisa who was, by now, twenty years old had been drafted into what was called the "Arbeitsdienst" (labour force) and sent to East Prussia to work on a farm. I was ten years old and we children had more freedom than ever since Lisa was gone and Mom was stuck with the baby and all her other work. Granny helped her. With the usual, "you are the oldest," I was responsible for my younger sisters. We went to the little beach at the lake but remembered the warning not to go in too far or the "Lake nymph" who was just waiting for little girls would get us.

We did not give up asking if we could invite other kids to our house to play.

"No, you are three, you can play with each other," was always the answer.

Now, on our own at the lake, I started to understand why Mom always gave us that answer. The village kids had built tents with their blankets. They had their panties off and played "doctor"; they used feathers to tickle each other and wanted us to play along. I was very embarrassed, disgusted and afraid of more bullying by not complying and did not want to go to the beach anymore. I could not tell my mother why and became very moody. From now on, we played outside on our own little playground and gave up asking for other playmates.

We each had a little garden under Peter's window and we could plant what we wanted, even dandelions. Dad had built a type of carousel with an old wagon wheel, which one of us had to push. We had a teeter-totter and my favourite was a swing under the huge pear tree that was much higher than the barn.

This tree was once split in half by lightning and our grandfather had put a strong iron chain around the trunk about ten feet up. This was before any of us had been born. He had needed four men to hold it to get the two halves together. This tree had about four hundred pounds of pears each year that tasted like lemon. I have tried but never found a lemon pear tree again. Once, when I was swinging high up, a pear fell on my head and, on my way down, I fell out of the swing. Mrs. Richter saw it and came to check if any bones were broken. She sent her son Paul to get a very cold spoon, which she pressed to the bump on my head and explained that this would prevent the bump from getting bigger. I felt somewhat dizzy and could not walk right away. Nobody even mentioned or thought that I could have had a concussion. Children were expected to be and maybe even were, much tougher than kids are nowadays.

Attack on the Führer

It was not the first time someone had tried to kill the Führer. High-ranking generals and officers had repeatedly plotted to kill him but Adolf Hitler always got away. Either, he was late for a meeting, did not turn up or closed it earlier than was his custom. July the 20th 1944 became a very sad day for many people in Germany. Because of an attempted bombing assassination, everyone involved was executed, even the children in the families of the conspirators, their relatives and close friends. Shockingly, it was not the socialist or the communist underground movement who were behind it but again high-ranking generals and officers. People started to think that Hitler had incredible foresight, a strong guardian angel or a pact with the devil and superstition of the country folk grew in leaps and bounds. They never forgot another occasion when he had insisted on driving himself and had his chauffeur sitting in the back of his car. There was an ambush and they shot the chauffeur instead of him. He got away, badly shaken but alive. Like so many times before, he was not killed on that fatal day, July the 20th 1944 but several thousand people were shot consequently.

For us in Stresow, far enough away from the actions in the cities, nothing changed after the shock had worn off. Nobody talked about the attempted assassination publicly. It was all very much hushed up in order, "not to let the enemy know about it."

Life as usual

Many summer days were just too hot to be outdoors. We played in the playroom in the house. The shutters were closed but the slits were left on a slant. Father had built a great two-storey dollhouse for me when I was little. The lower floor was a kitchen with everything. There were dishes in cupboards, cutlery in the table drawer, a stove, a kettle and two pots the size of a cup and a frying pan. When Lisa was still around or now Granny or even Mom with the baby, we were allowed to cook something with a tea candle in the stove under the pots or kettle. One day my cousin Renate came to visit from the city. She, Christel, Ingrid and I played house. We pretended to be cooking and put different fruits in the pots to make dessert.

A few days later, I was looking for something. The room was quite dark because the shutters were closed again and I had to feel my way to the dollhouse and noticed that one pot was heavy. I wondered why. I took a tiny spoon out of the drawer and tasted to find out what it was. Yikes! It tasted awful. I ran to the hall with the pot to look and saw rotten cherries and dozens of wiggling maggots.

I spat and coughed and almost vomited, but I still love cherries!

A soldier hiding in the rotting straw

We had two gardens with many fruit trees and bushes. Christel and I were now old enough to help with berry picking in the mornings. The berry bush garden was on the gable side of the barn. Close to the barn was a big pile of old rotting straw; it had covered the rows of strawberries during the winter. The cats liked to sleep on the straw in the sun and Granny always put a bowl with milk and a plate of bread or potatoes out for them. Lately she had wondered why the cats now ate it all so quickly. Usually it had lasted all day or they did not eat it at all.

While picking our berries I noticed that the straw moved and gave a little shout. A soldier looked out with a pistol aimed at us and demanded that Grandma give him civilian clothing. Christel and I crouched where we were like frozen statues; Granny kept her cool and mentioned that she would have to go into the house to find something. He agreed but demanded, "All right, but the children stay here. I will not harm them."

She left but on the way to the house saw a neighbour in the next garden and whispered to her in passing to urgently get the Master.

Before Granny came back with some clothing, Dad had turned up very casually as well.

He talked to the man quietly and then told him, "You better hurry up and disappear before you put yourself as well as all of us in mortal danger. My God, where will you go? Where is your regiment? I strongly suggest you try to find your way back to it and claim you got lost. You know what they would do if they catch you. It's your only chance."

The young soldier cried, "Sir, I am dead if I keep running and I am dead if I go back. You have no idea what it is like. The war is lost but they don't see it. I just cannot do it anymore. I just can't."

I did not hear more of the conversation between my father and him because Granny was taking us to the house. I only know that the next morning the soldier was gone. A few days later, there was talk of a young soldier found dead just a few kilometers away. Apparently, he had shot himself. It really shook up the village people and caused quite a bit of upset.

Food for several years

Mother was a great one for preserving all she could. There were hundreds of glass jars with all this delicious fruit in a secret cellar under the children's room. A carpet covered the trap door. There was row upon row, not only with fruit and veggies but also different types of sausage, meat, liver sausage, blood and tongue sausage, all marked with dates of several years. Every Sunday she allowed me to go down on the rickety ladder and choose a glass jar of fruit for dessert. I loved currants, gooseberry, cherries and pears. It was so hard to make a choice. Only occasionally was I allowed to bring up one with liver sausage for sandwiches.

My mother raised chickens, geese and ducks and looked after two milk cows, some rabbits and four or five pigs (two became food every fall). We never went hungry during the war. I held a bit of a grudge towards her, thinking of all the glass jars in the cellar and the four or five hams and over thirty salami and other sausages, hanging in the chimney to cure in the smoke. Throughout the week only my father and previously his men, but now he and Peter, were served a meal with meat and sandwiches with sausage or ham. Mother and we three girls just had potatoes with cottage cheese, herring or just plain homemade butter and salt; sometimes mashed potatoes with sweet and sour gravy and boiled eggs. Rice cooked in milk and sprinkled with sugar and cinnamon was a feast. Rarely did we have fish and if we had fish, it was either fried or cooked "brown".

I loved "fish brown"! All we needed was a sliced onion or two; then cook it in water with peppercorns, allspice, bay leaves, and a touch of salt and sugar. When the onions were glassy, the liquid was thickened with flour, it had to boil up and then the prepared clean fish pieces would be added. Just a brief boil again and when the fish turned white it was done. The best was still to come: Mother added Elderberry paste she had made the previous fall. Elderberry paste looked like tar but smelled much better. With the fish, it tasted fantastic. She used as much as she needed to achieve the brown color. It sounds weird but it was always stored in cups either without any handle at all or with broken handles and covered with a piece of cloth from old sheets, tied on top with string. Cling wrap was a thing of the far future. Today, I use *Dr. Duenner Elderberry* concentrate, available in Health Food Stores, when I make my "fish brown." Three tablespoons full of Elderberry concentrate in a glass of hot water is also good to prevent colds and flu. My advice: Drink it with a straw.

We had a big baking oven built out of rocks heated with big pieces of wood until they were almost falling apart but still glowing-red hot. These were then pushed to the sides of the oven and the prepared huge loaves of sourdough rye bread placed in the middle on the hot surface with a long, wooden paddle. A heavy iron door closed the oven and I was reminded of poor *Hänsel and Gretel* who were to be baked in an oven like this.

Have you ever had warm, freshly baked, crisp, cracked rye bread with bacon drippings and salt? It is delicious! Homemade sugar beet syrup and jam were on the breakfast table during the week while honey from Father's bees was just for breakfast on Sunday morning. Sunday was also the only day when we had a boiled egg and sometimes we were treated to white bread or reheated wheat buns. I helped to make butter from our own cow's milk and loved the fresh buttermilk. All fruit, veggies, potatoes, sugar beets, turnips and clover for the animals grew on our two acres of gardens around the house and a field along one of the lakes.

I did not like to go down into the cold root cellar under the barn to pick up something Mother needed for cooking. The cellar smelled musty. It was cold and there was not much light. There were mice, too and sometimes Dad would lock a cat in there for the night. Carrots were kept in big boxes of sand. Several types of potatoes were piled on the earthen floor divided by boards in a corner, and piles of turnips, red beets and other staple foods were stored there.

The rest of our land was leased and the leaseholder gave us grain for flour. Mother made candy from sugar beet syrup and poppy seed, called "noute." She made soap from bones. I think she hardly needed to buy anything besides sugar, salt or rice. Rarely were chocolate or candy in her shopping bag, which she had made out of an old piece of carpet. She also made different sizes of little bags out of old sheets or pillow-cases. She stitched "Sugar", "Rice" and "Salt" labels on them. If you did not have bags, you would not be served at the grocery store. Nothing came prepackaged as it is today. Talk about your ecological footprint or garbage. I do not remember that we had any garbage. Everything was used – either on the manure pile, in compost, or it was burned. They even put the ashes on the manure pile. We, like most of the village people, were living off the land. We gave back to it and, to a large extent, were totally independent.

Yes, we had electricity for lighting but no gas or running water. A pump was between the house and the barn. Sometimes you had to swing the handle five times before water came. Several lanterns burning kerosene were handy for power outages, going to the outhouse or to the stable. A very muddy pathway led to the outhouse between the manure pile and the barn. The door to it was next to the big barn doors. A small door was strategically placed to pull the box out from under the seat when it was full and emptied onto the manure pile where the contents would be covered with the existing rotting straw on that pile. A nail inside the outhouse held ripped up newspaper. When you had to wait a long time for someone to come back out, you knew that he was reading the old news.

It was frightening to go there if you had to do "big business" after dark. We kids would rather try to "hold it" until the morning when it was light. Number one was allowed using a pail in a kitchen corner or potty at night, parked under the bed. Bedrooms were not heated. It was healthier to sleep in a cold room but we had big fat feather pillows and covers. When you had a fever, they put a double set of covers on you to sweat it out.

"Bugs don't like heat," we were told, "don't complain, you'll be well tomorrow or the day after."

Oh, how could I forget the "Feather Feast"! That was a week or two in fall, when all the geese and ducks were slaughtered. No, I don't remember what they did with the birds, the only thing I do remember was that the breasts of the geese were put in the chimney for smoking and all the fat was made into "goose fat" to spread onto bread. It was considered a delicacy. The neighbour women organised the Feather Feast get-together, every evening in another house, to rip the soft parts of the feathers off the middle hard quill. The feathers were used to make pillows and covers for the kids. The down was used for baby beds, the parents' bed or the Hope Chest for young brides. Down are the feathers of the underbelly. They are so light, floating in the air and they covered everybody. We kids were supposed to sit still and listen to the stories the women were telling, but can you blame us for occasionally exhaling really hard, coughing or sneezing? Usually, we had freshly baked donuts rolled in icing sugar during a break!

7: Lots of Cat Babies

One sunny afternoon we older kids were sitting on the broken steps leading up to our house and talking about this and that. The weather was very warm and we were bored. Looking up I saw my cat, Mooshie, coming towards us carrying what I thought was a mouse. She came right up to me, put the little thing down in front of me, looked me in the eye and said, "meow" with a question mark.

"Mooshie"! I called out, "what is that?" She looked at me again and, after another "meow," left us, walking away purposefully.

We were amazed, not bored anymore. I picked up the little squirming thing and everyone agreed that it was a baby kitten. It did not even have its eyes open yet, was naked and looked weird. After a few minutes, Mooshie came back with another one. She repeated the scenario with the "meow" and she left again. This happened two more times. When she had brought four of those little critters, she stayed with us and started licking them. Mother had heard our excited voices and had come to see what caused the racket. She was very helpful and understanding when I said I needed to have a bed for the little cat family. She brought a carton and an old baby blanket. We made a little nest and placed the kittens in the middle. Mooshie jumped in and curled around them. The babies found the food supply and suckled. It was fascinating and we watched for a long time.

It must have been a week later when Christel's black cat, "Moorly", a sister to mine, had babies as well. She had been smart and had them in Christel's doll carriage in the house. She refused to move out of it, scratching and biting. None of our cats was allowed to stay in the house overnight. Even when it was raining or snowing, they were grabbed from the warm cozy place on the sofa or on a lap and heartlessly placed outside the house door. Father or Mother, whoever did the deed that evening, would put us off with, "There are enough warm places in the stables and barns; they know and they'll be all right."

Christel agreed to have her doll carriage put in the barn so that the cats could stay in it. The bedding was all ruined but that was no big problem. It was simply replaced when Mother knew Moorly was in the house for her milk. The cats always got milk and the same food we had.

For Führer, Folk and Fatherland

During spring and summer 1944, more Stresow families had received those dreaded telegrams with the words: "For Führer, Folk and Fatherland, your son/father….has given his life…." The bombers flying over our village increased in numbers as well as the frequency of the siren calling everybody to run to whatever shelter they had. When the planes had emptied their deadly cargo they would come back, not sounding like mad hornets anymore but more like honeybees and, now empty, flying much higher. One night we saw one with a fiery trail of fire coming towards us where we were lying in the ditch. It was like a huge big shooting star but you would not even think of making a wish, your brain stopped and you just stared towards it and unconsciously wished it would not hit you.

It came down a few hundred feet from us on the mill hill. The crash resulted in a huge, high, yellow flame and we waited for a big explosion. But there was no more noise; or was it drowned out by not just our own but the screams of all the other people hiding in the bushes along the trail? It was quiet and it stayed very quiet. The only thing we saw was just smoke, curling up into the night sky.

The next morning I asked my mother, "Do you think we can go up to the crash site and look if the fire is out and see what's left of the plane? I would really like to see it."

It was an overcast morning. The sky looked dark and smoky over the mill hill. The radio announcer had said that last night the air attack had been the most ferocious ever. Many thousands of people, mainly women and children, had been killed in bunkers under collapsed buildings, either by leaking gas or by simply being burned by the fire of the phosphor bombs when they scrambled out of collapsing or burning houses. Mother was not sure if it was safe to go. "What if it explodes while we are there? We have to be sure not to go too close."

The plane was totally burned out. It was actually quite small; one wing was gone. There was no tail either. In the cockpit sat a burned human figure, slumped over the controls as if sleeping.

"He is dead, isn't he? He doesn't look like a man, he looks so young. I feel sorry for him; I can't hate him for what he did. Can you, Mom?"

As I looked into my mother's face, I saw big tears running down her cheeks, "He probably did not like to do what he did. All soldiers get orders and they are shot if they don't obey them. His mother will never see him again. She will never find out what happened to him. They will just tell her that he is "missing in action." She will not be able to bring flowers to his grave, just like so many people around here. Oh God, what is the world coming to…?"

She took my hand and we walked back home. She talked to me seriously as if to an adult and I felt very special.

That afternoon I sneaked away on my own, picked wild daisies, buttercups and horsetail and bound it all together with a long piece of grass. I felt drawn to the plane and went as close as I dared, threw the bouquet into the open cockpit towards the dead man and told him, "This is from your mom."

I stood there for a moment actually feeling silly because he was dead, he could not hear me and then, suddenly it hit me that my parents could be shot if anybody had seen me and reported it. I turned and ran as fast as I could down the hill, stumbled, fell, scraped my knees, got up, cried and hoped that I would get away with it.

I was much more scared about the war now and had a premonition of terrible things to come that up to now had always happened far away from us.

Otto Puff

Stresow had a funny character who folks called the village idiot. He was around twenty years old and known as "Otto Puff." Puff was not his real name. Otto would walk up and down the village road, swing one of his legs and let go of one of his wooden clogs and call out, "Otto – puff," while doing it. Then he would walk up to his clog, put it back on and do it again, all day long. The village kids would run after him and yell with him, "Otto – puff."

Once I was in the group chasing him. My father saw me and warned me that he would take his own wooden clog to my behind if he ever saw me teasing Otto again. He explained to me that Otto was mentally retarded. Surely, he did not use those words. He said, "He doesn't have all his cups in his cupboard." It is the equivalent of the English version, "He is not the sharpest knife in the drawer."

He lived with his grandmother in the Almshouse. She was afraid of the day the dreaded men in the brown shirts would come to pick him up. People whispered about this happening to physically or mentally challenged people in the big cities. They would bring them to concentration camps or certain clinics and there they were put to sleep. It was part of Hitler's aim to "clean up the Aryan race."

Our Otto Puff met a very different type of end.

8: The Fall of 1944

September saw us back in school with lots of new children because of the refugees who had found a place in the village and stayed. Some were just sleeping in barns and helping the farm women who took them in. They were happy to have food and shelter. I was now in grade five, felt proud and very grown up because of helping my father with his daily bookkeeping. He allowed me to add up the long pages in his journal. He hardly ever found a mistake and no, there were no calculators or adding machines to make the chore easy. I thought it was fun.

A number of people wanted to leave the village and go further west to stay with relatives but nobody was allowed to leave. With exciting talks about "Wunder-Waffen" (miracle weaponry), the Propaganda Minister Goebbels tried to pull the wool over people's eyes but most of them knew by now there was no way Germany could win the war. You would be dead if you even breathed about what you were thinking and everyone pretended in conversations.

The country was fighting on too many fronts and had lost too many men. The worst mistake was the invasion of Russia. People would whisper, "Did they not learn from Napoleon's experience? Russia in winter is impossible to take."

The war was becoming a war of desperation. The Hitler Youth were still enamoured with Hitler and so the army enlisted younger and younger men. The air defence was mainly done by schoolboys, fourteen and fifteen years old. Many years later, I met one of them. He was fifteen years old, his whole class was in the trench in Hanau close to Frankfurt shooting at the bombers and every single one was killed the day after he had been taken to the field hospital with pneumonia. He told me that he had felt embarrassed and ashamed that he survived. His brother had died in a submarine. The German front retreated, moved back through Poland and spilled over the borders into Germany closely followed by the Russian army. My Aunt Irene was drafted to become a Red Cross nurse. Her small grocery shop not far from the Polish border had closed.

Jewellery and valuables

It was a Sunday afternoon and Father had asked the refugees staying with us to come to our living room. There was Aunt Erika and her daughter Ingrid from Berlin and the Grandfather with Betty and Helen from East Prussia. I did not like Helen, I had caught her repeatedly trying to seduce my father and she had succeeded in becoming very close to Granny. The relationship between my mother and Granny had cooled off because of it.

My father explained to everyone that the battlefront was coming ever closer and he suggested they bury all jewellery and valuables in the garden. He wanted everybody to be part of this and asked how each one felt about it. They agreed it should be done and they would be witness to the digging so each one would know where it was. I could not understand why they should all know because they did not even have anything to bury. It turned out to be just our stuff; Mother had very little jewellery except one bracelet I had my eye on and the family silver. We children were not to be part of it and I always felt it was not fair in case I ever had to unearth it in future years when the war was over. I knew so much of everything and now I was left out.

Christmas

Home economics and crafts were new activities in school taught by a volunteer woman. We learned to make dolls from old silk stockings and balls from rags. We stuffed them with wood chips or shavings, sawdust or small pieces of leftover snippets from the tailor. He had a wooden leg from WW I and therefore was never drafted. The toys we made were collected by the newly formed Stresow "Red Cross Women" and were meant to be given to children who would otherwise have absolutely nothing under the Christmas tree, if they even had one.

I had my own eye on a woman with five children of different ages, all less than ten years old. I made something for each one at home and put all of it in an empty potato sack. We sisters donated some of our own toys; Granny gave us some of the boy cousins' things and my mother put some clothing in it as well. I dressed in Father's big sheepskin coat, which almost drowned me. I put his fur hat on and, wearing a false homemade beard, went to the house not too far from ours where this family had two small rooms and a kitchen. The family who had lived there before had lost their father early in the war and the mother had applied for and received permission to move to her sister in the Rhineland. How lucky she was!

It was Christmas Eve. It was snowing very lightly and I felt very Christmassy. We had gone to the church service earlier that evening. I was Josef in the Christmas play and had actually wanted to be an angel. But I got my "kick" by going to "my family's house" with a ho-ho-ho. My voice was not loud enough so they did not hear me and I had to knock on the window with my cane. When they finally all stood in the open door, I emptied the sack at their feet. The children's eyes were so big and the woman started crying, hugged me and whispered, "Thank you so much you dear child." Didn't she see I was Santa?

That made me cry too and I quickly left. Unfortunately, some of the village bullies were out by then. They saw me, and called, "Look at that little Santa, hey little Santa, little Santa wait…."

They started chasing me, throwing snowballs and saw me running up my father's long driveway. Now they knew who I was and after the holidays were over, they teased me, pushed me and rolled me in the snow, rubbed my face with it and stuffed it into my collar.

Thinking back, the year 1944 had an exciting spring because of baby Edith; a hot summer with lots of new responsibilities and shocking experiences. The fall was strange. Somehow, people became very quiet and I saw many people crying in the church and in the grocery shops when I was there to get something for Mother. Almost every family had lost a father, a husband and one or even more, sons.

The LAST YEAR of my childhood was 1944. But I did not know that then.

9: The Russians are Coming

During the month of January 1945, the Russians made rapid advances into Germany. They came from the south through Czechoslovakia and Bohemia, crossing the upper Oder River. From the East, they advanced through East Prussia. They came from West Prussia and Saxony heading towards the lower Oder River in their push to reach Berlin before the Allied forces did, as demanded by Stalin. Eisenhower let this happen. The German army was forced to retreat, and they blew up all the bridges once they crossed the Oder River. Not all the German soldiers made it and they were just mowed down. The fighting was cruel and the losses on both sides were massive.

For my eleventh birthday on the 24th of January, none of my aunts or cousins came from the city to visit as was customary. There was the risk of being robbed or even killed by German deserters. People whispered about having seen some lone men in German uniforms here and there and it was reason enough for everybody to stay safely at home.

A few days later, on Saturday, January 27th, our teacher announced that the school would be closed, permanently. He explained that the Red Cross would turn it into a field hospital in order to treat casualties as the front was coming closer. Mr. König had tears in his eyes when he, with a breaking voice, said to us, "Goodbye, children. May God be with you and your families. We might never see each other again."

When we left the school, Mr. König shook our hands instead of looking at the usual "Heil Hitler" from our side. We all cried on the way home, even the boys. That afternoon the church doors were wide open despite the cold and the organ was played with "all the stops pulled", as the village folk said. Mr. König had been the village organist for a very long time and had played the organ every Sunday. Now he played it every day and, as a matter of fact, that is where the Russians found him, his wife sitting by his side.

Christel was very much afraid of thunderstorms; she always took cover somewhere and cried. She was a nervous wreck and did not stop shaking because there was constant "thunder" for the whole week and every day it got louder. Granny, sighing deeply, said, "Aaah, I wish it would be just that, thunder." We were not allowed to leave the house or go sleighing on the mill hill.

Granny had a big framed photograph of her son Curt in his fancy German army uniform. Father told her to destroy it because if the Russians would see it they would just as soon shoot all of us. She promised, but she just could not do it. She confided in me, "Gila, I feel I am killing my own son if I burn his picture."

She had taken it off the wall and Dad believed the deed was done. I had fed my Hitler postcard to the stove fire a long time ago and I had watched it curl in the flames.

My father and I were in the smithy when Fritz, the pub owner and my father's long-time friend, came by in his carriage, with his mother. He stopped in front of the big door. We both went out to meet him.

"I am leaving, Erich. Forget everything, take your family and come along. The front is very close. Let's still try to get away."

Father was quiet for a moment, looking at Fritz and then answered, "Fritz, they will shoot you," meaning the 'Volkssturm', people who were our neighbours.

"No, Fritz, I'll stay and hope for the best." He held me tightly by my hand.

Father and Fritz were part of the Volkssturm too, but neither had ever lifted a hand or listened to complaints, they had always been way too busy helping where help was needed. People knew it.

Fritz left but he was back within an hour, pale as a ghost and stopping at the smithy again.

"Erich," he said, "it's too late. We are surrounded."

I saw them, Daddy, Daddy, I saw them

It was the second of February 1945. My parents were in the kitchen and we children were alone in the living room. The "thunder" was louder than ever. I climbed up on a chair in order to look out of the upper part of the window. I could see the road from the city towards our village. My heart stopped as I saw them – long rows of tanks, cannons, all kinds of big army vehicles, trucks and jeeps, all flying red Russian flags seemingly endless. I was so shocked that I tumbled down and my pleated skirt caught on the back of the chair. I could not free myself. I called out for my mother and Christel cried out in her loud way. Both my parents came running this time. Dad freed me from the chair and scolded me for being up there in the first place.

"You know you should not be at the window. If you are seen, you'll be shot. They shoot at everything that moves!"

I was shaking and stuttered, "I saw them Dad, I saw them, lots of cannons. Daddy, Daddy, there are so many, they are like a long black snake all the way to the city…"

Father took one look and immediately took charge, telling the children to stay put. He ordered Mother to get all the others to the living room and told Peter to find Granny. He grabbed my hand and pulled me towards the stairs to the attic.

"You will help me fix the big white bed sheet to the windowsill upstairs."

"Hurry," he called out to my mother, "Else, hurry – hurry!"

It was "verboten" to leave the village and it was "verboten" to put white bed sheets out of your windows. The villagers knew that. If Master Erich was the first to do it, then it was safe for everybody to follow suit. He was the only one that had a glimpse of the road from the city at this end of the village. But everyone also knew that now they were not facing the Volkssturm but the real enemy.

Dad shocked me by hugging me tightly after he had nailed the bed sheet to the windowsill. Hugging was rare in our family. When Dad and I came back to the living room, they were all there: Aunt Erika with her daughter Ingrid, the old grandfather with Betty and Helen, Peter, my sisters, and my mother but not Granny.

"Master, I can't find her, she is not in the house; I have been calling but she doesn't answer."

Erich ran out to the yard and yelled, "Mother…." At that moment, she came out of the garage. I could tell that Father almost choked, "My God, Mother, the Russians are almost here, what have you been doing in the garage, you were supposed to be with the children."

He sounded very upset and angry. She continued walking, gave him a kind of sideways cold look and mumbled, "That's my business."

Pale and quiet, they all sat around the table. Mother sat in one corner of the sofa with the baby in one arm and my sister Ingrid in the other. Granny took the other corner. She held Christel, who hid her face under Granny's arm close to her. I was somewhat standing alone but close to Dad who advised everybody to just sit still, be very quiet, not scream, cry, or yell, and not say anything.

A lot of shooting went on when they entered and moved into the village. We did not know what they would be shooting at but I remembered Father's words about "anything that moves."

We first heard them coming from Granny's part of the house; they came with heavy booted but halting footsteps through one room after the other. The way the floors squeaked, I knew exactly where they were. All the doors had been left open. The last door between the master bedroom and the living room had been removed a long time ago and had been replaced with two heavy brocade curtains from either side so that, when left open at night, the heat from the living room could dissipate into the bedroom. Right now, this curtain was closed.

Uri Uri

The footsteps stopped just on the other side of the curtain. Then, very s l o w l y the barrel of a machine gun poked through and the point of a bayonet above it slowly pulled the curtain aside. They stared at us as we stared at them. My father raised his arms as did Peter and the old man. The Russians pushed into the room; there were seven of them. Some held us at gunpoint while others searched the men. They looked very different than we had expected. They had slanted eyes, darker skin and thick uniforms. Later we learned that they were from Mongolia.

One started to speak and it sounded very different too, guttural sounds with lots of rrrr's and pppp's coming from deep within his throat. They wanted something and kept asking, but we couldn't understand them and just did not know what it was. Dad looked very helpless; I had never seen him like that and so I started to cry. One of the Russians said something very harsh to me and I just couldn't help it, I soundlessly cried more. Large heavy tears rolled down my cheeks into my collar but I kept my big hazel eyes on the soldier. Suddenly he turned around, looked at my mother for a long moment, gave an order and then they left towards our hall and the kitchen beyond.

It only took minutes until other heavy footsteps came through all the rooms and we saw them through the now open curtain. These were younger men with lighter skin and held their guns with bayonets at the ready. One was blond with blue eyes and he held out a bag in his hands.

"Uri uri!" he said with urgency in his voice, "Uri uri!"

We had no idea what he wanted. Just then the grandfather clock chimed three times: Quarter to three.

"Uri uri!" he repeated, pointed at the grandfather clock and made a sign of it getting smaller. Father got it. He wanted watches. Three were offered. "Uri uri…," it was not enough, my father lifted his hands, let them drop for the sign "no more." Aunt Erika offered her necklace and it was accepted. Then they took the wedding bands from Mom, Aunt Erika and the grandfather. Because of his type of work, Dad never wore one. Another soldier came through and had Dad's alarm clock in his hand, playing with the buttons and screws on the backside.

"Uri uri?" He asked. (Uri – in German Uhr – clock)

Finally, they understood there were no more. He put the alarm clock in the bag as well and they left through the door to our hallway. I watched them and suddenly the alarm clock started ringing. They threw the bag to the floor and gunfire hit like a whip. Father pressed my face into his stomach because now I started to cry hysterically.

The bullets left holes in the brick floor.

Screams in the middle of the night

Somehow, the day gave way to a nervous evening. The Russians carried off quite a few sausages and hams. With longing eyes, we watched them go, and I looked at my mother. She knew what I was thinking. A few soldiers stayed and had their guns poised. That night our whole family, Father, Mother, and all three children slept in my parents' big bed snuggled up to each other, glad that it had not been worse. Baby Edith slept in her crib next to Mother's bed, with just the nightstand in between them. Granny slept on the sofa in the living room, and Peter, rolled up in a blanket, slept on the floor. Aunt Erika and Ingrid, who normally lived in Lisa's old room, had brought a mattress into the living room. The Grandfather with Betty and Helen occupied the converted dining room on the other side of the hallway, next to the kitchen. The big sideboard had been moved from the dining room into the living room to make room for beds when we had taken them in. Granny's suite, Lisa's room and our children's room were full of Russians.

It was very dark when some horrible screams woke me up. At first, I thought I had a bad dream. I was wrong – the others were awake and had heard the screams too. Father hushed us up and whispered, "Please, please be quiet."

He pulled us closer. Christel and Ingrid slipped under the blankets and covered their heads with the feather duvet. Father had his arm around Mother's shoulders with the baby now between them and I was on his other side. We were all very close together. Mother begged Father not to do anything and to just let happen what would happen to her, as long as we were alive after it.

We heard some loud cursing and then the front door opened, only to shut with a loud bang a moment later. Several Russians came from the children's room through our bedroom with flashlights. One soldier stopped and walked around to my mother's bedside. He sneaked into bed beside her. The others went on to the living room. Something was going on in there because Granny was crying "No, no" and Aunt Erika made noises as if someone was hurting her. There was a shout, like an order, and then, the Russians who had come through our room went out into the hall. It was a very noisy night. When I touched my father's face, it was wet with tears.

Our hearts felt like they had been beating at a hundred beats per second.

The screams had come from Betty and Helen. Several soldiers had raped them. The old man had tried to protect his granddaughters but he was brutally beaten. When he was unconscious they just threw him out the door, while the others stood in line and went on with their business. Aunt Erika had been smart enough to just submit to it.

To our horror, Betty and Helen's grandfather was dead and frozen stiff when we found him in the morning.

Congregation around a manure pile

During the late morning, with guns and bayonets they herded everybody into a neighbouring farmer's yard. More than half of the villagers must have been there. People carefully whispered to each other about things that had happened the previous day. One of the twins, who had helped to wean me off the baby bottle, had been standing at the window and had been shot dead. Ruth, who was a girl from grade eight, who so far had sprouted only one breast and had been teased about it by the bullies, was dead. She was raped so many times that she died in the process and they just went on raping her. Not one woman, no matter how old, was spared. Even children my age and younger had been raped. Men, fathers, brothers, or friends who had tried to intervene were simply shot.

A small group of underground communists had lined up to welcome the rescuers from the Nazis, but machine gun fire mowed them down. Otto Puff, who had donned his Sunday suit and stood in the middle of the road at attention with his right arm raised in the Hitler salute to greet the oncoming tanks, was flattened. An SS man had forcefully entered a house, demanding civilian clothing. He was in his underwear and hid under a bed when the Russians came in. They saw his uniform, shot several women in the household, as well as three children and then poked the bed with a bayonet until they had him. They kept stabbing until the blood ran out from under the bed. Mr. König was forced to keep playing the organ in the church while the Russians stood in line and raped his wife next to him.

All of us were standing halfway around the big manure pile waiting for whatever was going to happen. They brought Freddie, the farmer's son, his little sister and his mother out of the house. They were placed by themselves so that they could see all of us and vice versa. Nobody knew that the father was at home having deserted from the army. He was naked when they brought him out from a stable. The poor man could hardly walk. His back had bloody streaks across it. I remembered our whip and thought we should have burned it. He was shamefully hanging his head. A sound of anguish went through the crowd and his wife could not suppress a cry like a wounded animal. They placed him on top of the manure pile and bound him to a pitchfork that they had stuck in it.

A Russian spoke to us in German, explaining, "This man is a bad Nazi and he has denied it. He hid his uniform but we found it. And now we will punish him as a deterrent for everybody."

The uniform was not an SS uniform but that did not make any difference. A couple of Russians went up to him and started whipping him. First, he tried to just take it but then he lifted his face up to the sky, opened his mouth and let out a terrible scream. I was reminded of a picture of Jesus on the cross when He cried out, "My God! My God! Why hast thou forsaken me?"

Two Russians held him up, one on each side and a third one cut off his penis, threw it onto the dung crushed it with his boot and then proceeded to cut off the rest of the genitals. I did not see the rest of the punishment because my dad had pushed my face into his tummy. I was sobbing.

The screams of this man and his family followed me for years in my nightmares.

Rob, rape and kill

When we walked home, dazed by what we had witnessed, Granny was very pale. The next few days just saw more of the same. Raid the cellars and the smoke houses, drink the wine, rape the women and kill the men. All were activities ordered by Stalin. His soldiers had never been allowed to go home on leave since they had been conscripted. No relief and their hormones and the order to do whatever they wanted drove them to destruction.

They were like mad animals.

No, animals are much better than these men were. When our rooster was chasing a hen, the hen would be running like crazy and when he caught up with her she would duck; he would jump her, bite into her head and do what roosters do. What he put into her we would see in our Sunday egg or, if a hen would breed, resulted in a cute little chirping chick. The hen would get up afterwards, shake her feathers, cackle a bit and go back to her flock. The rooster would walk around as if he was the biggest gift to the hens. Maybe he was. They all got their turn, one at a time. But the Russians just couldn't get enough, and did not even mind standing in line while their superiors came first. There seemed to be a hierarchy even within the same army rank. There were not enough women for these thousands of needy men. So the same woman was raped over and over again. If she would beg to be put out of her misery after a dozen rapes, the next Russian, disgusted by this request, would say, "We don't shoot women."

One of the Russians sleeping in our house came with a faucet. He held it against the wall and motioned to my father to attach it to get "water from wall." He got angry when Father tried to explain that this is impossible.

They discovered Father's car and came to fetch him and start it. Since he couldn't, he talked about the bad Nazis who had taken the battery by showing them the empty spot. Quite unhappy, they left but soon came back with a horse. With my mother's laundry line, they tied the horse to the car and then pulled it out of the garage and away. We children were standing at the window watching this spectacle and thought it was funny. Father had tears in his eyes. A car pulled by a horse? Yes, talk about horsepower. We had no idea what they did with it.

We were practically prisoners in our own house but at least we were not turned out. Yet.

Granny shot

Oh God, they had found the big photograph of Curt in his fancy army uniform. Granny had hidden it under the hay in the loft above the garage. We saw them come across the yard carrying it. My father turned snow white and looked at his mother – she lifted her hands and her shoulders and let them fall again, eyes to the ground.

"Oh Mother," was all Father said.

They came into the room, looked at my father and exclaimed, "You – Nazi!"

They took all of us into the children's room with the dark blue wallpaper with the silver and brown specks. The officer who had raped Aunt Erika (who had not resisted him) was there. She smiled at him. He was very serious and said that he has to report us to the "commandante" and we would all be shot because we were hiding this picture.

Our Polish man, Peter, started anxiously to speak out in his language, pointed to my dad and repeatedly said, "Master nyet Nazi, Master karashow man, Master karashow, Master nyet Heil Hitler, Master nyet this man," shaking his head and pointing to the picture…

After a while, the officer looked at Granny, "Sin?" Peter answered for her, "Da da, sin, malysh, Matka malysh" nodding his head repeatedly and pointing at her. (Nyet-no, karashow-good, da – yes, sin – son, malysh – baby)

The officer said something to the soldiers who had brought the picture. They pulled their pistols and pointed them to Granny's head. She was wringing her hands, looking down and saying nothing. She did not even know what was happening and it all happened so fast. Two shots rang out. Blood spurted hitting the dark blue wallpaper with the silver and brown spots. Granny fell. They had just grazed her cheek and temple, but she was bleeding profusely. She looked at Dad and whispered, "Sorry, Erich. I am so very sorry." Then she blacked out.

We stood there – frozen – expecting to be shot next.

Sixteen to sixty to Siberia

The women had to cook and work for the Russians staying in our house and barns. They held guns to any of the women's back and took them to the outhouse. They pointed for them to clean it. None of us could understand why the seat was always covered with feces. We were allowed to use the pail in the kitchen since the Russians came. Aunt Erika had made "friends" with the highest officer and we were now protected by him. I was sure my mother had not been raped again and I convinced myself she had not been raped at all. There had been no noise or movement when the Russian had sneaked into her bed. I heard her tell Father it had been a very young man and he had just snuggled up, lost it and cried. I was not quite sure what she meant but I was always around watching.

My mother had to milk our two cows and we were allowed to keep some of the milk. Mother was still nursing Edith. The Russians were smart enough to know it wouldn't be wise to kill all animals and besides, there was enough to eat. They knew they only had a few days of respite and other hungry comrades would come when they went on their way towards Berlin. The "thunder" had not stopped yet and the fighting was still going on just a few kilometres away at the other side of our village.

On February 5th, everyone had to come to the village square. Men and women from sixteen to sixty were separated from nursing mothers and apparently unfit or sick people who had to step aside. We children were very happy when our mother came back home. Nursing mothers were not taken away, so because of baby Edith we still had our mother. Aunt Erika had kept her officer company and escaped the tragedy. Helen also had a high-ranking officer friend. Betty never came back. Father was gone. We never saw Peter again. All the chosen villagers were loaded into trucks and taken away on the road to the city.

Nobody knew where these people would be taken but the talk was about Siberia. Years later we found out they actually spent four weeks at the military airport in Königsberg, (now Chojna) fourteen kilometers away, removing the rubble from the bombing and making the runways usable. Then they were taken to Siberia.

10: Frau Komm

Only Mother, we three children, the baby, Granny, Aunt Erika and her daughter, Ingrid, were left. Our father was gone and we never saw or heard from Peter again. Betty and Helen did not come back to our house either. It was a very sad day and we all felt more than a little lost. The same Russians were still in our house. We felt safer because of it and somehow there was a strange sense of normalcy. When they wanted a woman now they would just look at one and say, "Frau komm." (Woman, come…) This was not the rough raping of the first few days; there was no denying this request. It was an order with usually a pistol pointing in the direction the woman was to go.

My mother had started to put silver paper from cigarette boxes (very thin aluminium foil that used to be an inner cover of cigarette boxes) over some teeth. She pulled her straight, almost black hair tight over her scalp and braided it into a bun at the back with a dark scarf over it. The scarf was put on the way Orientals do, covering the forehead down to the eyebrows. She looked years older than she was and the Russians started to call her "Matka" (Mother). Granny had become Baboushka and we kids loved the sound of it. She was still weak and pale but the facial abrasions from the shots had started to heal. The women had to continue to cook and clean and even wash the Russians' underclothing but we were not starving. That was a great gift.

A few days after our father was taken away, the atmosphere changed and everything seemed different because it was unusually quiet. The constant "thunder" which had troubled poor Christel had stopped. The Russians grew restless and got their trucks ready; Aunt Erika's officer friend shouted orders and said "Dosvedanya" (Goodbye) to us. He mentioned Berlin and we understood there would be many new Russians coming, all heading for Berlin. After they left, endless rows of trucks, tanks and columns of soldiers went through our village for hour upon hour.

First eviction

The newcomers ordered us to vacate the house and leave the village. With a handcart and the baby carriage, we walked off, not knowing where to go. On the back road, we joined the other villagers who had also been evicted and just aimlessly kept walking. It was February and the earth was frozen solid with not much snow. After three or four hours trekking we came upon a row of small houses with fenced back gardens: broken windows, damaged roofs, no doors and no people. My mother called out, "Gila don't look to your right, keep your eyes down and watch where you step…."

I was pushing the baby carriage and because of the warning, I surely did take a look to the right. I stopped dead in my tracks and stared at a German soldier sitting against the fence with his head beside him on the ground. He had no legs either. Those were on the other side of the baby carriage. From the legs, I looked across the field. There were dozens of dead German soldiers, also heads, arms and other pieces of bodies. Thank God they were frozen. This was the area where the "thunder" had been coming from for the last week. It was here where the last of the German army had fought the mighty Russians, who outnumbered them by six or seven to one while trying to get to and cross the Oder River on the way to Berlin. The retreating German army had blown up all the bridges to slow the Russian advance and therefore many German soldiers were caught on the east side of the river and did not make it across either.

I had to move on like so many people with handcarts before and after me. We had to keep going, pushed forward by the people behind us. After about five kilometers and with the light failing as the evening fell upon us we came to another village. We saw a small house with lots of women and children standing around it. We joined them and asked if we could stay the night.

"The more the merrier," replied one woman, "at least we might get away with just one Russian raping each of us."

There must have been forty or so women and children in the not very large living room. The Russians who locked us in occupied the rest of the house. Everybody slept on the bare floor rolled up in a blanket very close together like sardines in a can or sat against the wall. I felt very lucky to have a place under a table with my sister Christel and several other children. My friend Ingrid did not leave her mother's side. Under the table, nobody could step on us.

The women talked about the fighting that had gone on close by. The Russians had taken care of their own dead and buried them but nobody was allowed to touch, remove the dog tags from their necks or bury the Germans. The topic uppermost on their minds was the raping. A horrible story one of the women related and she had witnessed, was that her neighbour had whispered to her would be rapist, "Syphilis, syphilis …."

He had just shot her and turned to the next woman. One of the Russians in the house spoke German. One older woman asked him why the Russians would rape young children as well as old grandmothers. He shrugged his shoulders, spread his arms and replied matter of factly:

"Frau is Frau. (woman is woman) Has hole."

A ghost at the window

The two windows in our room had shutters and in the middle of the night, one of the shutters was opened from the outside and a Russian voice kept urging us, "Frau, open up, open up. Now just one soldier, in one minute, two minutes, lots and lots of Russian soldiers. Open up, Frau, open up."

Everybody was afraid this man might shoot his way in and kill several of us in the process. This soldier might not have known that the rest of the house was full of his comrade Russians. The woman who had invited us in banged on the door of our locked room. One of the Russians on the other side opened it and looked at us. Many women started screaming and pointed to the window. Then all hell broke loose.

They did not come into our room but went outside to where the soldier was at the window. The women were very anxious and afraid of raping after this interlude. Shouting and shooting lasted maybe a minute and then all was quiet again and our door was re-locked without anyone coming in after all.

In the very early morning the Russians started up their machinery, unlocked our door and the German speaking man told us to leave, "All go, dway, dway." (hurry, hurry)

This time our path went through a forest. We saw dead soldiers here and there curled up behind boulders or old trees, injured, who had bled or frozen to death. We children were admonished not to look at them. After some hours, Granny recognized the Stresow forest where she had often been mushrooming. She took us to the bottom of our mill hill. Home again? Really? But now, what's next?

As far as we knew there was not a single German person left in Stresow. We had no idea what was going on in our house and what kind of Russians would be occupying it. After some time discussing what to do, Granny offered to check it out. She just walked up the narrow footpath taking the risk of being shot while we waited down by the caved-in bunker. It was a cold overcast day with not even a glimpse of the winter sun. Everything around us was dull and grey. The trees stretched their empty branches towards each other and we were shivering inside and out.

A feeling of doom and gloom settled over us and the quiet conversation between my mother and Aunt Erika petered out. After what seemed like an hour we saw Granny coming down the footpath, smiling! SMILING! That truly could only mean one thing and we all looked at her expectantly.

Home again

The Russians had converted our house into a field hospital. A young Russian soldier had taken Granny to the doctor because of her facial wounds, one of which had become infected and was starting to fester. The doctor spoke to her in German, "How you wounded? When happen? How you know here hospital and doctor?"

She told him the truth and he looked at her for a long time. He treated her and was amazed to learn that she had not known that there was a doctor and that this was not the reason she had come to the house. He listened to her story about finding out if she and her family could stay somewhere in our house or even the barn because it was cold. There were small children and a baby and we did not know where else to go or what to do. She told him that all three women would be willing to work, clean and do anything they could to earn their keep.

"There still must be a God," she exclaimed as she returned, "and this was the reason why I was shot. He led me to this doctor. We can stay in the attic of our workers' house. We must not be seen during the day, but we will be able to come out in the late evening to stretch our legs and get some fresh air as long as we do not go into the village and we keep the children from being boisterous. When it is safe, a soldier will come to pick up us women to help with the cooking, milk the last cow, feed the remaining small pigs and do other work as needed."

Imagine what an utter relief this must have been for the three women with five children in their care. They were overwhelmed with joy and we children envisioned living in the attic as a big adventure.

11 : Life in the Attic

There was only one small window in the gable of the attic so we would sit close to it when we needed light. The roof slanted and touched the floor on both sides. Mother warned us not to push against the tiles or snow and rain would make it very uncomfortable for us. We had to be careful to walk on the beams holding up the ceiling of the room below in order not to crash through. Large boards had been put in place and straw from the barn was spread across it to sleep on. We thought that previously the Russians must have used it for sleeping quarters as well. With the blankets and pillows we had carried on our handcart, we were reasonably comfortable.

A wooden ladder with wide rungs leaned against the wall and a trap door had to be pushed up to open for us to enter the attic. There was a big heavy chest full of workmen's clothing and old dresses from Mrs. Richter. We were supposed to pull it on top of the trap door for our own protection. We did use some of the garments when we took our own off for the night. Sometimes a Russian would come up the ladder and knock, calling "Frau come" but we were not allowed to acknowledge that we were up there and always kept as quiet as mice.

During the long boring days in the attic, we would pretend to be "monkeys" and take turns to check each other for head lice. We did have a very tight little comb from the nice doctor but mostly we picked the lice and cracked them between our thumbnails, looked for nits and tried to get them off each other's hair. It was not easy since my mother, Christel and I had very long braids. The idea of cutting them off did not even enter our minds. Aunt Erika, her daughter Ingrid and my sister

Ingrid had short hair but they had lice as well. We would take our clothing off, turn it inside out and check all the seams for lice. We had no chance of washing either ourselves or the clothing we wore. Hygiene was something that got lost during those weeks. A pail had been provided for our bodily functions and in the evening, we carried up a pail half-full of cold water from the pump to be able to at least wash our hands and faces.

The first evening when we were allowed out, I noticed many of our photographs on the manure pile. They used to be in a big silver bowl on the sideboard in the living room. I climbed up onto the pile and collected as many as I could and cleaned them. Some had cracks in them but it did not matter. They became my personal treasure and they are the only pictures of our life before the war that exist in our family.

Are they any different?

My friend Ingrid and I had seen so much raping going on without actually ever having seen the "thing" because the Russians never pulled their pants down. Sometimes they opened the pants in the front or not even that, just did it through the fly. Since we were all girls, we had never even seen a naked boy, let alone a fully-grown man. We were wondering what the Russians' genitals looked like that caused all women so much trouble and how they had even killed with it. One evening we happened to see a Russian enter the outhouse. Sneaking up and quietly opening the lower door, we looked in but did not see anything, just the shit falling down into the box. The splash it made caught us in the face. My mother would have said, "that serves you right," if she had known about it.

We learned nothing about how Russian men were "built" but we did discover that they stood, or squatted, on what for us was the seat which accounted for the feces all around the hole as their aim could not have been accurate, even if they tried.

Faithful in adversity

One day when Mother and Aunt Erika were picked up in the very late afternoon by the appointed Russian to accompany them to work, my friend Ingrid and I begged him to let us out to help them muck out the stable. Since it was not long to our allowed evening outing, he agreed and we promised to stay close to our mothers. The women did not know but we managed to follow and watch them. Two soldiers, both called Ivan, had become friendly with Ingrid and me. One Ivan was twenty-eight years old, tall and blond and I had a crush on him and did not like it when he disappeared with Aunt Erika into the barn. The other was a few years older and dark haired, more of a father type. I think he was envious of the blond Ivan. Aunt Erika fell for the young blond one. That evening when my mother was milking the cow, Aunt Erika told her about the blond Ivan, how good he was at "it" and excitedly recommended him, "Else, you should try it."

Ingrid and I were listening and watching them. Mother shook her head and answered in a low sad tone, "Erika, I really don't want to do that kind of thing. I love Erich. He promised he would come back and he keeps his promises. Yes, you are right, he might not come back, but I have no desire. You know I have four children. The whole situation is bad enough. If you need sex and enjoy it with Ivan, I do not blame you for it. But don't you think of your husband – what and how much will you tell him?"

"Else, I have not seen or been with him for years because of this damned war. I am thirty-five and not getting any younger and I like to have some kind of life, even if this life is not what I had hoped for and, for heaven's sake, at least it's not rape. I am just making the best of a very bad situation. And think about it, Else, my friendship with ONE officer has kept Gila and Ingrid as well as you safe and all of us from being ravished by a whole company of rapists."

Ingrid and I stole away because we felt very guilty listening to this intimate conversation. Ingrid was very embarrassed and ashamed of her mother and, almost crying, promised, "I'll tell my dad everything when we get back to Berlin after the war."

For me, it really drove home the fact that Aunt Erika was very important for our safety. I warned her, "Ingrid, don't do that. I think it would be much better if you don't tell your dad because if he gets mad at your mom you can lose your family."

The blond Ivan called me "Gisillisi" because he could not say "Gisela" but for all the others I was Liza. One day Ivan brought me some bows for my braids. I remember thinking, "Which family in Stresow would have wrapped their presents with such fancy bows?"

We surely never did.

Ivan, crouching in front of me to be at the same height smiled and asked me, "Gisillisi, do you want to go to the barn and play with me? I will show you something very exciting."

I was old enough, wise enough and had seen enough to know what that meant. I looked down at the bows in my hands and shook my head. He did not press the issue just kept smiling and said, "...if war over, I come marry you. You kid now but old eyes."

Often I saw the dark Ivan watching the blond one and shaking his head.

Stress relief

Granny helped the Russians in the kitchen and we never saw her during the day. Several soldiers were busy cooking meals for many dozens of men. They had what they called a "field kitchen" and it was placed not far from the pump. The food was always some kind of thick soup with barley. We called it "Russian soup with calf's teeth." One day it was turnips and potato with barley, the next day it was barley with potato and turnips. On the third day, it would be potato with barley and turnips. Our stores of food in the smoking chimney and cellars must have been quickly depleted. To add meat to their cooking, they started by killing one pig and just a few days later, another. When our pigs were gone, they brought some from the village.

Since we had come back, we had not seen any of Mother's beloved chickens, geese and ducks. The artificial eggs placed in each nest to entice the chickens to lay theirs there were still in place. I cannot even remember if there were any pigeons flying around. In the evening, we could hardly wait for Granny to come back from work because she always brought a canister full of hot soup or stew for us. We were starving! After six p.m., we were allowed to go outside and spend some time running around. The village was totally off limits. "Our" Russians would have been in big trouble if their comrades had seen us.

The fence between our yard and what used to be a pasture next to it was down and lots of trucks and tanks were parked there concealing the view of the village road in either direction. The Russians sat on garden chairs and old benches they must have picked up somewhere. One played my father's accordion and another one a balalaika. They sang Russian folksongs which I got to know and love. Some of my favourites were *Stenka Razin* and *Kalinka* and a third one of which I still remember the melody, but not the title or the words. Russian folk music is beautiful, somewhat sad but very romantic. Sometimes the music got livelier and they would dance the krakowiak. I tried to learn it. It was very difficult to throw my legs and arms into the air, hop with bent knees from one leg onto the other and back and forth like that or even be on the ground with my legs horizontally in the air and switch from holding myself up by one hand to the other – and fast! Needless to say, the guys sometimes killed themselves laughing at my antics.

One of the Russians brought us an old, totally rusted bike without tires. We took turns riding that thing around the yard, it creaked terribly and they had fun watching us fall and laughed. This bunch of soldiers seemed to love and enjoy us children. Maybe having us around made them forget the horrors they had gone through for a few hours, and maybe they were also thinking of the end of the war, going home and seeing their own families. Several of them were old enough to have children like us.

It was a very exciting evening when I saw my cat Mooshie under one of the trucks. I tried to grab her but she moved to hide behind another tire but always looked at me. I crouched, called, held my hand out, pleaded with her, placed a little plate with milk for her, but sadly my cat would not come out for about a week. I could not even sleep because I was thinking of what I could do to make her trust me again. I loved her so much and thought about the day when she brought her first four babies to me. She was always there when we were outside the next day, but she was now very shy. A little stray dog joined us too and never left again. For some unknown reason we called him Bruno.

Helen returns

This somewhat, dare I say, "idyllic" life must have gone on for nearly two months. The field hospital in our house remained while the flow of the Russian army through the village went on and on, which was why we had to remain hidden during the day since we were the only females and civilians for miles around.

Spring came. Trees and shrubs got leaves; the snowdrops bloomed and the crocuses came out. Then one day we had quite a shock. Helen, one of the granddaughters of the old man the first Russians had killed, walked across the yard with an officer. This officer talked to the doctor standing at the house door. After listening to the two of them, he lifted his arms, dropped them, nodded and went back inside. Helen and her officer disappeared but came back with a wagon pulled by an old, tired looking horse. It was during the day when we were not allowed to come out therefore we could not go to greet Helen. She and the officer took spades from the wagon and proceeded to walk around the house into our fruit tree garden.

"My goodness," my mother exclaimed, "she is going to dig out our valuables!"

Helen knew the location. Sure enough, it did not take very long and they came back with a couple of wooden boxes, which they placed on the wagon. Some other boxes were already loaded. They knocked on the door again, went in and came back out with my parents' rolled up rug from the dining room my parents had only used for special occasions like birthday parties or visits of relatives to see a new baby. They unrolled it and placed it over the wagon; then both climbed up and off they went. I looked at my mother and piped up with tears of anger in my eyes, "See Mother, now she stole all of our valuables. Why did Dad let all of them be part of the digging and I wasn't allowed to see it. They should never have known about it! I never liked her."

The war is almost over

It was a happy but very unsettling day when the doctor took Granny aside, "Baboushka, tomorrow we will dismantle hospital and continue go to Berlin. You can move into house again."

With that, our tranquility had been broken. Everything was so familiar now, we felt safe but we did not know what would happen next. The future was far from certain. Next, the doctor offered, "Erika, you and daughter want to come to city, go on train with us to Berlin? War is good as over. You go home, da?"(yes?)

The war was as good as over? This was indeed good news. The best news! All of us were very excited about it and thought that maybe Dad would come back soon. But we were very much afraid for Aunt Erika and Ingrid on their trip to Berlin with a train full of Russians. They had no idea if their home had been bombed or was still standing; no idea how they would find it in the rubble that was once Berlin after the bombing and the fighting. Would they starve because of lack of food or would they be subject to worse raping in Berlin than had ever happened in our area and that had been bad enough. The blond Ivan had told Aunt Erika about it. During the weeks with us, he had learned quite a bit of German just as we had picked up enough Russian words to communicate. He had also told her that now ten-year-old German Hitler Youth were fighting the Russians in Berlin because there was no army left.

Ivan was sure it was just a matter of days until they would be winning the war. As far as we were concerned, we thought they had won it already!

Aunt Erika and Ingrid, who had become my soul mate or my twin sister, had lived with us for several years and through some unbelievable horror. They had become closer than family and we were devastated to see them go. We could not envision our life without the optimism, the humour or the sheer "joi de vivre" with which Aunt Erika faced adversity. I know that without her my mother would never have made it. She had a way of always seeing the bright side even if there was none: riding out the storm or choosing the way of the least resistance. She always tried to cheer my mom, "Come on, Else, chin up, after this time there will be another better one."

We tried to convince them to stay with us until the war was truly over. Still, they decided to risk it and we felt terribly lost and lonely.

My mother cried a lot.

12: The End of an Era

Sleep in our own beds again

Our house was a mess. Granny and Mother tried to get everything back into a reasonable order. The sideboard in the living room had been tipped over and turned into a bed; some army blankets were still on it, full of lice. But it did not matter, we had them anyway. We all helped to get the sideboard upright again and stared at each other in shock when we heard the noise of the breaking dishes inside. Had my mother's "good china" been in it when it was tipped over? Yes, that's what happened – they had tipped it over with everything in it.

"Fine china doesn't mean anything to the Russians", my mother said. "What would they have used it for? And they couldn't take it to Berlin and God knows how long they would have to hide it until they could go home."

There was not one piece unbroken, no plate, no cup, no bowl. Father's desk must have been used as the operating table; there was lots of dried up blood on and all around it. The bedrooms were reasonably okay but some had more beds in them. The floor in the master bedroom had been lifted but was nailed down again. Once upon a time, there had been a cellar under it and the floor always moved and creaked when you walked across it so the Russians must have thought there were valuables hidden under it or, perhaps, more food. Grandfather had closed it off a long time ago when my father was a young lad. He had told me that he and his brother had had fun picking up rocks in the garden and dumping them down there but they never had enough to fill the old cellar.

Granny had worked in the kitchen so here things were not too bad. The shelves in the cold room were almost empty except for a box with long outdated, pudding powder. Several half-full barrels with legumes and flour made us very happy. We wondered about some odd items in small bags or cans but resourceful Granny would lick her forefinger and stick it in to taste it. One item really pleased my mother, "Salt" she was incredulous, "the body needs salt!" This bag became her "white gold."

Behind the wooden ladder to the attic were many cartons; some contained old toys, others cleaning rags, torn clothing, underwear and such. We cleared them out – and surprise-surprise! Under, and mixed in with a lot of junk, we found several salami sausages. They had the typical grey-whitish coating on them but since they were cooked and smoked, that did not affect the quality.

"My goodness, whoever has hidden these here? That must have been Father. Wow!"

Granny had taken over and she made sure we ate just a little bit of it each day in order not to get sick. Our stomachs surely were not used to this kind of food anymore. We enjoyed potatoes boiled in the skin and salami that day, what a feast it was. The sausages and hams from the smoking chimney were gone and the hundreds of glasses with preserves my mother had saved so diligently must have been very much enjoyed by our enemy. We still found a big pile of potatoes, a lot of them starting to rot, sugar beets and turnips in the cold cellar under the barn, and some carrots and red beets in the big sand boxes. The one cow my mother had been milking every day was still in the barn thanks to the nice doctor. Life did not look too bad.

Other Russians would sleep in all those beds every night on their way to Berlin, but after the masses that had moved through earlier it became a mere trickle now. The raping had almost stopped except for Berlin as long as there was fighting, part of the tactic the Russians used to wear down any resistance. The soldiers coming through our village now seemed very exhausted and tired. Every morning we heard the one in charge shouting orders to get them moving again. They usually brought their field kitchen with them and we would get some scraps. When we were alone Granny would bake bread and to save on flour she would mix cooked and grated sugar beets or turnips into the dough.

We would gobble it up when it was still warm. It surely gave us bloated stomachs and a lot of gas, but who cared?

It felt wonderful to change our clothing especially our underwear. Amazingly enough, many of our things were still in the chest of drawers. Father's suits and Mom's dresses were hanging in the big wardrobe as if nothing had happened. Dad loved sweaters but they were gone. Mom found some scented soap in her drawer that she had placed there to keep the moths at bay and she and Granny would heat water in the big "tip-kettle" to clean us all up and wash our hair. It was a real treat. It did not go over well with Christel though as she had thick wavy hair and the longest braids so it tangled and she cried bitterly. Lots of chopped wood was still piled up outside so we had no problem cooking or heating. The pump had held up and it still gave us clean water. Granny discovered bones from the slaughtered animals behind the barn and she and Mother proceeded to make soap to wash clothing. My cat was with us again and Bruno kept close and alerted us when someone came up the long driveway.

"Our" Russians had left about a week ago and there were not many new ones coming. Granny decided to risk a walk into the village to find out if other families had returned. My mother refused to leave us children because she was afraid that something could happen to her and she would not be able to come back. Granny met a few women and was surprised to learn that they also had lived hidden in their barns with the Russians and just like us had thought they were the only ones. She came back very excited, full of news and we had high hopes that, just maybe, there was a life after going through hell.

She had found out that there were still "storage mounds" in quite a few fields containing potatoes and yellow and white turnips. These mounds were common in Pomerania. Potatoes or turnips or sugar beets would be piled up, protected with straw and then covered with lots of earth. In spring, these mounds would be opened up and used for food, or in the case of potatoes, for planting. We wanted to go and raid them right away! We needed feed for our cow badly because her milk was just a trickle and it was important for baby Edith. Mother's milk had dried up some months ago. Granny and I sneaked off to save our family. We were not the only ones at the mound we went to but we heard some more news and went home with as much food as we could carry and tales to tell. These trips were repeated regularly. Our cow was a lot happier and we were too. In time, we became more daring and went openly with our handcart. Once when I was searching in the covering straw a mouse bit me in the right middle finger above the second joint and held tight. I screamed and shook my hand like crazy but it would not let go. Granny finally gave me stern advice, "Stop that! Place your hand on the ground and keep it still – the mouse is just as afraid as you are. It will let go if you don't move."

She was right, the mouse let go and I took my bent finger to my mouth and sucked on the bite, spat and sucked again and again. I guess I was lucky that I did not get an infection because I surely did not have a tetanus shot, but I do still have the scar.

We started preparing the garden to plant potatoes in order to grow something for the coming year. The fruit trees were in bloom, the bees were busy and Granny predicted, "If nothing else, we'll have a lot of fruit to live on until things get better again."

With all our hearts, we believed they would, if we only could get some seed for other vegetables! Granny found some turnip seeds in a large container in the tackle room and handled it like gold. She was planning to ask the other women coming to the storage mound if they had other seeds and were willing to exchange some.

A new army is coming

It was around the 20th of May 1945. We were not sure about the date because we had no calendar. We were busy in the kitchen when two soldiers in different uniforms from the Russians came in.

"Out, out" they commanded. "Ten minutes – out! And no come back. Polski rodzina come." (Rodzina = family)

They carried machine guns and one of those two had a gun with a bayonet pointed at us. We were stunned and did not know what was happening. We could not comprehend what they wanted us to do. Out? What did they mean by 'out'?

Well, they made sure we understood when they poked Granny with the bayonet, nodded towards the door and repeated, "Ten minutes – OUT!"

They grabbed my mother by the arm, shoved her towards the door and pushed us children in the same direction. It had not sunk in but Bruno made a lot of noise and was underfoot when my mother ordered, "Gila, lock Bruno in the barn, bring the handcart and hurry back; get some clothing for all of you, some warm things as well. I'll get some food and blankets and what else we might need. Granny, please help get the baby carriage out and settle Edith in it, her things, baby bottle, some food for her, you know, keep the kids close to you. Put the salt bag in the baby carriage on the bottom, we need salt. Oh God, Granny, what's happening now, ten minutes, we have to hurry I hope we think of everything."

It was pandemonium. I just flew through our rooms and drawers, grabbed things, even pulled some of Mom's dresses out of the wardrobe, I also got Christel to grab some stuff. I stuffed everything into several pillowcases that still had been there and threw them onto the handcart. I came flying back in, grabbed my little doll suitcase with the treasured photographs, added some cutlery and before I knew it we were all outside by the handcart and the baby carriage.

Then Mother exclaimed, "I need a cook pot!"

She started towards the house, tried to go up the stairs but the two soldiers barred the entrance, one hit her with the machine gun over the back and she fell, tumbled down the stairs, but she shouted, "Don't cry he'll shoot" and crawled towards us through the dirt. With difficulty she got up, she was snow white and shaking like a leaf when she whispered, "Granny, I guess we'll just have to go."

"I am not leaving, no matter what," said Granny, "When Erich comes back someone has to be here. How else would he ever find us?"

"Mother," my mom cried out, "You can't stay here. You heard them. They won't let you. And you can't go alone when they push you out. We need to stick together. You have to come. Please, Mother, please…. The children need you. Granny, don't do this to us."

We were all sobbing and Christel and I grabbed her arms, pulling her. She gently pushed us away and repeated, "I am not going. If they shoot me, so be it. You better get going. Bye…." With that, she turned, walked a few steps and stood with her back to us, facing the ground. Then she half turned and made a gesture like shooing us away and pleaded with a choking voice; "Go. Don't make this any harder on me."

She walked over to the side of the workers barn facing our yard, sat down on an old piece of machinery, put her hands to her face and cried.

Had she reached the end of her tether?

Oh, God. Poor Bruno locked up, barking and crying full of despair.

On the road to nowhere

It was awful to just walk away from her, down our long driveway, making a right turn once we passed the smithy onto the village road, and then joining all the other people who had come back to Stresow. They were similarly outfitted with a handcart; some with a wheel barrow and some even with old unused prams. Some just had a rucksack or a bag in each hand. Everyone went in the direction of the city of Bad Schönfliess (now renamed to Trzcinska Zdroj). Someone in charge must have given this order. I asked Mother if we could go to Grandmother's house.

"I don't know, Gila," she mused, "they are probably evicted too."

Tears were rolling out of her eyes but she did not brush them away. She did not have a hand free for it anyway. She pulled the handcart with Ingrid sitting on top and Christel held onto her other hand. I pushed the baby carriage. It felt heavy because in addition to baby Edith Granny had loaded it with all kinds of things.

I thought of the day when I had spotted the Russians coming down this road and now we were going in the opposite direction. When we came to the last hilly part of the road, I turned my head and looked back. I could see the church tower and the roofs of a few houses surrounded with big trees looking just the way the village had always looked when we went to or came from the city. It had looked like this at night when the bombers flew over and we were crouched in the ditch by the useless bunker. I looked towards the mill hill and tried to find our house. Some kind of unearthly silence lay over the familiar landscape with a low iron-grey sky above it. So much had happened but it hadn't changed a bit. It seemed to have always looked like this. Maybe it would continue to look like this. Maybe it didn't matter if we or the Russians or Polish people lived in those houses. I will always remember how it looked at that moment. Sometimes I wish I had artistic talent and could paint it.

"Gila, don't dream, watch where you're going," –my mother's voice.

We walked down the black sidewalk where I had run over the ladies with Mother's bike in what seemed like a hundred years ago. We passed the grand house owned by the man that was supposed to have become Mother's husband. Toward the end of war he had been hanged by the Nazis on his own door frame because he had a long-gone, Jewish Great Grandmother and he had been hiding friends who also had Jewish blood in their family. We turned onto the street that brought us by Grandmother's great garden outside the city wall. The fence was on the ground. The garden had become a huge parking place for tanks, trucks and other war machinery. Lots of it looked quite damaged. My eyes watered for all the trees and berry bushes that were gone and the wonderful jam Grandma used to make with black currants and plums. Grandfather's arbor was gone too, but the century-old, city wall with the big, heavy door was there as it had always been.

Next was the city gate and I asked Mother again about checking if we could stay in her parents' house, at least today so that we could take a bit of time to get better organised. It was the first house through the gate and just around the corner.

Several soldiers were guarding the gate and nobody was allowed through.

So much for that idea..

We continued on the long trek on the road to Königsberg (today called Chojna, Poland). The road was leading towards the Oder River and, once you crossed it, on towards Berlin. You could not see the beginning or the end of our raggedy column. Next to us were the Russian trucks, jeeps and the occasional tank; all going in the same direction. The trucks were packed with Russians. They had a soft roof over their head but the backdrop of it was rolled up and open. They all had guns across their laps and they were looking at us. Sometimes I met a soldier's eyes but nobody smiled or waved. You could not make out what they were thinking. On this, our first day on the road to nowhere, we walked the fourteen kilometers to Königsberg. Hundreds of us stayed in a bomb-damaged, empty, huge hall not far from the former military airport. Here we finally had a chance to check what Granny had packed into the baby carriage and were hugely thankful to find some bread and the last of the salami. Edith's bottle had been filled with milk. It was cold and Mother let her only drink half of it and gave her a piece of bread to suck on when she cried.

We talked about Granny and couldn't even imagine what she was going through right now. Was she dead? Was she alive? Did she have anything to eat? Would she be allowed to sleep in the barn with Bruno?

"Oh God, Gila," whispered my mother to me, "what are we going to do?"

That night we cried ourselves to sleep, rolled up in a blanket on the cold, hard, concrete floor close to Mother between the pram and the handcart.

Quite early the next morning a Russian officer told us in German that thousands of Polish families were on the way to move into our cities, villages and homes. We should not entertain any hope of ever returning. The war was over. Hitler had committed suicide and this part of Germany was now part of Poland. He also told us that the Russian army had built a moving bridge on boats across the Oder River and they would help us to get to the other side. We had to move on because crossing was a slow process and hundreds of thousands were going in the same direction and, naturally, the Russian army had priority. They brought a truck with a huge barrel of water and we were allowed to fill whatever canisters or bottles we had. No, they did not give us any breakfast. It was the last time that we were spoken to or received anything to ease our plight.

After this, every day was the same, walking in the endless trek and sometimes pushed to the very edge of the road or even into the ditch by a passing Russian truck. If one had to pee or worse you just stepped beside the road, did your business and tried to catch up with your family. Most nights we just settled under the overhang of a commercial building when lucky or slept under the sky with hundreds all around us. Once I placed myself on a big cornerstone beside a garage door at a railway station. I refused to move. I could lean into the corner and nobody could step on me. I had to go pee but I was afraid I would lose my protected space and begged Mother to keep it for me. She refused, because she might have lost her own space. People were not considerate. Someone would have just pushed the pram or the cart away. Everybody was trying to find the best spot. First come, first served. Nobody knew each other anyway, so there were no guilty feelings. I did my business just next to my seat, tried to aim for the edge of the driveway and the cobblestoned place next to it. I tried to sleep sitting up but found it impossible, so I slept in front of "my rock."

I don't know how many days later we arrived at the Oder River close to a small city called Zeden – the Polish name now is Cadynia. At the narrowest spot of the river, the Russians had tied several larger boats together and built a platform across it. They pulled this ferry platform back and forth across the water all day long. Only about 10 or 12 people could fit on it, depending on what they brought along or just one army truck. Masses of people were waiting here. We joined the line-up and it took four days before it was our turn, moving slowly with the line and sleeping on the road in order not to lose our space. Thankfully, it did not rain but it was cold at night and the sky was full of twinkling stars. When I looked up before falling asleep, I wondered if God was sitting up there looking down on the misery of His people. Why would He allow all this horror? What was our sin?

We hardly had anything to eat now. Somewhere along the way, dozens of people had raided one of those storage mounds and gotten away with two or three turnips. We ate everything raw and never had a chance to cook some of the outdated pudding powder that Granny had packed into the pram. Mother hunted down some water when we were settled each evening and added a little of the powder to the cold water in Edith's bottle, shook it and gave it to her. Our stomachs either growled or hurt most of the time. Thankfully, Edith slept a lot.

Once we realized that it would take several days until it was our turn to cross the river, Christel and I went exploring the area. Not far from where we were "parked," was a long kind of carport, similar to the one my Grandparents had for their carriages. This one had a row of carriages under the roof and another row in front of it. We climbed all over them and tried out each one. We sat on the bench and said "ho-ho" to an imaginary horse. I let Christel handle the horse while I played the butler standing on the back step, opening the built-in boxes of each one and, lo and behold, maybe in the eighth of them I found a bag with grain.

"Christel," I whispered, "come here and look at this! It's grain, can you feel it?"

We could feel it! It must have been at least ten or fifteen pounds, maybe more. I could hardly lift it and certainly could not carry it. Christel raced to get Mom while I guarded it. She came to bring our treasure home to our spot. We had to be careful that nobody noticed because people might kill us for it. Incredibly, Mother had packed a coffee mill and now was glad because she could grind the grain, which happened to be barley! What else? Russian soup! All we needed now was a cook pot and a place to make a fire. Granny had hidden matches under Edith's mattress. We were hungry but my mouth watered just knowing that soon we would get a hot barley flour soup with salt! For the next few days, we just chewed a handful of the grain as it was.

Crossing the Oder River

After four days, we were lucky to be on the first crossing of the day because it gave us a head start towards wherever we would spend that night. It might have been on this day or the next that we arrived in Bad Freienwalde. This city is still part of Germany. Mother suggested that we finish walking early because we were exhausted. God and all the Saints were with us. Turning off the main road, we came into a side street with little or no traffic and small houses like the one where the headless German soldier had sat against a fence. We spotted a slightly open door, knocked but received no answer to our "hellos."

Very carefully, we entered, afraid we might find dead people. We checked every room but it was totally deserted. White, frilly curtains were on the windows in the cozy living room and the beds were made in the master bedroom. There was a bright yellow children's room with twin beds and toys on shelves but several empty drawers. Our inspection of all the wardrobes suggested that the owners must have fled very recently. We moved our few belongings inside the hallway, even the handcart so that it would not be stolen. Mother and I took it apart because it was too big to fit through the door. After the front and back covers were pulled off, the side boards could be taken off, the bottom board lifted and then a large pin was pulled and the two parts with two wheels each were easy to manoeuvre. We locked the house door with the dead bolt so as not to get a surprise visitor. We half expected that the house owners might come back at any moment.

"Don't go close to the windows, stay far away," warned our mother. We remembered about 'the shooting at any movement' back in Stresow and obeyed.

The first thing on Mother's mind was to check for a cook pot. She found several and a frying pan as well. Some food, cans and preserves were still in a cold room off the kitchen. There was wood and coal in a basket next to the stove. She muttered about taking the absent strangers food and prayed they might forgive her. She cooked something and it smelled good. Christel had the job of grinding barley with the coffee mill. Mother roasted barley in the frying pan and announced happily, "We have coffee! I'll give Edith barley coffee instead of just water. I found a small can with coffee cream and that'll help for a few days. I hope we have a chance now after we have crossed the Oder River to cook more often."

Ingrid played quietly with the toys in the children's room. I got the order to put water in the bathtub – what a luxury! It was cold, yes, but it did not matter. I could wash Edith's diapers and our panties. Up to now, we had just rinsed the diapers in a ditch and let them dry on the handle of the pram. Plenty of towels were hanging on hooks, which I used to roll the laundry in and pressed hard so that it wrung out most of the water. Left to dry in the kitchen, warm from cooking, every-thing was almost dry in the morning. While we had our first warm but simple meal after more than a week, all the pots on the stove were filled with water to heat up. One by one, Mom stood us in the bathtub and scrubbed us until our skin was red. She was last and sat in the soapy dirty water, fighting sleep.

All of us had a wonderful rest that night. We slept on top of our "hosts" beds covered with our blankets and left them as we found them. For breakfast we had oatmeal with raisins, compliments of the absent house owners. Mom fed Edith a bit of it with a small spoon. She did swallow it and it did not come back up. Would we ever have loved to stay in that house another day but Mother was afraid the Russians would come checking or perhaps neighbours might have seen us and reported us so she therefore felt it better to move on.

Ingrid wanted to take a doll she had slept with. Mom did not allow it. She explained, "Food is different, but we don't steal things."

However, she did take a medium-size cook pot and a small frying pan. When Ingrid questioned that Mother told her, "I am only borrowing it and will give it back as soon as I can."

Once we were turning into the main road again, Mother stopped, took a deep breath and looked at me, "Gila. Gila, I don't know what to do. Where are we going? I'm afraid we will not be so lucky and find such a nice place again. Edith is starving. She is so thin already, unresponsive and does not even cry, she has diarrhea and she will die. Oh my God, Gila, what can we do?"

The way she talked to me reminded me of the day when she and I came from the crashed plane on the mill hill and she had spoken to me as if I was a grown-up. Looking right into her eyes I said with conviction, "We are going to Aunt Tutti."

I hadn't even thought of it up to now but at this moment a picture of a sunny day at the beach in Stresow with her and the boy cousins flashed through my mind. They were the only relatives we had on this, the west side of the Oder River, except Aunt Frieda, Uncle Curt's wife in Holstein.

Mom took another deep breath. "You are right", she said, "We'll just have to find the way."

Now our walk had a purpose to it. Again, we were part of the endless trek and the Russians were still streaming past us.

Calamity strikes

Within a day or two, my throat began to hurt. I did not want to tell Mom, but she noticed that something was wrong.

"You seem to be unsteady, are you feeling dizzy?" She put her hand on my forehead and was shocked, "My God, Gila, you are burning up! You have a fever. We better find a place to stay, you need to rest."

By that time, I could hardly breathe and it got worse by the minute. We saw a sign with the city name "Wriezen" and my mother, desperate to get me settled, asked some people for a place to stay. She was directed to an old flour mill. Quite a few people were already there. The whole floor was covered with straw, the sun shone into an overhead window and I could see the dust motes dancing in the rays of light. She placed blankets under and over me. I did not know anything after that. Maybe I fell asleep or I fainted. When I woke up my mother carried me across her two arms; I saw a street with unfriendly looking grey houses and then all went dark again. The next time I woke up, I could hear my breath coming noisily in short bursts. A man in a white coat over a Russian uniform was talking to my mother. I saw a baby crib in front of me and many narrow beds with mainly old people with hollow cheeks in them. Mother was sitting in a chair holding me.

"Your daughter has diphtheria. It is rampant. I need to open her trachea but I have no bed for her and she is too big to fit in the baby crib. I have one ampoule of serum. If I don't give it to her, she will die; if I give it to her she might live, but someone else will die."

My mother begged him for mercy and I had heard it all and looked at him with what the blond Ivan had deemed my "old eyes," never leaving his. After a few seconds he made a decision, "Frau, go through that green door, down half a stairway. There is a toilet, take her in there and pull her panties down. Wait for me I'll be with you as soon as I can."

When we were in that small room I saw the water tank high up on the wall with the pull chain hanging down with a white ceramic handle on it. The door, the walls, everything was an awful green. A small, white-framed window was high up in one wall. I did not want my panties pulled down but Mom placed me over the toilet seat and just got me ready for the doctor. He did come with a syringe in his hand and stabbed me in the bum. He looked carefully out of the door and ran two steps at a time, back up the stairs. I looked after him and thought, "Did he do something that was 'verboten'?"

The next time I woke up it was very quiet. I was not sure where I was and why I was where I was. I saw the yellow golden straw around me, lit up by the sun and deep shadows in the far corners, two huge round millstones and the dust motes dancing in a long sunbeam. I seemed to be floating between being and not being. I closed my eyes and just waited to fall asleep again. After a bit, I heard whispering voices and careful footsteps. The next sound was like suppressed sobbing. I opened my eyes again and looked straight into a woman's eyes and only after she started speaking did it slowly dawn on me that she had my mother's face. She stood there, a few meters away from me, with folded hands.

"Oh," she said quietly, "you are alive. I came to say goodbye. When I heard your wheezing stop last night, I thought it was over. Sorry, I had to put you far away from us but the other people were afraid they would get sick too. They want us to leave; most people are gone already. Can you walk?"

I could not. She helped me up but my bum and the leg on the side where I got the needle hurt so much. She half carried me outside to a fence, next to an elderberry bush in bloom, where I could relieve myself. I could smell the blossoms, pointed to them and croaked "tea." My mother picked a few of the flowers. The handcart, the baby carriage and my sisters were ready and waiting. They were very quiet and did not speak to me at all. Mother, Christel and Ingrid had swollen red eyes and I wondered why they might have been crying. Mother left us for a while and then came back with a rather thick stick that she had found somewhere behind the building. She pressed it into my hand and begged me, "Gila, you have to be a strong girl, we don't want to leave you but they won't let us stay. Please try. We'll go slowly."

It did not work. Ingrid had to walk and I was placed on the cart until we were out of the city and back with the endless crowd of refugees. When the road went a little uphill I offered to walk. It was not too bad. The longer I walked the easier it got. I was just so weak, so terribly tired and still a bit dizzy but the stick helped.

Next to the road was a very deep, grassy bank down to a narrow ditch with some water in it. I felt that I needed to pee again and with my hoarse voice, I said so. Mother could not stop, there was no room to get out of the line of people and she called, "Catch up with us; we'll wait for you when we next have a chance."

I carefully went down the bank several feet, pulled my panties down and squatted, facing the bank across the water below and the forest up on the other side. My stick was by my side, as I knew I would need it to get up again. I looked left, I looked right, and to my delight, I saw something small and red and recognized wild, ripe strawberries. Stretching out my hand I picked one, put it in my mouth, it was aromatic and sweet. I reached for another one and toppled over. I either blacked out or fell asleep with my panties around my ankles in the midst of the strawberry patch.

After several kilometers, Mother saw a path that went over the ditch into the forest. She parked the rest of her family there, admonished nine-year-old Christel to take care of everything and came back to find me, walking against the stream of people and half on, half off, the bank. She told me later that she thought I had died after all when she saw the way I had fallen over. Talking about death or dying was natural because we saw it all around us.

It had taken her an hour and a half to come and it took us longer to get back. The kids were all right, nobody had bothered them. We made camp right there under the big fir trees and I could see the stars in the sky. Mom carefully made a small fire to boil some water from the ditch for Edith's coffee. That was all she could keep inside her now. She boiled the fresh elderberry flowers for tea but we ate them as well. Elderberry is good to reduce fever and prevent colds. We had Russian soup but I could only get very little down. Swallowing was very difficult.

I cannot remember how or where we slept the night after that or the next ones. But I could walk much better. My stick was my best friend. Mother had turned off the main road leading to Berlin when she saw a sign to Eberswalde. It went west but the sign also listed a road to Angermuende, which was northeast. It was further but the road we had to take. We aimed for the road north from Angermuende to Pasewalk in order to get to Aunt Tutti on the Island of Rügen. Mother remembered that she had relatives living in Angermuende from her mother's side and hoped that we could find them. It was good not to be in the endless trek with the Russians alongside us anymore. We could go slower, rest and make a little fire more often. When we came by some of those vegetable storage mounds Mother and Christel always went but found them empty. Our barley grain kept us alive.

The train, the train

We did find Mom's aunt, but the uncle had died. Her house was full with people like us but she let us sleep in the living room on the floor with me on the sofa because I was not well. We could wash ourselves with warm water and rinse Edith's soiled diapers. She cooked some potatoes and we supplied some of our precious salt. We departed the next day and now walked north to Pasewalk, finally in the right direction. This was the first larger city we encountered and were surprised to hear trains were still coming through occasionally. Nobody knew when they would come, or where they might go, but everyone had hopes of catching one, no matter where it was going. So we decided to go to the train station, find a place under an overhang and wait for a few days. It would be a rest and just maybe we might have a chance.

After two days, towards dusk, we heard a train coming. Everybody jumped up and got ready. It was not a passenger train but one with boxcars. It went back and forth changing tracks until it finally stopped. It was long, with more than twenty cars. People took their belongings and ran along the tracks to board the train. Nobody asked questions. They all just wanted to get further away from here.

Someone called out, "It's going north in the morning."

We walked a little farther away from the crowd and got in as well. We had to take the handcart apart to be able to lift the parts up and someone helped us to get the pram in. We all clambered on board. The train slowly moved onto another track and onwards to a small station with a sign "Scheune". Here it parked for the night.

We were alone in this boxcar with another family, an elderly lady, her daughter and a cute four-year-old little blond girl with big blue eyes. They were on one side of the car and we were on the other. Ingrid liked the little girl and played with her. The women talked about where they came from and where they hoped to go until both parties rolled out the blankets and eventually settled down to sleep.

It was pitch black when the sliding door on the other side started to open a crack and a Russian with a flashlight came in. Mother gathered us close to her and said "Ssssh." The light went over us, then over the other people. The soldier walked over to them, crouched down by the young woman grabbing her. She put up quite a fight, was squirming away, managed to get up and screamed, "Stalin say nyet, Stalin say no more, no more, go away...."

With the light shining on her he pushed her over, took his bayonet and thrust it right up between her legs. The two women and the child were screaming horribly. He pulled the bayonet out of the woman and pushed it first into one then the other eye of the little girl. The blood was spurting and I cannot understand to this day why she stopped screaming. He turned around and shone the light on my mother. She whispered, "Don't cry, don't scream or he is going to do that to you too. Be very still."

He came, stood over us, opened his fly and his penis practically jumped out and he proceeded to rape my mother. She let it happen and was quiet like a mouse. We cuddled next to her. It was the first time I had seen a man's penis and I could not believe such a young man would have such a big one. No wonder Ruth from grade eight had died after so many Russians had pushed a thing like that into her. It did not take long and he got up, took his gun, wiped the blood off the bayonet with one of Edith's diapers hanging on the pram handle and left the way he had come.

The old woman across from us was sobbing. She had a towel wrapped around the girl's head and cradled her in her arms. The young woman was crying and moaning with pain. We were in shock and shaking. Mother cried noiselessly. I don't know if she slept that night but we children eventually did. When the grey of the morning crept into our boxcar we looked over to the other side. Only the old lady cried now as if her heart would break. The two others were quiet and nobody had to tell us they were dead. The towel around the girl's head was red and a thick patch of blood was all around the group and their blankets were soaked with it. We needed to pee and went, one after the other, to the farthest corner of our side of the boxcar. The boards of the floor were damaged so the urine could run off or drip down. We did not know what to do or say to the old lady, so we just let her cry and we stayed close to our mom and waited for the morning light.

There was a jolt and then another. We thought the locomotive must have been attached. It was exciting to know we would get going, rolled up our blankets while Mother opened the sliding door. She saw people further up in the cars closer to the station building, jump out of the train, which now ever so slowly started to move.

Someone yelled, "It's going back to Poland."

I have never seen Mother move so fast. She just pushed the pram with Edith out the door and incredibly, it landed on all four wheels.

She screamed at me "Jump" but I froze. I was afraid because it was so far to the ground.

She pushed me out, then Christel, followed by Ingrid. One by one, the pieces of the handcart were flying down and all the stuff that was to be loaded in it. I was afraid that she would go to Poland because the train had started to pick up speed. Finally, she jumped with an armful of blankets, fell down and sat there for a few seconds but thank God, she picked herself up. Some of our things were close to the moving train; others were lying in the next railway track. It was spread out over about a hundred metres. Needless to say, we were not the only passengers who sat stunned or tried to move their legs and arms. Mother came to where I was with the pram and my sisters. She checked if we had broken any bones but it was just scraped knees and elbows. Leaving Ingrid with Edith, the three of us then proceeded to collect our belongings. Other people did the same.

Strangers exchanged a few words of how horrible it would have been to go back to where we had all come from and how lucky nobody had broken anything.

Mother left us at a wider spot between two railway tracks to prevent us being run over if a train passed on either one and went to the station. She desperately needed to boil some water for Edith's coffee and she wanted to speak to someone to find out about another train or if we should start walking again. The information she received was that they did not know if or when another train would come or where it would be going until the last minute. The kind, elderly man she talked to was shocked to learn how a baby could be kept alive this way and filled the baby bottle out of a thermos with his own warm, grain coffee. Grain coffee had been the only coffee for the Germans during the last years of the war. He could not believe that a girl with diphtheria was not in a hospital bed for six weeks but on the road walking. He asked her to bring us closer to the station and promised to give her a sign if there was a train going west or north away from here. His advice was to get further into what was still Germany since it would make it easier to find a train going to Stralsund, our ultimate aim. From there it would be only five kilometers across the bridge to the Island of Rügen where Aunt Tutti lived.

Incredibly, on the same day, there was another train and it was stopped for several hours before our new friend gave us the thumbs up. A little later, a woman came, introduced herself as his wife and helped Mom to get us in through the normal narrow door of a large passenger compartment. It had few seats but lots of room for luggage. She left us some sandwiches with lard and salt, wrapped in old newspaper and an old beer bottle with more warm grain coffee for Edith. We were over-whelmed with gratitude but prayed that her husband was right with the direction the train would go. It would have been very difficult, if not impossible to get out the way we had from the boxcar. It was a tearful goodbye.

We had four seats, two each across from each other. The room got crowded before the train left. Ingrid and Christel had to vacate their seats for older people. They wanted to sleep on the floor anyway. The train rolled along with the typical click of the wheels over the rail joints and a burst of steam every so often. We looked out of the window and were amazed to see fields with wheat, rye, barley and oats growing. Red poppies and blue cornflowers grew at the edges just like at home. Long rows of potatoes, sugar beets and turnips promised a good harvest. We saw small communities of gardens with people working in them and lots of fruit trees and bushes. Sometimes these gardens were close to the train track and we could see ripe currants and gooseberries. When I saw cherries ripening, I started to cry, thinking of all the many cherry trees we had at home – at home in Stresow. Every garden sported a little arbor or summerhouse like a shack. Other gardens had washing lines with laundry flapping in the wind. Women were sitting on benches holding coffee cups and children played in sand boxes. Was I dreaming? It looked so much like a fairy tale and could not possibly be real; life just was not like that, at least not anymore. Maybe they did not have a war over here.

Mother knew that lots of the grain would have been sown in the fall. She pointed out, "It's the same in Stresow; the mill hill and all the fields will be green. Only now the Poles will harvest it."

She went on to explain that the Russians came much later to this area and therefore the local people had planted potatoes and put in turnip seeds during the spring when things here were still pretty normal. Also, there was no more fighting between the Russians and the Germans, that all happened in our parts east of the Oder River. Thinking ahead, she said on Rügen it would probably be even better since the Russians arrived much later and, depending on when we arrived, we might be able to get some early potatoes. Since nobody had money to buy anything and there was no shop or place where you could even buy something, she promised, "I'll work for it."

She had another idea, "Once the farmers have harvested their fields we can go and find potatoes that fell through the machines."

Occasionally the train stopped in the middle of nowhere to wait for another train coming in the opposite direction. The engineer in the locomotive would always give a whistle warning before he would start moving the train again. Once people figured it out, they would hop down to empty their bladder and hurried to get back on. More than once, we saw people running to grab on to the handlebar and held our breath wondering if they would make it. The train would stop at lots of small villages. Sometimes people would get off and others got on. We still had no idea where we were going. We did not see any familiar city or village names. Did it really matter? We seemed to be in a much better world and, come evening we ate the rest of the sandwiches, which had been so generously provided. Mother gave Edith one quarter of the coffee in the baby bottle and we settled down to sleep.

It was dark outside when I woke up and noticed the train had stopped. I woke Mother. A few men with lanterns were walking back and forth. Whistles were blown and the train jolted into action again after one lantern was lifted high. My God, we were going in the opposite direction! We had been facing forward – now we were going backwards! We could do nothing. Most people kept on sleeping, some just mumbled, "I couldn't care less. Leave it up to God. Nothing could be as bad as what we had before."

After many hours, the night gave way to a glorious sunrise. People groaned and stretched and lined up at the only, by now, dirty toilet where "things" would just fall down onto the tracks. The faucet at the tiny sink did not spout any water. The Russian came to mind who had been demanding "water from wall". That seemed like more than a hundred years ago.

Later during the morning a man in the typical railway uniform came through and informed us we would be arriving in Stralsund at about a quarter to one if all goes well. Did he say Stralsund?

STRALSUND, oh my God, we were on our way to Stralsund all this time and didn't even know it!

He also announced, "It's the end of the line so make sure to take all your belongings with you. Ladies from the Red Cross will be there with warm drinks and some baked goods. They will help where help is needed."

Mother pulled me close with the arm she had across my shoulder and we both started to cry but this time our tears were tears of happiness. Christel and Ingrid could not comprehend why we cried and anxiously looked at us, ready to cry too. Smiling with tears dripping down our cheeks we told them that soon, very soon now, we would arrive at Aunt Tutti's house because we had come close to the end of our journey.

A few red cherries save five lives

Slowly the train rolled into the station under a huge glass dome with no glass in it because Stralsund had seen its share of the bombing. Let me add that beautiful Stralsund is now rebuilt and is one of the World Heritage Cities.

The train bumped against big steel buffers. The locomotive gave a last puff of steam and it sounded as if it, too, breathed a sigh of relief. The platform was packed in no time with people tumbling out of the train. Mother had lowered our window and we just waited because she could not manage to get the pram and the parts of the handcart out by herself. She was shaking and I started to get worried. I was forever afraid something would happen to her and then what would we do? I did not think I could look after my sisters on my own. We were quite hungry by now as well.

After all the people from our compartment had left, Mother started to bring out what she could carry and piled it up in the middle of the platform. Our three little faces hanging out of the window were noticed by a lady with a Red Cross band around her sleeve. When I caught her eye I waved frantically. First, she thought we were by ourselves but then Mother came and spoke to her. Together they got the pram out and the larger parts for the cart. The lady excused herself but promised to come back. Mother proceeded to put the cart together and loaded it. Finally, she asked us to come down the steps from the train and she made sure we did not fall under the railcar, which could easily have happened.

We patiently waited for the Red Cross lady to come back and lead us towards the station building and FOOD! Our eyes got bigger and our mouths watered when we saw a table set up with Danish pastry, hot (barley) coffee with milk and apple juice. Several Red Cross ladies were busy serving people, many with children. Our lady warned us to chew well and eat slowly in order not to get sick.

She reminded us, "Your stomach is not used to food like this anymore. We don't want you to vomit, right?"

Mother filled Edith's bottle with the coffee and milk mix. She brought it up immediately. The lady could not believe when she heard that this small baby was over a year old and had survived on just barley coffee for several weeks. She got some, handed it to Mother and warned her, "Don't give it to her now, wait until later. But you must be prepared – you might soon lose her."

Mother nodded and just whispered with tears in her eyes and a breaking voice, "I know."

We enjoyed the warm drink with the sweets and had a glass of apple juice before we left. The lady made sure that we "chewed" the apple juice before we swallowed it. It was the best food we had had since we couldn't even remember. We were almost afraid to leave to start on the last few kilometers not knowing what to expect. We were now amongst the last people with the wonderful caring Red Cross women. They handed us four packages with two Danish for each of us and a small pointed bag of red cherries. I was longing to eat them but the lady, probably a nurse, shook her head, "No, wait till later, your tummy has enough to do right now. Your mother will share them with all of you later."

The nurse asked if we needed accommodation. Mother told her that we wanted to go to Rügen to Aunt Tutti who lived just across the bridge close to the small railway station where her husband worked. She advised us that the drawbridge leading to the big bridge called the "Rügendam" had been blown up by the Germans but the Russians had built a temporary one on boats around the damaged part and that we might have a few hours' wait and also needed a permit. Telling her of the four days waiting for the Oder River crossing, a few hours' wait seemed minor to us. They gave us directions and explained where to get the permit. We departed and thanked them for their help and the incredible reception.

The office for the permit was in the old Rügendam station building. Trains could not cross the Rügendam anymore because of the damaged bridge. In peace times, the train would go all the way across Rügen to Sassnitz; drive onto a huge ferry and cross over to Sweden. A Russian with a German man translating interviewed Mother. They wanted to know where we came from and why and where we wanted to go. When they heard our uncle worked for the railway station on the other side of the bridge and lived with his family in a railway house close by, they stamped the permit we had filled out earlier. The German wished us luck.

We set off up to the drawbridge where only about twenty people were in front of us. Here was a checkpoint with two Russians checking all permits. We watched as they let some people through without a problem and others had to wait on the sidelines. When we came closer, we noticed some people put something down with their permits and they were the ones let through. Watching that, my mother realized you needed a bribe and without hesitating she put down one of the packages from the Red Cross ladies with our permit and sure enough we were waved on to the temporary bridge built above a number of larger boats. It was much bigger than the one at the Oder River. It was not a platform and did not need to be pulled but was more like a narrow road and wide enough for trucks and tanks going one way connecting to the Rügendam.

Looking over the left railing, we could see a village and Mother told us, "That is the village of Altefähr with the church tower. Your cousins go to school there."

How exciting! We walked along with renewed energy. It was all so very beautiful: Stralsund with several church towers damaged and many bombed buildings on the one side. The wide channel leading to the Baltic Sea with white caps and a few fishing boats beneath us; Altefähr on the other side on what was the Island of Rügen. I had dreamed about coming here since Father had aborted his plan to visit his sister, who was my beloved Godmother, after the accident with the horses and the motor bike a number of years before. Yes, I was only half as old then as I was now.

After about a kilometer, we came to another checkpoint. Again, we had to show our permit and the soldier toyed with it. Mother just handed him another of our packages and, voila, we could pass. Greedy bastards, we needed that food much more than he did – but? This happened two more times and all of our four packages were gone. What would we have done if we had not had them? Did the Red Cross women perhaps know what we needed them for when they warned us not to eat them "until later"? We hoped this was the last checkpoint. The bridge over the open water ended soon, then continued on an earth bank at the same height and slowly sloped down to the road by the station. We could see the houses of the railway people; one of them Aunt Tutti's house, oh my God, it could not take us much longer now than thirty or forty minutes! Shaking with anticipation, we marched on but lo and behold, there was a beam across the road. We had not thought of the fact that this was the entrance to the crossing coming from Rügen and heading to the mainland. Naturally, there would be a bar and yet another checkpoint. A Russian with a gun and the frightening bayonet pointing up to the sky looked towards us.

Mother showed him the permit. He looked at it a long time, put it in his pocket and said, "Nyet, nyet – no go."

Mother started to sob, we joined in but he just kept shaking his head. He made the sign of "going back…" pointing to where we had come from. My mother lost it.

She screamed, "I will throw you all over the railing and then jump, we can't go on like this, I'm at the end, I'm finished, I can't, I can't…."

With that she took Edith out of the pram, the little blanket fell down, she held the baby over the railing but before she could let go Christel, Ingrid and I pulled on her dress like crazy and she stumbled back onto the sidewalk. The Russian had watched us with a curious expression and then called, "Stop." He pointed to the small pointed bag with the cherries in the pram. It had been under Edith's blanket. He picked it up, opened it and smiled, "Da da, karachow" (Yes yes, good). He handed me the permit still smiling and opened the beam. I looked back at him when he closed the beam after we had passed. I cannot remember if I smiled back. I felt as if I was floating and my head felt very empty. My legs had a mind of their own; I stumbled several times because the left one went over the right and vice versa.

Aunt Tutti's house

Coming down off the bridge, the road went straight ahead with a smaller one to the right under a railway overpass. Since the houses we could see were along the road to the right, we decided it must be the right one. Mother remembered the house number. We went into the yard and Mother sat down next to the cart. Her legs simply gave up and her whole body was shaking. She was exhausted. I entered the two-storey house, looked at the nametags beside the doors inside and found theirs up one flight of stairs. That's it! I was trembling when I rang the bell. A young woman opened, I recognized my "babysitter-sister-aunt" Lisa, gave a shout and put my arms around her, sobbing as if the world was at an end.

She cried out, "Gila! My God, Gila!"

Three other women came to see what was going on: Aunt Irene, Aunt Tutti and one I did not know. Later I learned it was a cousin twice removed called Aunt Helen. The women talked to me all at once, asking questions and when I had my sobbing somewhat under control I stuttered, "They are all in the yard."

Everybody ran down the stairs followed by our three boy cousins as if the house was on fire. They crowded around my mother and my sisters and kept on talking all at once. Aunt Tutti took one look into the pram and carefully lifted Edith out. She looked at her and said with tears running down her face, "Oh, my God, this little girl will not live another day."

We were very quiet. Mother had fainted. But we had survived. We were alive – so far.

13: Arrival on the Isle of Rügen

Bathing and de-lousing

"How and when did you leave Stresow? What happened to Erich? Why did you leave? Where is Granny? Did Granny die? Why is she not with you? For heaven's sake, how could you have left her behind?"

Lots and lots of questions from all of them came at once; they did not even wait for answers.

Mother was slowly coming to after her fainting spell but she stayed on the ground. She was very pale and her hands were still shaking. She held one with the other to hide it but she did not succeed. Christel and I were weak too but in much better shape than she was and gave most of the answers, as we knew them. I got very dizzy and lowered myself to the ground in the bit of shade the handcart provided. Aunt Tutti had the baby in her arms and just could not believe this skin and bones, small and starved human being was still alive after living on cold water or barley coffee watered down for weeks! She promised, "I will take care of her. I want her to live. I'll make her live. I will do whatever it takes. I'll not let her die. We must slowly, with one drop at a time, get her on milk again. Fritz must get some."

Fritz, her husband, was a railway man. (No, he had absolutely nothing to do with the other 'Fritzes' previously encountered. Fritz happened to be a popular name at the time.) Tutti's sister Irene quietly warned, "Tutti, don't get your hopes up."

She knew Tutti had lost her firstborn, little Dorothea, in 1932. Her baby girl was buried in a grave next to her father, my grandfather, in the

Stresow cemetery. She always wanted a girl again but instead had three boys by this time and later another one. Just like her brother, my father had wanted a boy and had four girls.

The excitement to see us so unexpectedly slowly gave way to more practical considerations. Aunt Irene took charge, probably because she had been trained as a field nurse in the German army, "Else quickly needs water. She is not only exhausted but also dehydrated. Let's get her out of the sun. Siegfried, go upstairs and mix water with a bit of raspberry concentrate but make it weak. Bring enough and also cups for all of them. Manfred can help you. They might be hungry but they need to drink first."

Then she looked at Lisa and Helen, "You two get the tubs in the laundry room ready, heat a lot of water in the big kettle we normally boil the laundry in. Let's clean up these gypsies, they haven't bathed in weeks and their hair is full of lice. I suspect their clothing is too. We might have to burn it all. Then one of you go upstairs and find some clean clothing. Bring pyjamas from the boys for the girls and a long nightgown for Else or one of Tutti's old dresses. Those will fit her now she's lost so much weight."

We still hadn't truly taken in the activity around us and were just overwhelmed they ALL had come here. It was like being in a dream, trying to wake up but the dream continues.

After Siegfried and Manfred brought the refreshment, they were told to go to the station and find their dad, "Tell him everything and ask him to get some petrol or kerosene because we need it to get rid of the head lice."

I had visions of having my hair burned off but Aunt Irene explained, "Don't worry I'll not burn your hair off. But we might have to shave it off. Trust me, my treatment will work. I'll use the kerosene to wet your hair and then wrap an old towel tightly around your heads like a turban. You sleep with it for two nights and then the lice will be dead. Wouldn't that be wonderful?"

Yes, it would. After all the things we had seen and done, this couldn't be so bad, just smelly. I have always had a sensitive nose and the idea of having the kerosene smell around me for two days and nights was not very appealing. However, it needed to be done if we did not want to have our hair shaved off. We understood they did not want us to bring lice into their home and we surely did not want to do that.

"We can sleep in the laundry room or the small shed!"

But no, they wouldn't hear of it. Aunt Tutti made plans, "Helen, you stay in the attic room. Lisa and Irene, you can move into the living room for now and they can all be in your small bedroom."

They had a three and a half room apartment: Living room, master bedroom, the children's room and the half room plus the kitchen with a sink and running cold water "from wall." A toilet was half a stairway down and shared with the people in the main floor apartment who had to go half a stairway up. It had the water tank high up against the ceiling and a chain with a ceramic handle, just like in the schoolhouse hospital where I got the serum shot that saved my life. I was glad it was not green but a pleasant, light-yellow colour.

"How come your toilet room is light yellow?"

Aunt Tutti answered, "Uncle Fritz painted it."

Thirteen people now lived in this apartment and shared their life. There were seven children and six adults: Tutti, Irene, Lisa, Helen, Else, Fritz and the children Siegfried, Manfred, Dieter, Gisela, Christel, Ingrid and Edith.

Food for a small army

Mother and I each had single beds previously occupied by Lisa and Irene. Christel and Ingrid slept on a mattress on the floor between us, Edith in her pram just inside the door. It was tight but we thought it was pure luxury. Fortunately, one door went out to the stairs so we did not disturb anyone when one of us had to go to the bathroom. We were warned that occasionally a Russian would still turn up and call "Frau come…."

"Don't ever open the door at night. Use the potty. It happens that someone forgets to lock or re-lock the front door. That's when they come in."

Irene had come with the retreating German army across the Oder River and headed to her sister after her release. Lisa had been put on a train with dozens of other young girls from the "Labour Force" in

East Prussia when it was clear that the Russians pushed the Germans back through Poland and west back to Germany. She had decided not to come home to Stresow but also to get much further away from the oncoming front. Wounded soldiers in the train gave them ominous warnings for which they could have been shot.

Mother shared her worries with me about how Uncle Fritz could get enough food for all of us. Every day after work, he would take a rod and go fishing with Siegfried. There was no school for them either since the teacher had fled to the West before the Russians came. The boys had to dig for worms before their father came home. Since he was a railway man, he was allowed to walk on the tracks to check for safety or damage even though there were no trains crossing the bridge now. Trains were only commuting from Altefähr where we were across the island. Just before he came to the (what was for us the unforgettable and scary) check point he was able to lift a small trap door in the middle of the tracks and climb down to the first wide pillar holding the bridge to do repairs from underneath. From here he fished, unseen by anyone. Once, when I was steadier on my feet again, he took me along.

I held a rod, and I caught my first fish!

"Uncle Fritz, what do I do now?"

He took it off the line and I tried again. I was so excited that I almost fell off the pillar. My fish was rather small but it helped to feed our big family together with the ones he had caught. We were used to eating little or nothing. My mother still had some of the barley and they learned to make "Russian soup". The salt came in very handy.

A farmer had just started harvesting early potatoes in a field across the road, raking them up with a big machine. Most of the people living around here in the railway houses including us kept an eye out for the farmer to finish his work. A few minutes after he was gone everybody ran and just like a flock of birds settled down on the field. With our bare hands, we grabbled in the earth feverishly and picked up even the tiniest potatoes. Naturally, the big ones were all gone. It didn't matter… the small ones taste much better anyway. The first evening Aunt Tutti cooked a big pot full of our harvest and everybody was digging in.

Christel piped up, "Now I can't eat any more. I had fifty-four!"

I only ate thirty-two of the delicious little marvels, some as small as peas. The boy cousins could not keep up with us. With extended tummies, we went to bed, for once really full.

Lisa and Siegfried collected any scrapings and crumbs, took them to the small shed and put them just inside the door on the ground for the birds. They had a string tied to the door, which they left open. Quietly hiding inside, they waited for the birds. When they had a good flock in there, they pulled the door shut, and then caught one after the other with a butterfly net. When we found tiny little bones in the Russian soup, we wondered how they would get in there and if maybe they were from mice. One day Uncle Fritz proudly came home with a skinned rabbit.

Mother gave it one glimpse and teased him, "Looks more like a roof rabbit to me", meaning a cat.

We would never know. Actually, now that I think about it, I don't remember any cats or dogs running around. People could not afford to feed them, having hardly enough for themselves. But then, what happened to the ones that used to be around?

I hunted for berries along the fences of the community gardens. Currants or gooseberry bushes sometimes grew through the fence with fruit on them. I loved berries, I still do. – It was hard to pick them into a small bowl to share. Mostly there weren't many anyway so I would eat them. When I was convinced nobody could see me, I would push my small hand through or over the fence and pick some. What terror when the owner of the garden spotted me, got mad and called me all kinds of names. Yes, it was a sneaky business. One day I was at the bottom of a deep ditch looking for stinging nettles. We cooked it like spinach and then it did not sting at all. The women would also use it like parsley and put it in the Russian soup.

Aunt Irene declared, "Nettle has a lot of iron and vitamins. It's good for us."

We ate the stems of the dandelion blooms, which are sweet. We used young dandelion leaves for salad, added plantain and coltsfoot, which we had always considered "weeds." What is a weed anyway? It is a plant that grows where you don't want it! We used camomile, peppermint, raspberry leaves and the elder flowers; all made a healthy good tea.

Many elder bushes grew along the ditches and Mother looked forward to the berries.

I was sent out to bring some greens home but instead I found a pair of ladies' shoes with semi- high heels and a black ladies' coat. Was the clothing hidden? No, it looked discarded. I thought winter will come again and I don't have a coat or shoes. I tried the coat. It was too long and too wide. It had a big bust stuffed with horsehair under the lining and was flared from the waist down. There were two very large holes on the backside but I thought they could be fixed. I took both things home. Aunt Tutti had some green pieces of leftover material. She dyed them with something. I proceeded to sew patches over the holes and was quite proud of myself. The shoes were too large but one could stuff rags into the toes. Trouble was the height of the heels. It was as if I would play "Theatre" again as I had done when I was a child.

When I was a child? When was that?

The flour mill

Uncle Fritz talked about a flour mill three kilometers away. We could not bake bread because there was no flour. Lisa had been at that mill a few times but the miller did not have any more flour.

Maybe I can try. I knew that my "old eyes" had some kind of power if I looked at people a certain way. My face was small but my eyes were huge surrounded by deep dark circles. I had been able to get a baby bottle of milk for Edith daily from the farm across the potato field. The first time I had accompanied my Uncle, who had explained the situation, and after that, I went on my own. The woman always wanted to know how the baby was doing. I reported everything to her. Sometimes she gave me a piece of bread. Edith had always vomited after even a little milk and they had to give her the burned barley coffee with a drop or two of milk in it. Aunt Tutti started to dip her finger in the milk and just stroked Edith's lips with it again and again and again. She would say, "Come on little angel, open up your "Schnutchen."

In German, that means "little snout". Schnutchen became Auntie's pet name for her. Everyone was excited when one day Edith's little tongue came out to lick the milk off her lips. Auntie then used a dropper.

Ever so slowly, the baby became responsive, could even eat a little solid food, focussed on the person looking at her, she wiggled her legs and arms and learned to smile. We knew then that she would live and she got better, a little every day. When she started to speak a word or two Aunt Tutti was a happy woman. She had managed to save this little girl's life and always thought of her as the daughter she never had.

One day, without anyone knowing, I took the empty barley bag and wandered off to see the miller. It was a sunny day. I was barefoot because my shoes were too small, were torn and they hurt my feet. The road was not paved and in rainy weather would probably be quite muddy. Today the ground was dusty and the deep ridges from wagon wheels were crusty but it felt warm under my feet.

We had learned that our ordeal, the walk after our eviction from our home in Stresow to Aunt Tutti, had taken three weeks. We had arrived on the tenth of June and we had left around the 20th of May. I looked up at the blue sky with a few sailing white clouds. In my imagination, I always saw something in them, faces, animals, figures, angels. I saw the swallows flying high in the air. I heard them singing.

"The weather will hold if they do that," I thought, "when the air is heavy with rain the bugs fly low and, for the swallows to catch them they fly low too. A sure sign that rain was on the way."

I liked swallow song because we had several nests in Stresow under the overhang of our house as well as in the barn. The neighbours used to say to us, "So many swallow nests. You must be a very happy family. If they nest close to you they bring luck."

One nest had just been next to our front door.

Wandering along on this still summer day I thought back to our house and Granny, poor dog Bruno and my cat Mooshie, how life had been then and how within ten minutes it was all gone. It was not that long ago but it felt like years. Was I really only eleven years old? Or did I miss a birthday or two? I felt very much grown up. My mother relied on me and needed me; she always asked me what to do. I knew she felt badly that we were a burden to the relatives. Six adults and seven children living in a small apartment and all had to eat. Sometimes Mother wondered if we should have taken the accommodation in Stralsund the Red Cross woman had offered. They might also have been able to find work for Mother. Coming closer to the miller's house, I got very nervous. I thought of Lisa's unsuccessful visit and that he does not have any flour until the next harvest and I felt ashamed and embarrassed to even try.

He was in the room with the big millstones. Rays of sunlight came in through two push up windows in the roof. I saw the dust motes dancing again and remembered the day when my throat hurt so badly.

The man, I rightly assumed to be the miller, turned to me and I uttered, "Hi."

He looked at me and I did not avert my eyes. We were communicating with our eyes; no words were spoken. He then stated a fact, "You are small. – Take that dustpan and the brush, crawl under and around the stones and sweep all the flour together. It's not white but good with the bran in it. A bit of dust does not hurt. Did you know you have to eat four hundred pounds of dirt anyway before you die? Your mother can bake bread with it. I don't think you have milk but she can cook it in water and maybe add some fruit if you have some and you can have it for breakfast. Along the road to Poseritz are apple trees. They belong to no one. You could wander up there tomorrow. They are not quite ripe but good enough for cooking."

He kept on talking to me while I was sweeping what looked like dust onto a pile. Then I took my barley bag, and with the dustpan I put as much into it as I thought I could carry. I crouched by the pile left over, looked at him thinking, "He is nice as if he were my grandfather."

I felt my throat restricting and was afraid I would cry. He must have noticed because he asked me if I was hungry. What a question! I was always hungry and nodded.

"Good," he said, "I don't like to eat alone. Come with me into the house and we will have a sandwich."

Fleetingly, I thought of the Russians but this man could not be like that and I would be safe with him. I had to trust him but with all the experiences I had had, it was not easy. We entered a neat, very sunny, little country kitchen.

"Sit down, kid. While I fix us something, tell me about you."

I did not know where to start so he asked me questions. At first, I just gave short answers but little by little, I opened up and told him about everything. It was like some flood gates had opened. I never even stopped to take a breath.

I told him how it was with the Russians; and when they were gone, the Polish army came and threw us out and we had to leave our house within ten minutes; that Granny did not want to come with us and the aunts blamed my mother for it; the week-long walk west and the waiting for four days to cross the Oder River and sleeping under the stars; the barley I found in one of the carriages; the baby sister just drinking roasted barley coffee and most of the time cold; the murder of the woman and the little girl next to us in the boxcar and what the Russian then did to Mother and how the next morning she pushed us out of the moving train because it was going to Poland; the Russian doctor and the needle for the diphtheria; the sleep in the strawberry patch with my panties around my ankles and always the Russian columns of trucks and tanks and jeeps beside us and finally the unexpected arrival in Stralsund; the nice Red Cross women and the food packages they gave us; the checkpoints on the bridge and how the guards had to be bribed and we lost the food again and when we could see auntie's house already and did not have anything to give at the last checkpoint; how my mother lost it, sobbed and wanted to throw us all over the bridge railing into the water because she couldn't go on anymore and when she pulled the baby out of the pram the blanket fell out and the soldier saw and took the small bag of cherries we had forgotten and it was "karochow" (good, all right) to carry on and he opened the beam.

This kind elderly man just stared at me, one hand on the bread before him and a knife in the other. He looked pale and very serious. "My God," he said and then he was quiet for a very long time. He seemed to think of something as he kept looking at me and finally asked what kind of work my mother could do. I told him about house and farm work when she was growing up.

"Can she milk cows?"

I nodded "yes".

"Would you like to come back and get the rest of the flour you swept up? I have an idea how your mother could get work and help feed you all. But first, I have to see my friend and check with him. My wife is helping him now. Let's say, you come back the day after tomorrow about the same time, all right?"

I could only nod with tears sitting very close to the edge of my eyes. After that, we ate very quietly, each trapped in our own thoughts. When I left, we shook hands. I could barely speak because of so many emotions. I would have liked to throw myself into this kind man's arms – hold on to him and cry and cry and cry. But that would have been utterly unthinkable.

"Thank you, thank you so much," was all I could manage.

Mother starts working

I felt like running home but the bag of flour dust weighed me down, it kept me grounded. Aunt Tutti couldn't believe my luck as she called it and all the other aunts just looked at me, smiling. More Russian soup and bread! I wasn't sure if I should tell about work for Mother, some feeling kept me from doing so. I slept fitfully thinking of it and when I noticed that Mom did not sleep either, I crept into her bed and whispered the whole story to her. She kissed me on the forehead, "You are a smart girl, Gila, let's keep it our secret and pray that it happens."

That night I fell asleep in her bed and I slept well.

It did happen. Not far from the mill was a large farm and the farmer's wife had died not long ago. He needed help desperately, especially someone who could look after the household, cook for several field and barn workers and generally take over the chores of his wife. He had two young grown-up sons, one nineteen and one twenty three years old. He would pay her with food and at the moment worthless money. She told him, "that's not necessary," but he insisted. "There might be shops again, and then you'll be glad you have a bit in your pocket."

She started work the day after she went to see him.

Bed bugs

Uncle Fritz got another unused attic room at the top of the stairs on the third floor ready to be our living room-kitchen and my bedroom.

Someone had given him a folding bed with a thin mattress. At night, it was my bed and it was a sofa during the day. It was a new experience to sleep in a room by myself. We had a table and two chairs. He "organised" (that's what trading was called) a three-legged, little stove with a hole on the top, covered with iron rings. To fit the size of the cook pot one could take away as many rings as needed. Naturally, it had to be fired up with wood. It was Christel's and my job to look for sticks and branches to burn in it. It was not easy to find because everybody needed wood to cook. Uncle came home with some pieces of old lumber one day to build walls for another small room in the attic, a bunk bed and, because the roof was slanted, one wider bed. He traded fish for straw to serve as mattresses. In lieu of a closet, we pegged our few pieces of clothing on a string in the open part of the attic.

Mother was very happy with this new arrangement. She had to go to work every morning leaving at five a.m., walking more than three kilometers. She would not come back before about eight o'clock in the evening. After a couple of weeks the older boy lent her his bicycle and she could leave half an hour later in the morning and was home half an hour earlier at night. She always brought milk, bread, occasionally butter and veggies, all of which we shared with everybody. I had to take care of myself, Christel and Ingrid while Aunt Tutti looked after her pet, Edith.

Unfortunately, I developed some very itchy spots since living upstairs. Aunt Irene looked at them and knew right away, "Bed bugs"!

We could not find any when we checked the mattress. But it did not stop and there were blood spots on my sheets. Someone had the bright idea that I should use a flashlight to look under my cover at night. Uncle brought one from the station. I saw the buggers, not just under my cover but also on the wall next to me; yes, they came out at night to feed on me. The boys teased me. "Sleep tight and don't let the bed bugs bite… hahaha!"

Lisa figured, "They must have been in the old mattress on the folding bed."

I was to kill as many as I could but as soon as I switched on the light, they scurried away in all directions. We got rid of the bed and mattress. I slept in the upper bunk bed in the other room, Christel in the lower and Ingrid with Mother in the wider one they called a "French bed." Aunt Helen slept in the next room and we would hear her cry almost every night. She was a widow. Her husband was killed quite early on in the war.

I don't know exactly how we got rid of the bugs but Uncle smoked them out with something and in the process almost burned down the house.

Looking back, Aunt Irene's treatment of the head lice had worked. My turban had to come off early because I was crying with pain and blood kept seeping through the towel in the back of my head. The kerosene had run down that way and eaten away on my skin. Below the hairline, it was raw and infected from one ear to the other. My forehead was not quite as bad and healed reasonably fast. The treatment was camomile rinses and sunshine because there was no other medicine. It took a very long time to heal and during my whole life, whenever I had a perm it would break open again. My sisters and Mother had no such problems.

Red Cross calling for vaccination

A rumour reached us about several cases of typhoid fever. To avoid an outbreak in Altefähr the Red Cross women had received the order and enough serum to vaccinate everybody. We asked where it came from and the nurses confided that Sweden had donated the product. Sweden was just a few hours ferry ride from Sassnitz across the Baltic Sea. At one time, the Swedes had even owned the Island of Rügen.

Aunt Irene was now part of the Red Cross. The vaccination was compulsory. It was a series of three shots, one a week. It was the first time we went to the village we had seen from the bridge. I was happy for all of us to walk the two kilometers together. The needle went into the upper arm just below the pockmarks we had from vaccinations in early childhood. Ingrid was crying because it hurt. I remember skipping along and laughing about it on the way home.

"Ingrid, remember when I had that awfully sore throat? I got a shot into my bum and it hurt so much I couldn't even walk but without it I would be dead now."

I convinced her that she would be all right. Ingrid was such a nice, quiet and undemanding little girl. She never complained, hardly cried and somehow always just fit into every situation.

Not even one week later and before the second shot I was unconscious in a make shift hospital in the old village school in Poseritz, six kilometers away. I had typhoid fever. I did not regain consciousness until four weeks later. When I woke up I was in a room with eight women and they all started yelling, "Nurse." I had no idea where I was or why I was in this room with so many strangers who all looked at me and seemed to be excited about something.

A nurse came and sat down on my bed. She looked at me for a while, felt my pulse and asked me, "Who are you?" I told her and she nodded.

"Are you hungry? Do you want something to eat?"

I wasn't sure and just closed my eyes to think. She shook me and I heard her say, "Stay with me, don't slip away, you have slept enough, wake up, wake up."

To please her I opened my eyes and admitted, "Yes, I am hungry but I don't know if I can eat. My stomach feels funny. I am afraid it might come up again and I'll soil the bed."

The nurse laughed and shocked me with her answer, "You have done that and more, like a baby for four weeks and one more time doesn't matter at all."

Four weeks? Why would I have done that? I felt very embarrassed.

Never in my life before did I have a slice of bread with cottage cheese and strawberry jam on top of it. It was delicious and the nurse fed me one bite at a time. It stayed with me and from then on, I asked for it every day. I could not understand why all the women and the nurses watched me eat and were happy about it as if I did something really spectacular. Weird! I had to stay another two weeks because I was very weak and could not even stand or walk on my own.

Finally, Uncle Fritz came with cousin Siegfried and our handcart to pick me up. They had upholstered the cart with pillows and I felt somewhat silly to lean back in it like a Chinese Queen!

I was shocked to learn that Christel got typhoid fever after the second shot and was in Bergen, the capital of Rügen, in a real hospital. Our mother got it after the third shot and was away too. She had a different type of typhoid fever to do with her head and she lost a lot of hair. The only one who did not get sick after the three shots was Ingrid. I don't know if Edith had any shots at all. Maybe she had been too weak in the first place. None of our relatives got sick. Their immune systems must have been much better than ours were.

Helen was lucky during this time to be able to see a real doctor. He cured whatever ailed her and caused her to cry every night. He had given her quinine not because she had malaria or something. She had been raped a number of times and did not get her period. She had been devastated and ready to kill herself. I had a good idea what had been wrong. The crying stopped and a new woman emerged after a few days. I happened to overhear the aunts talking about those terrible days. Lisa had gone through it six times. Irene was not spared and Aunt Tutti, who had a heart condition, was raped on her sofa several times until she fainted and Uncle had been held at gunpoint to watch. They all expressed gratitude that they were all right and were supportive of Helen. I closely observed my mother from then on thinking of the happenings in the train. I was sure she would not do what Helen did but it would have been terrible. Another mouth to feed and what would Daddy think or feel when he came back?

Harvest fields and beach

With Mother away sick, we had less food again. I heard them whisper about the possibility she might not make it and how could they raise us four kids plus their own three. It was a very worrying time for me. I felt responsible for my sisters. Christel was still in hospital with typhoid fever but she was doing better than Mother was. Still weak, I pushed myself to go along the garden fences again to find something, along the ditches to pick weeds and I saw that the elderberries were starting to ripen. I could not yet walk the three kilometers to my miller friend but I did visit the farmer woman across the field. I found her in the barn sitting on a three-legged stool doing the milking. She nodded to me, indicating I should wait. She later filled my little milk can and she put some veggies in my held up skirt. I had no bag and she did not either.

"Tell you what," she said. "My husband is starting to harvest the wheat field tomorrow, next to the empty potato field. By the way, why don't you take a hoe, you might find more potatoes. When the men are done setting up the sheaves of wheat, you can go and pick up any ears that the machines did not rake up. Just don't go close to the sheaves. The men will have guards out there with dogs. I warn you, you don't want to be caught."

It was very tough to go out on that stubble field with bare feet. We learned to shuffle our feet against the stubble to press it down but we found many wheat ears this first evening and stuffed it all tightly into a pillowcase. Lisa and Irene were with us kids and we went home happy. Later that evening we sat around the table, talked animatedly and peeled the grain out of their covers while Aunt Tutti put it through the coffee mill and made flour. We tried several more times but by then other people had been there as well. I took a rake and went to the elder bushes in the deep ditch. I held the branches down and picked the ripe dark elder umbels. We added these to our watery flour soup. Aunt Irene announced, "All the iron and the vitamins and minerals in these will keep us healthy." At first, we did not like the taste of the elderberry too much but it was growing on us. Hunger is a great motivator. Nature provided plenty more.

Aunt Irene and Lisa had taken the train once a week to check on Christel and Mother in the hospital. Finally, Christel came home and, a week later, Mother. The aunts went on the appointed days to pick them up. I was very relieved. Mother still had to take it quite easy because of constant headaches that she suffered with for the rest of her life and dizziness. She had to postpone her wish to go back to work. Christel was not interested in playing and just sat around a lot, staring into space and was always very tired. Her legs were very thin and she had to hold on to something or she would stumble. Mother and I talked about her and we were concerned she might not be all right in her head anymore. Luckily, we were wrong. She just needed time to get over this awful disease. I had spent six weeks in the makeshift hospital in the country while she was only four weeks in the real hospital in the city. Maybe I had better food once I could eat again. She surely did not have bread with cottage cheese and jam.

During the day, we started to go to the beach not too far from the bridge on the train side. The boys had bathing suits but Ingrid and I just went into the water in our under pants. Warm September days, lots of sunshine and a bit of fun splashing each other helped to forget for a few hours how gruesome all this time had been. Lisa and Irene were not allowed to come with us. Russians in jeeps were controlling the roads and young women were not safe. Often they had to hide under some junk in the far corners of the attic. We forgot the time and did not notice how low the sun already was. I had picked some hard beach grass to make myself sandals by braiding it, forming soles and sewing it together with thinner grass. Lisa came to get us to come home but she quickly had to hide in very prickly blackthorn bushes growing along the cliff. Did she ever get herself scratched up!

A Russian on a motorbike had come along the narrow path by the cliffs and continued on to lower ground towards a former lonely "Gasthaus" (Pub) at an old unused ferry stop further down the beach. A woman with two daughters a bit younger than Lisa and a son about fifteen or sixteen lived there. When the biker was out of our sight, we grabbed our clothing and ran home.

Uncle Fritz worried, "A single Russian? That does not sound good. Hope the girls in that old guest house are okay."

Since the next day was a warm sunny day again, we went back to our "spot" playing in the water. All of a sudden, Siegfried, turning towards the cliffs, pointed and yelled, "Look! There is a motorbike in the bushes…."

We rushed out of the water, reached for our things and headed off towards home in a hurry. Afraid there might be a dead or injured Russian, we did not even dare to take a closer look.

The next few days many Russians ransacked every house and asked many questions, checked every nook and cranny, they dug deep into every freshly turned earth in the community gardens and made a lot of threats. After about a week they discovered an old unused dried up well in a grove of bushes, not far from the lone house at the beach, filled with lots of rusted farm implements and whatever fit in there, straw and kelp, sand and big rocks. They unearthed it all and there he was. The family from the guesthouse was missing.

School and brown sugar

Some political activity was going on in the village of Altefähr. Uncle Fritz received an order to come to weekly meetings. A few men had formed a communist party and they were trying to restore some order and organize the civic affairs. They chose a council, a mayor and a secretary for him with an office on the ground floor of a nice-looking house on the road to Bergen, the capital of Rügen. The first order of the day was to check and list all empty houses, suites or rooms in the village and to get people like us, evicted refugees from the eastern side of Germany, which was now Poland, into agreeable living conditions. To the delight of everyone, a family of four came forward, a couple with a five-year-old boy and the wife's father. Both men were teachers. They offered to get the school cleaned up, organized and going again. The former teacher's house was empty with all the furniture left in it when they had fled to the west of Germany. This family moved into the "Teacher's House" and got busy doing what they had promised. A number of women volunteered to help with the cleaning of the school and the school grounds.

At the beginning of October 1945, the school was ready and all the school-aged children were registered for the appropriate classes. Nobody could buy pens or paper, books or other school supplies. The first three grades were taught by the older gentleman, Mr. Drawe; the younger man, Mr. Scheider had all the kids from grade four to grade eight. The old chalkboards were still there and broken pieces of chalk were on the narrow shelves.

The teachers found ways to make the school time interesting and somehow the parents of the local pupils came up with old school books and all kinds of paper, wallpaper and even brown packing paper, letters and envelopes with the back-side empty and old scribblers with empty pages in them. Uncle Fritz found a stack of newspapers in the attic and we used the white edges to write on. There was still ink in the inkwells in the school desks and for the appropriate pens we made quills out of feathers we found on the beach. I actually loved to use them. We learned the multiplication tables, every number from two to twenty by heart, we had to stand up and rattle off the ones we had learned. I can hardly imagine that many children nowadays can do that. Do you know off-hand how much eight times nine is or seven times eight or twelve by twelve? You get the drift – that was math class!

For singing lessons, we had to remember every verse of the songs by heart. We had to repeat after the teacher verse by verse until we remembered the words. I still know many German folksongs as soon as I hear the melody. Literature? There were ten books in the school, all classic ones like, "War and Peace" by Leo Tolstoy or "Faust" by J.W. von Goethe; not really books read by youngsters. The teacher would read portions of a story and then we would discuss it. I borrowed and read all ten of them, one after the other. I was a voracious reader but I also wanted to impress Mr. Scheider. He did not really believe that I read them but when he asked me questions, I could give him the answers.

Once he expressed his sentiment, "I can't believe that you read those books, I haven't even read them all."

I had a crush on him, probably because he was the first male who made an impression on me since I had lost my father, who had been my hero until I was eleven years old. I forgot, but yes, I was still eleven years old. Our school was closed in January 1945 when I had been just a few months in grade five, so now in October of the same year I was placed in Grade five. With no books, we did not really know what we had missed but we were all eager to learn.

Mother had gone back to the farmer for work. Since she had to leave so early in the morning, she would wake me and I was totally in charge to get my sisters and me ready for the day. It was my responsibility: washing, dressing, combing and braiding our hair; breakfast and then Ingrid to go to Auntie who looked after Edith, and Christel and I off for school. Going along the road we had a two kilometer walk to school every morning. School started at eight a.m. and was finished at 12.30 p.m. We walked together with our three boy cousins. If we went across the train tracks, we cut off almost half a kilometer. It was "verboten" to cross the tracks but since Uncle Fritz worked for the railway, we dared to race across with the promise not to trip and break our legs and also to watch for unexpected trains coming. That never happened anyway and we knew the schedule of the very few regulars but then they often were late and only once one surprised us.

We had a beautiful warm fall. One day on the way home, we decided to go through the middle path of the community gardens close to the village, trying to shorten our way a bit more. The gates were still locked in the morning but then open all day.

I did not like to use the always-dirty, outdoor toilet on the school grounds and felt a need for some privacy.

"Go ahead," I told the others, "I'll follow shortly."

When finished I walked just a few steps when I got terribly dizzy. I sat down leaning against the fence. With the warm, noon sun on my face I felt drowsy and fell asleep. A woman coming from her garden found me, woke me and asked where I lived. She wanted to know why I was lying here. She shook her head, "You tell me you came out of school at 12.30 and you are sleeping here ever since? Have you had some food or anything to drink since breakfast? It's close to three o'clock!"

She gave me three plums and a small apple and insisted I eat them right away. Then she walked with me all the way through the gardens until she came to hers. She opened the lock, we went in and sat down in the shade and she gave me some water from a little pump.

"Easy now," she said, "one little sip after the other, keep it in your mouth until it's warm before you swallow. Water after fruit is actually not a good idea but you do need it."

On the way home, she kept me company until we could see Aunt Tutti's house and I just had to cross the tracks.

Christel and I had no shoes for the colder weather ahead. Uncle had fashioned us some wooden soles with a strap across for school days. What a surprise when he came home one day in early November with a big smile on his face and handed each of us a pair of brand new Dutch clogs.

"Here is an early Christmas present," he said, "it might be all you get."

We had never seen the likes of such funny clogs and marvelled how they could have gotten the form of a shoe inside this piece of wood – but they fit with room for thick long socks handed down from the boys. At first we both had trouble walking in them but got used to walking more flat footed because they don't bend. I never had cold feet that winter. I have never had any other shoes that kept my feet warm in rain, snow or ice.

I had to wear that funny ladies coat with the patches and the big bust. I was teased a lot by the local kids but I had no other coat.

"Grin and bear it," said Mom.

With that voluptuous lady's coat and the Dutch clogs – what a sight I must have been wearing them. By the next spring, the patches had faded and become green again. I wish we had photographs! My Aunt had a chest with old clothing in the attic and she offered that my mother could make us something out of whatever she found. We still had not advanced to wearing pants. I had picked a piece of bright green felt. I folded it, sewed it together and it made a nice warm hat which kept my ears warm. I stitched little stars with orange yarn around the front and had bands on each side to tie under my chin. It looked like it belonged to one of the *"Seven Dwarves...."*

One stormy, very cold, winter day I came home on my own across the tracks and saw about half a dozen men busy at several boxcars on a side track. A truck was parked next to them and that had never happened before. Curious, I walked closer. They were unloading big bags like potato sacks from a boxcar into the truck. I watched them for a while and then asked the closest one to me, "What's in the sacks?"

"I don't know, kid, but it smells like...," when one of the other men gave a shout, "Oh shit, it just slipped right through my hands, godamnit."

The sack had burst and a whole pile of brown sugar was there on the ground between the track and the truck. The men kept working as if nothing had happened. I was nailed to the spot and stared at the sugar, my mouth watered as it does right now and then the man who had the accident grinned at me, "Take your hat off kiddo, fill it and if you want to lift your skirt, I'll put a few hands full into that too."

I had no qualms about it and accepted both offers. Coming home with this treasure the boys raced over there and got some for their family. Every night now we had boiled potatoes in the skin cut open and brown sugar on top. The watery flour soup in the morning tasted delicious with brown sugar as well.

14: Phoenix Rising from the Ashes

Political developments 1946

Life during the winter of 1945/46 was quiet. My aunts were busy unravelling old sweaters to knit socks and mitts and Mother had time to sew dresses for us out of old clothing and even made underwear. We had no radio or newspaper so we heard little or nothing about what was going on in the rest of Germany. People still disappeared leaving everything behind and hoped to find a better life in the western parts of the country. Uncle Fritz brought us news from those meetings he had to attend about the happenings in Berlin, the political centre. On June 5th 1945, the Allied Forces agreed to divide Germany into four areas of control: The Russian, the English, the American and the French zones, with Berlin like an island in the Russian part. Our area remained controlled by the Russians. They also divided the city of Berlin into four parts. Later, "Checkpoint Charley," the divide between the east and the three west "sectors" became famously "infamous."

In the big cities, women had started to clear the ruins. They cleaned the mortar off every brick and piled them up. These women became known as "Trümmer-Frauen = rubble women." The German women provided the start and the base for rebuilding the cities that were now nothing but piles of rubble.

Early in spring, 1946, my mother had applied for a community garden and been granted a small piece of overgrown land covered with lots of rocks close to the beach. It was about one quarter of an acre in a triangular shape bordered on one side by a tall blackthorn hedge and a narrow path along another side with more blackthorn bushes separating it from the cliff down to the beach. Nothing had ever grown on this piece of land except tall grass, thistles and other weeds. The school was closed for Easter holidays so we children, including Ingrid, who would turn six in August, spent many hours each day collecting the rocks and piling them up along the third side. As long as there was light in the sky, Mother came after work and started digging. We helped to pull the weeds out of the dug up earth, careful to get all the roots. It was very hard work especially in this first year but in the end, we could plant enough potatoes and some veggies to help feed us. I remember feeling a certain pride when this field was all green and the potatoes were blooming! Mother's employer had provided the seed potatoes and the seeds for the veggies, mostly turnips and sugar beets.

Then one day Uncle Fritz came home with more news. At a conference held in Potsdam in the beautiful luxury castle of the Prussian Kings on August 2nd 1945, the expulsion of several million Germans from the eastern quarter of Germany was mandated in order to seize this part of the country for Poland, with the Oder and Neisse Rivers to become the new permanent eastern border of Germany. Our hopes of ever going back home were suddenly dashed and we now felt truly homeless.

To make matters worse, Uncle Fritz told us that he had met a man from Stresow, Max V. who had escaped with two others after the roundup of all able men and women in February 1945. The Russians had shot at them. He had taken the first shots in the leg and arms. He fell down and the two others were killed and fell on top of him. When the Russians checked the men on top of him, he pretended to be dead as well. He had told Uncle Fritz that he was a hundred percent sure that Erich, my father, was dead. He claimed that he had personally seen when and how Father was carried out of the large hall where hundreds of men slept and that Father never got to Siberia. This was a terrible shock for us but my mother shook her head and declared, "No way, I just don't believe it. I am convinced I would feel it if he were dead. He promised to come back and I still believe that."

At that time two political parties existed: The KPD (Kommunist Party) led by Wilhelm Pieck and the SPD (Socialist Party) led by Otto Grotewohl in Berlin. In April 1946, both parties were united under the name SED = Sozialistische Einheits Partei Deutschlands = United Party of Germany. Mr. Pieck and Mr. Grotewohl became Co-Chairmen. This party, under the watchful eyes of the Russian occupiers became the most Stalinist party in the Eastern Block. Without being a member, people could not advance in any career or, by being reported by someone for not toeing the line, people would disappear. This was not much different from the "good old days..." as people, who trusted each other, sarcastically said. Altefähr also got their SED party.

To organize the young people the FDJ = Freie Deutsche Jugend (Free German Youth) was founded in summer of 1946. It was very tightly controlled by the SED. The younger kids had their own organisation until they were old enough for the FDJ, the "Young Pioneers." At the beginning, the programs were geared towards leisure activities. Actually, everything was very much like the Hitler Youth. Membership was not mandatory but without it, many disadvantages awaited the unfortunate and unsuspecting pupil. At this point, we did not know that. Most children had to help their parents in the fields and had little time for leisure, except maybe after supper kicking a soccer ball around on the village street.

Industry and commerce were nationalized. Plans to divide the large estates and farms into thirty-acre plots were underway. The large farms closer to Altefähr were the first to be divided and were given to whoever applied for land and then they were organized into a "Co-op." The new farmers had no say in what they wanted to grow: Each one would get an order of what and how much of it he was to grow and how much of it he had to deliver to the "Co-op," who, in turn would sell it to small shops called "Konsum." These shops sold it to the general population. The big farmhouses were also divided up between the new people who now farmed the land. Many fights broke out because of sometimes six or even ten parties having to share a kitchen. Quite a number of the former owners left for the western zones. If they stayed, they also only had thirty acres now instead of their former hundreds or even thousands. Everybody was to be "equal" and we Germans were told to be proud to be part of an "Arbeiterstaat," (a workers' state) like our friends and brothers in the Soviet Union. The intellectual class was to be "equalized" as well. Titles should not be used, just first names and the familiar term "du" like the French "tu". It did not work well with the Germans, used to formality.

The Red Cross announced that, in order to provide a means to find lost relatives or friends again, all displaced people should register with them and also provide the names of people they would like to find. The postal service had a very slow start but a start nevertheless.

Even the church bells had started to ring again to invite the people for Sunday services since a new pastor had turned up, just as the teachers had materialized. The older generation said, "The Lord provides for His own." Funerals, baptisms and weddings could now be arranged. Altefähr had only a Lutheran church. The new pastor also offered classes for twelve-year-olds for confirmation at fourteen. My cousin Siegfried, Annemarie, a girl whose family had moved into the main floor suite in the house where we lived and I, happily signed up and had to attend weekly confirmation classes in the pastor's house. If you joined the confirmation class, you could not be a member of the FDJ.

A new subject in school

We looked forward to starting school again. Ingrid was enrolled in grade one and our little group had become larger with her addition and Annemarie, who was my age. We always sat next to each other for the next two years. To our surprise, Mr. Scheider introduced a new teacher, Miss Kerstins from Lithuania, and announced that she would teach us the Russian language. It was a compulsory subject and nobody could opt out. Most of the boys hated her from the start because of her squeaky voice and her subject and made her life miserable by being obtrusive and pretending to be dumb. Sometimes she lost her temper and screamed at them but that made it even worse. She could not help having to give them good notes in the report cards when they did surprisingly well in the examinations.

I truly enjoyed learning another language. Within the school year 1946/47, I mastered the Cyrillic alphabet and could read simple stories from a Russian book each one of us had received. I thought it fun to write something nobody else could read! By now, four of us girls had made friends and we were sending little notes in Russian to each other. Early "texting!"

All four of us were in the confirmation class. There was Rosie and Wally, local village girls, and Annemarie and me as newcomers. I was proud to have an "A" in language in my report card. The village boys bullied us and once, after geometry class, I was really hurt by the worst of them, Bubi Warsow. He ran by me and drove the sharp point of the drafting compass into the right side of my bum. I was standing in front of the announcement display across from the mayor's office to find out when it would be our turn to pick up our ration cards. I sank down to the ground. He never stopped running. I had trouble walking and a lot of pain for more than a month.

"Gila, you would have lost the use of your leg, if he had hit the nerve," Aunt Irene said.

She treated the infected flesh wound with an herbal concoction and luckily, it healed up. I was very wary of that boy, who was also in our confirmation class. He had warned me that I would be very sorry if I would ever tell.

A first letter and a proposal

Altefähr had a female postman, sorry, a post woman. She often asked us to take the letters for the people who lived in the station houses to save her the four-kilometer walk, two each way. Today she gave us a letter and it was for Helen. Aunt Tutti probably knew what it was about but nobody ever mentioned it. Helen subsequently left without goodbyes when we were in school. I still have no idea where she went and she has never attempted to contact any of us. She probably wanted to leave her past behind and the people who knew of her severe unhappiness. Aunt Irene now moved into Helen's attic room.

One early spring evening we were all sitting together, chatting. Aunt Tutti looked at Mother, "Else, what's the matter? You are too quiet and you look troubled. Are you all right?"

"I am not sure how to tell you this," Mother answered, "my boss has offered to marry me. He wants me, and my children to move into his house. His sons are okay with it …."

They all exclaimed at once that she should accept, that this was a great opportunity, that she was a very lucky woman. When Mom finally had a chance to get a word in she explained, "He told me that I would have to declare Erich deceased and get a death certificate. I cannot do that. I still think he is coming back."

"My God, come on Else – remember Max V. has seen him dead. He is never coming back again; you have to finally face it. Don't be ridiculous. You owe it to the children to give them a real home and a family again. You can't live in the attic forever!"

I just stared at my mother. Declare Father officially dead? NOOO! To move to that farm and be more than four kilometers one way away from school? How would we get back and forth during the winter months, through snow and ice with no real shoes or warm clothing? Did the aunts just want to get rid of us by pushing her so hard? My tears started to flow.

"I am sorry. I told him that I like and respect him and appreciate his offer but that I still love my husband and know in my heart that he is coming back. He is disappointed and said that I am running his house like a wife and he thought it just right to make me this offer."

"But if you declined, can you keep working there?"

"Yes, he understands and said that he will ask me again next year."

I heard my mother cry that night and I went to her, sat on the edge of her bed and told her that I am very glad that she did not accept the proposal.

"Gila," she said, "I don't want you girls to grow up on the farm and become unpaid farm hands. I want a better future for you. You should get an education or learn something for an office job or nursing, anything but a farm. I remember my own young years working for my father. No, I surely don't want that for you."

A post card makes me fly

It was a cold grey day in March and a strong wind was blowing. It came straight on to my back with such sudden gusts I could not even keep walking, I had to lift my feet and run in order not to be pushed over. The postal woman called me when I passed the post office, "Hey, Gisela, can you take this card home with you? It's for your mother."

I took the card, glanced at the address. Yes, it was Mother's name and it hit me like lightning, "It's my father's hand writing! Oh, my dear God; it is my father's hand writing!"

My eyes almost fell out of my face. I looked at the women and she smiled at me. I realized that she had read the card and I hated her for it but only for a moment. I was shaking with shock, mumbling, "It's from my father." I looked down at the card in my hand and heard her say, "Your mother will be so happy. You better get home fast, every minute counts."

I did not take the time to read the card. My heart was in overdrive, my feet were flying over the ground and halfway home a strong gust of wind caught under my coat and lifted me up. My feet kept making the running motions and I counted five empty steps in the air. I had to spread and wiggle my arms to keep my balance, I almost hit a tree and then I was back on the ground. Coming to the house, I ran all the way up the first two sets of stairs and kept calling, "Mother! Mother! Mother!"

I was crying hard, could not breathe anymore and collapsed on the landing.

The aunts heard the commotion and opened their door, "Goodness Gila, be careful; Gila, what's the matter?"

"Dad's coming home. Dad has written a post card – Dad is not dead...."

When I came to I was flat on my back on Aunt Tutti's couch, my mother was sitting in a chair crying her eyes out into a towel. The three aunts were busy with changing the cool cloth they put on my forehead and around my calves. All the other children were sitting perfectly still on the floor watching the scene. It took a long time until Mother was finally able to read the card to me. Dad was in a prisoner camp in Thuringia. He had found us through the Red Cross, and was hoping to join us within the next few weeks and be with us at Easter. He had to wait for his release papers and then it would depend on the train connections the Red Cross could get for him. He had water in his legs almost up to the hips and he was hoping to make it to Altefähr without it getting any higher. But the edema had been a blessing. It was the reason for his release from Siberia.

When Mother told her boss, he was incredulous and marvelled about women's intuition.

Afraid to lose my teeth

My gums were white and all my teeth were loose. I was afraid to bite on anything and avoided eating. I could handle soups, I mashed my potatoes with the fork and I did not chew anything but just carefully swallowed whatever food passed my lips. My teeth had been my pride and joy and now I was afraid they would all fall out. I fainted during a math lesson and just slipped down under the desk. Bärbel Moldt, a nice girl from Christel's class, offered to take me to her mother who would know what to do. The Moldts had a bakery just three houses away from the school. The teacher insisted that my cousin Siegfried would go along to hold me up, Bärbel on one side and Siggi on the other. Mrs. Moldt put me down on a couch, covered me and put a cool wet cloth on my forehead. She sent the other two back to school. I was cold, shivered and was very dizzy. Mrs. Moldt asked me about my daily life and declared after my confession, "Gisela, for your age you are way too small and thin. You are overtired, overworked, totally exhausted; you have scurvy, and you need lemons and much fruit with vitamins and good food. Don't be shy; come to me every day after school. Your sisters can go home with your cousins. Christel is now the age you were when you started to look after them, so let her do it for a bit. I will fix a special drink and a light meal for you and you'll see it won't take long and your teeth will be all right again."

Bärbel took me home with her every day for about three weeks. I'll never forget the enticing baking smell when entering the bakery. I was not sure of my feelings but it must have been a bit like sadness, jealousy or not even quite understanding that people still had such a wonderful life. Did I think that everybody lived as we did? I also felt guilty spending an hour in this always-warm cozy house and my sisters had to go home to help themselves to whatever. I will never forget the day when I had my first fresh bun with homemade liver sausage. I remember holding it in my hand and looking at it before I had to cut it into very small pieces and soak each one in my mouth before carefully trying to chew and swallow. I was too embarrassed to keep going to her and just stopped. But, yes, I am indebted to Mrs. Moldt in Altefähr for my teeth.

It happened on one of the first days after visiting Mrs. Moldt that I had to sit with my back against the fence again on the way home and fell asleep. But this time I woke myself up with a scream. I had been dreaming of the soldier with his head beside him and the legs on the other side of the pram I pushed. In my dream, he had lifted his head with both hands, held it out to me and begged me to put it back on his neck. It was the first time that I had this nightmare, but it was not the last.

A widowed seamstress with her own sewing machine, Mrs. Wienholz, moved into a makeshift living space in a workshop building in the middle of the train tracks. She made a dress for me out of two old ones and a skirt out of a used one from Aunt Tutti and promised to make me a new coat for the coming winter as soon as we could find suitable material. But, until then, I had to wear that old black ladies' coat with the now green patches and unfortunately also the ladies' shoes with the semi-high heels. The Dutch clogs had passed to the younger sisters. I loved spending time with Mrs. Wienholz and helped her by sewing on buttons and other such little chores and decided I might become a seamstress when I grew up.

Father is with us again

A second post card arrived about two weeks after the first one giving us the time of his arrival at the station in Altefähr. My mother refused to come along to pick him up and expressed her feelings, "I can't handle it. Tell him I will wait at home for him. I am afraid I'll break down. I am so weak my legs will just give up."

Yes, I understood her, but I wouldn't miss it for the world. Ingrid and Christel came with me, little Edith was still too young and besides, she did not have any outdoor shoes. Uncle Fritz was on duty on the platform. Only three people got off the train. Dad saw us right away and we ran towards him. He opened his arms but his first whispered words were, "Where is Mother? Is she all right?"

"Yes. Yes, Daddy. She is waiting for you at home."

Uncle Fritz joined us as soon as he had given the signal for the train to leave. The men shook hands and both had tears in their eyes. They could not even speak. Finally, Uncle dismissed us with a little wave of the hand and remarked with a shaky voice, "See you later at dinner. Everybody is happy about your homecoming, Erich. Your sisters Lisa and Irene are here as well."

Each of us wanted to hold onto Dad's hands but he only had two. Used to stepping back because I was the oldest, I took his only piece of luggage, a rolled up army blanket, held together with some string. He did not even have a warm coat just a ragged jacket over his shirt and the wind was still cold. He was limping. His more than well-worn shoes were open without shoelaces. He was very emotional and did not say very much at all while Christel and Ingrid chattered on. I walked beside them and never looked away from his face. He was not as handsome as he was when I was five and had wanted to marry him. But he had been in Siberia for close to two years and we had always heard that that was a death sentence from hell and nobody would ever come back from there.

It was a miracle! He made it – he did come back from hell.

How very lucky that Mom did not have a Russian baby and had not married her boss. That would have been absolutely horrible. I wondered if she would tell him. I surely would never mention it.

He did not want to see his sisters first but pulled himself up by the railing for the last steps to the third floor. His eyes locked on Mother who was standing on the landing looking down at him. I worried because she was so pale. They fell into each other's arms and held tight for a long time. They were swaying and I was afraid they would fall down the stairs. I pushed on Father's back and shouted, "Mother, step back, you'll both fall down the stairs and break your necks...."

Finally, Mother moved backwards into our small kitchen, never letting go of Dad. It was only the second time in my life I had seen my parents hug and kiss. It was my father who cried and my mother's tears mixed with his. I could not stand watching it, so I hugged my two sisters around the shoulders and whispered, "Let's leave them alone for a while. I'm sure they will soon come down to Auntie's kitchen."

There were more tears when they entered. His three sisters hugged him in a circle with him in the middle. Laughing and crying was all mixed up. He asked about their mother and was shocked to hear she had remained in Stresow to wait for him and now it was Poland. He only knew what the German guards who worked under Russian control in the prison camp had told him about the zones and all the divisions of Germany.

Ingrid now slept in a cozy corner on the floor because our parents needed that French bed. I could not fall asleep for the longest time because of Father's snoring but mainly because so many thoughts kept me awake. Would Father get well? There was no doctor to help him. Would he find work? Would we get a place to live in the village now that we were a real family? Mother had to go to work in the morning. What would her boss say? Thank goodness, it was still kind of winter; therefore, her hours were much shorter and she always came home before dark. I knew our life would change, but how would it be?

The next few nights I could not fall asleep because Father was telling Mother about Siberia when they thought we children were in dreamland. I could not believe the horror he had been through. Men died like flies and even before they were quite dead, the others would rip their clothing off their bodies. Every morning a truck would drive up to the door and a few men were singled out to throw all the dead bodies onto the truck. One had to grab the arms, the other the legs, swing the body and then let go and it would fall onto all the other naked bodies already on the truck. They died by the hundreds. Father recounted how most of the Stresow men had died during the first few weeks in the prison camp. Most of them just gave up, had no hope or drive to stay alive. They didn't even care when they were whipped and simply lay there. Many just went out into the night and froze to death. It was the easiest way to die. He had no idea about the women but felt sure none of them would come back home because of the way they were abused. He explained to Mother, "The men had it bad but for the women it was worse."

The men had to work the stones loose from the rocky walls of a quarry and chip and hammer them into required shapes. A Russian with a whip was always close by and when you got tired or stopped to take a breath he whipped you into shape. When you felt a natural need you just had to pee or shit into your pants. The hall where they slept was stinking to high heaven with no chance for washing. You used snow and ice to clean yourself and the only pieces of clothing you had you were wearing. You never ever took anything off. If you did, you kept it in your hands or it would be gone before you could even blink. The food was watery thin soup but if you did not have a container, you did not get any. Everybody was hunting for empty cans around the Russians' camp. They would throw them to you as if you were a dog and the Russians laughed when the men would fight over one.

Father had looked for some edible weeds, mostly nettle, to add to his soup when he found a rusty piece of metal from an old jeep and hammered it into a pot. A Russian watched him and asked him to make him one too. He brought him a piece of aluminum for a liner and there was enough for two. Dad had brought this container, rusty on the outside but clean in the inside, home with him rolled in the blanket he had received in the German prison camp. He also had fashioned himself a spoon and fork put together in such a way that it folded, the fork nesting within the spoon. Years later, I used both items for my canoe camping trips. The Russian guards saw these things and he had to make more. They brought him more suitable tools and he got extra food portions. Then he started making rings out of Russian money coins. The Russians admired his expertise and just loved the "jewellery." Dad stayed alive because of it. He promised, "Else, I'll make you a new wedding band out of a Groschen," (German 10 penny piece of brass).

He did. The ring was polished and looked like gold.

Uncle Fritz had asked for and received permission for Father to tinker in the railway workshop where Mrs. Wienholz lived. There he also fixed and rebuilt items for the railway without being paid but it kept him busy and from brooding too much. Years later, when he wanted to buy Mom a real gold ring she declined. She wore the one he made until she died. It was very thin by then but it was still on her finger.

Up to now, I had not hated the Russians on the whole because we had lived with some really nice ones in Stresow when our house was a field hospital. We sat in our laborer's attic during the day cracking lice or, in the evening, watched the Russians dance and sing those beautiful sad folk songs. The terrifying experiences of the first few days were pushed into the back of our minds and we never talked about them. But now, listening in the dark to Dad telling Mom about all the horrible things he had endured when his voice broke and he was weeping, I felt the hate physically and curled myself into the fetal position and stuffed the corner of the pillow into my mouth not to cry out. I did not want to learn Russian anymore. Miss Kerstins could not believe it since I had been her star pupil. I often broke out in tears over some words and she asked me repeatedly what was going on with me. My report card mark went from an A to D within a few months. I pretended to make some effort because I was afraid she would find out that it was because of my dad talking about Siberia. She was a party member and if she would report it to the SED, they would come for him and take him right back there.

15: A Home of Our Own

Moving and work for Dad

Father went to Altefähr to the mayor's office to apply for living quarters and to find out about a chance to get work. He came home with promises and full of hope. It only took about four weeks until we moved into an old house with our handcart and the pram holding all our earthly possessions. We had two rooms, a kitchen and a cold room with a cellar under it. It did not have a stairway or a ladder, just a pull-up trap door. It was not very deep. The Red Cross helped us by providing essential pieces of furniture that we were to give back as soon as we could find something ourselves. The kitchen had a red brick floor that sloped down to the living room and we had to learn to walk on it without losing our footing. A built-in stove was in the corner with an open chimney above it. I climbed up and could see the sky! A small window looked out onto a cobblestone yard and a brick shack for animals or storage. Two out-houses were side by side – one was for our own use, the other for two other families living in the house: an old woman with her elderly son lived across from our suite and upstairs was a younger couple with a two-year-old child.

Dad visited the closed-down smithy owner. He hoped to lease it – but it just didn't work out. He went to the chairman of the Co-op and ended up getting a former garage only three houses away from where we lived. It was part of a former, very large estate but the owners had fled to the West. The house had been divided up for several families like us and all the barns and stables were empty. In the backyard was a huge collection of farm machinery from ploughs to threshers; all of it needed to be fixed. Father had permission to look through the buildings to see if he could find anything useful to establish a repair shop in the empty garage. He did find workbenches and some other things, but now, he was excited about asking the old retired blacksmith if he could buy or rent his machinery. They came to an agreement and my industrious father was back in business. The Co-op paid him a kind of retainer for fixing the useless equipment and even provided oil and other repair items as needed. It did not take very long for other farmers to come and he was busy right from the outset.

One day he came home with a pretty little ring for me, made out of a brass coin like the one he had made for Mother, but mine had a little heart on top.

"Gila, this is for being such a great help to your mother."

His voice was shaky when he put it on my finger. I was so surprised and impressed. Love welled up and made me all hot and I was so proud of my father that he, actually a blacksmith by trade, could make such beautiful things out of coins. When word got out, he could probably have made a living from it. I never took that ring off, wore it for over two years until it was worn through and it was too thin to be repaired, but I did keep it.

The farmers had told him about all the rapeseed and flax they had to plant this year but they had no idea where to get it pressed for oil.

They grumbled, "We would have to bring all of it to the Co-op, not only what's requested but then we hardly get anything in return."

Well, Dad thought about it and built a press, which he installed in our little cellar since it was empty anyway. It was strictly illegal but when the time came, he was busy every night. The cellar did not have a window, a very important factor. I remember that he got six bottles for the farmer out of one-hundred pounds of flax and, in lieu of payment, one bottle for us. Since we could not use it all, it was a welcome item for trade. One farmer brought us a little pig and Mother insisted we needed a goat to have milk. We also acquired a couple of hens and a few small rabbits. By the end of the summer 1947, Father had found enough driftwood at the beach and usable items in the dump to build rabbit cages.

Another shack was attached to the existing one and a rusty wire fence was built across the little cobblestone yard.

We still had the piece of land close to the station where we planted staple crops. The farmer bordering onto the rock wall we had piled up the year before requested that we give it up and insisted it was part of his allotment. We lost it in the fall and were assigned a piece of very dry, loamy land close to the new cemetery outside of the village. Again, we had to pick up, and this time carry away, rocks and pull weeds in fall to get it ready for the next year. We were not very happy with it; it was harder work and lots of our produce was stolen.

Fall 1947

The Rügendam, the Germans had partially blown up in 1945, was finally rebuilt. The trains started crossing again and it had become possible to visit the city. A small ferry connected the village of Altefähr with Stralsund. It was shocking to walk through the streets of the former beautiful old city in ruins and just see a building standing here or there, sometimes only one on a long stretch of street. It was a joy to see that the famous front of the Gothic City Hall was still standing and the City Hall behind it was damaged but not beyond repair. Some small shops had opened in buildings that one would expect to fall down at any moment. I remember one buying and selling any type of used jewellery and watches. A few years later, I bought my first wrist watch there. In a lonely building along one former shopping street was a toy shop. Nothing new here either. Only used toys but people were happy to get any! For several years, children did not even know what new purchased gifts were like. They grew up with homemade things. Wertheim, a former department store, had re-opened and the heading said "Konsum." They had some clothing but you needed a coupon. There were many terrible looking dishes. Who needs so many dishes? But people were buying. I also found a small bookshop. It smelled very musty in there and they had many books – all used but one could get books.

Russian vs. English

During the summer holidays of 1947 and the fall harvest, I had worked for a farmer who lived next door to us. Mostly I looked forward to the breaks to get the tasty rye bread covered with bacon drippings and salt and the welcome barley coffee fortified with lots of milk. I also got five Deutsche Marks for each day of work. I needed it to pay the pastor for private English lessons. I had suggested it to my three girlfriends and jointly we had decided to do this and keep it a secret. I remember the sunny days, sometimes too warm for work crawling along endless dry and dusty rows of tiny turnip or sugar beet plants, which we had to thin out leaving only the strongest ones. Hard work for me was harvesting potatoes for the small farmer who had no machines. I was the only kid; the others were all women. It was a tough time. But I needed the money while the other three girls got it from their families.

One day during Russian class, I answered a question with a few English words. It was long before Dad came back and I guess I wanted to show off. Boy, oh boy was I ever surprised and thoroughly embarrassed when Miss Kerstins let loose a whole barrage of English on me! She also explained and wrote on the black board how the words I had used had to be put together in a different way. With a red face, I sat down and never uttered another English word in Russian class even if she sometimes asked me if I knew the equivalent word in English. She told us that she was fluent in six different languages and she would actually love to teach us more than just Russian. But that was not in the stars, neither for her nor for us. She briefly mentioned that her family was German and had lived in Lithuania for generations. They were evicted from their home during the course of the war. It made a big change in the behaviour of the "bullies" towards her.

At the pastor's, I had problems with the pronunciation of the "th." I had to repeat and repeat words with "th" until I cried. I was almost ready to give up. The pastor had even kept me behind when the others left after our two-hour lesson. It was too difficult to get my teeth apart and stick my tongue out at him to say, "THIS is THAT and THAT is THIS when we are TOGETHER." Now, after Father was back and I had lost all joy in learning Russian, I kept up my English lessons with no premonition of the importance of it for my future.

One day Father came home all excited and announced, "We have a chance to immigrate to Canada. I have seen a placard in Stralsund. The Province of Alberta in Canada welcomes several hundred people who are willing to either work on huge farms or take over some land and work it on their own. They also need tradesmen like me to repair farm machinery. Mother, I'd love to go and put in an application. If we are accepted we have a chance to make a new life and our children can grow up in a peaceful country."

"Canada? That's on the other side of the world. They speak English, we don't. Don't tell me we will learn, kind of on the job. No, I am not going. If you want to go, go. You don't transplant old trees. We are too old for such an undertaking. We'll be strangers among strangers. It's for young people. I am going to stay put."

I was on Father's side. I wanted to go with him. We tried to convince Mother. Father knew there were many German families who had gone to Canada already before the war, but she was like an old mule. She didn't even talk to us anymore. Father was very disappointed but he gave up.

A flirt, a baby and a wedding

Lisa and Aunt Irene worked for several different farmers that summer. I remember vividly how they often came home excited and laughing when the threshing season had started. A single man called Heinz had fallen for Irene and was constantly teased about it. He had a lot of humour and flirted with all the other girls as well. Going to work had become fun for my two single aunts. Irene looked rather well and gained some weight. In late summer Aunt Tutti, a woman who had gone through four pregnancies, had her suspicions, sat her down and questioned her, "Irene, I am your older sister. Please tell me what's going on with you. You have changed. It's not just your weight which is good but also your demeanour. Are you pregnant?"

There was a bit of a surprised pause and then Irene looked her sister in the eye and declared, "Yes, I am and I am going to get married as soon as the suite in Heinz' house becomes available for us. People live in it right now but the mayor promised they would be moved as soon as possible. Right now, he lives with his sister. She actually owns the house but she does not want it and will sign it over to him."

"What? How long has this been going on? And you never told me? What kind of man is this Heinz? And where is the house? Why did you never bring him here? Introduce him? Does Lisa know?"

"No, Lisa does not know. Nobody knows. Heinz is divorced but there are no children. The house is the one with the mayor's office. It has a one and a half room suite in the back and several rooms upstairs. The post woman and an older couple live upstairs, and they share a small kitchen area. There is a very large backyard and several acres of land not far from the village. We'll start our own business growing vegetables and flowers for sale."

"Irene! A divorced man! How could you get involved with a divorced man? We have never had any divorces in our family. Think of your reputation! Now you'll have an illegitimate child. No, Irene, you can't do that...."

Aunt Irene was very stern, "Tutti, I'll have a life! I'll have my own family. I'll live in my own house and will make it a go with Heinz. He is a few years older than I am and we get along very well. He is a good man. Can you show me one single man my age alive, one who could offer me all that? You cannot talk me out of it. I have made up my mind."

With that, she got up, left the room and went upstairs to her attic.

There it was. It was a shock for some and a huge surprise for others in the family. I think Lisa felt a bit jealous. Mother was very happy for Irene and she did not need to convince us, "She is doing the right thing. Most young men are dead. Now she will not only be an aunt but also a mother and does not have to live her life as a spinster. I hope Lisa will find someone, too."

We were all excited and looked forward to her wedding. We all applied for special consideration coupons for dresses or material. Aunt Irene was granted brown silky material with tiny white flowers in it for a wedding dress. Mother received two cotton pieces in grey, one plain and one with a check pattern. Nothing for us girls but our dear Mom talked to Mrs. Wienholz who was able to make two dresses out of the material, combining the two pieces and Christel and I had brand new twin outfits for Aunt Irene's wedding.

Since the "cat was out of the bag" so to speak, Irene invited Heinz for tea the next Sunday and actually everybody liked him. He was not a tall man but charming and funny. By gosh, did he ever flirt with me! We laughed a lot that afternoon.

In late fall Aunt Irene had become quite big with the baby growing in her. She had already lived with Heinz for a few weeks in the new home he provided to get it ready for the big day.

Lisa had taken over the attic room in Tutti's house. Therefore, Tutti and her family had their apartment to themselves again.

On the wedding day, Aunt Irene asked me to come into the cold room and help her to get dressed.

"The cold room?" I asked her.

She smiled and responded, "Until we have enough food to fill the shelves we took them out and made it a bedroom for now. We'll have privacy there, Gila."

I was proud that she trusted me. When she finished dressing and I had closed the small buttons in the back of her dress, she handed me a necklace to put around her neck and close the clasp. Heinz had given it to her; it was from his mother. His sister had kept it up to now but she said she had no need for it and she wanted Heinz to have something special to give to his bride. This brown wedding dress was not really the right color for her but at least it was new. Mrs. Wienholz had made a good job of it. After the pregnancy, she could easily change it to a Sunday dress. Christel and I were proud in our grey outfits. My mother wore one made out of her old pale green, summer coat I had stuffed into the pillowcase when we had been given ten minutes to get out of our house in Stresow. All the others looked nice too.

Funny that the registry office for the wedding was in Heinz' house in the front rooms! From the back door, they had to walk around the corner, up the front steps to the office to sign the legal documents. Then return the same way. After the informal wedding service in the church, we all went back to the house and had a wonderful chicken dinner at noon, which was prepared by Aunt Tutti and Lisa and a tasty crumble cake for the afternoon coffee hour. Yes, it was still roasted barley coffee, but at least with lots of milk, we children could drink it too. It was a very nice day. Now we had another uncle!

Father and Heinz took to each other and over the years were not only brothers-in-law but best friends, sharing cigars, the love of their honeybees and endless hours of talking.

I had a new coat! The army blanket Father had received and brought from the prison camp was dyed a cornflower blue and my dear friend, Mrs. Wienholz had helped me to design a coat for myself. Nobody can imagine my relief when I put the ugly coat I had been wearing for two winters back into the ditch where I had found it. When I pushed it under the bushes to rot I thanked it for keeping me reasonably warm but made a solemn promise to myself never ever be so poor again. "I'll work my butt off, but I'll always have nice clothing when I grow up."

I kept that promise to myself, even if I often shopped in second hand stores or flea markets organized by a church. You could find very nice things if you arrived early. The day came when I could afford designer clothing and buy a Mercedes Benz – but that is another story.

Granny

It must have been a week or two after the wedding in December when, one morning, a Red Cross woman accompanied by an older white haired lady rang the bell at Aunt Tutti's door. My father, Lisa and Aunt Tutti sat in the warm kitchen talking. The aunts were knitting socks and mitts.

"Yes? Can I help you?" Aunt Tutti was a bit short sighted and naturally focussed on the woman closest to her. The Red Cross woman turned around and pointed to the white-haired older one who was holding a small bag but she never had a chance to say what she was going to say.

"Mother? Oh, my dear God, Mother!"

Lisa had jumped up to look and just then, Aunt Tutti fainted but Lisa caught her and cried out for Father to help. Between them, they carried Tutti to the couch. The Red Cross woman felt her pulse and Granny got the usual cold wet cloth for the forehead and it did not take long before she came to again. Aunt Tutti told us the story over and over when we saw her again and always ended with, "I thought I was seeing a ghost."

Nineteen forty-seven and forty-eight were the years when every last German was transported out of the former homeland. Granny never talked about the first few days after we had left, but she did tell us that later she was taken to Wildenbruch six kilometers away and placed with a large Polish family. She had been working as their maid for the last three years and was treated fairly well except that she had to sleep on the hard kitchen floor behind the stove. Reminiscing she reflected, "At least it was mostly warm there. I was like a Granny for their seven children. I loved them. It was hard to leave because they cried."

It hurt to hear her say this. I remembered exactly how it was when we had to leave Stresow and how we cried because she did not want to come with us and how my mother had been blamed when we arrived in Altefähr without her.

Christmas 1947 and New Year 1948

We had a small Christmas tree! We still felt like being in a dream and afraid to wake up. The family was together again. Father had come home. On Christmas Eve, we met Aunt Irene and Uncle Heinz in the church. Christel and I had been involved in the Nativity play. The sky was full of twinkling stars and some light, drifting snowflakes would have made it perfect. The companionable walk back home on that frosty evening was memorable in itself. We felt so very blessed and thankful. It was wonderful to enter our own warm living room and look at the little Christmas tree, decorated with homemade straw stars and paper chains.

After the evening meal of potato salad and fried fish, we each got a present of socks and mitts. The Red Cross must have had donations of used toys because little Edith, Ingrid and Christel each got a doll. The girls looked like Christmas angels, their little faces glowing with joy. I received a used book *Gisela and Ursula* and a scribbler. I had started to write poetry and I still have the faded, yellowed little booklet, sixty-five years later. I had discovered that my Granny's father, who was born in 1855, had written quite a number of songs for the Evangelical Church Song Book and I tried to follow in his, my great grandfather's, footsteps.

My poems were not religious and perfect like his but full of longing for our Pomerania homeland and even the welcome relief of death for many older people.

Ever since we were little children, we had always received a present for the body, something we needed anyway, and one, even if it was a small one, for the soul (toys, books). I have followed this, my parent's tradition, all my life with my own family as the children were growing up.

On Christmas Day, we went to Aunt Tutti's for Christmas noon dinner. Lisa had received a letter from her old Stresow friend, Rosie, now living in Jena, Thuringia and contemplated joining her. She would have a much better chance for work, other than farm work, and maybe even meet a nice man. Jena was a University City. The world renowned Zeiss Company, now "people's property" meaning nationally owned employed many people. She left not long after the exchange of a few more letters.

At teatime, when everyone was relaxed, Father told us about his first Christmas in Siberia and no eye remained dry. "My prison camp was in the middle of nowhere. Escape was impossible. They had built a barbed wire fence all around the compound anyway with watchtowers on the four corners. Heavily-clad guards pointed machine guns towards us at all times. Before we retired at night, we had to line up and they checked how many of us were there because sometimes some had died during the day. Many of us had no shoes but just rags wrapped around the feet and with the Siberian cold, we were shivering. A red flag with the golden hammer and sickle logo was on a high pole and a warmly dressed officer stood beside it during roll call. It usually happened during the twilight hour, between the parting day and the rapidly approaching night.

"On that day, Christmas 1945, a bitter frost crackled in the air and our breath came in puffs like smoke, it was suspended over and around us. I heard a shy thin voice starting to sing, the sound got louder, stronger, steadier as all the other men standing in the square joined in, despite the warning shots fired around us, bouncing off the frozen earth. Loud and clear, it rang up to the sky, 'Stille Nacht, heilige Nacht...'

"You can't imagine what it felt like. It was an eerie scene, useless in the big picture of history but already part of it. We were lost. We knew we would most likely die and still thought of Christmas and sang with thoughts of our loved ones and home on our minds; hoped against hope for peace on earth and many a tear froze to an icicle on the lashes. But the big surprise for us was when the guards put down their guns and joined the singing in their strange guttural language."

Dad sat there, lost in his thoughts and memories. Mother took his hand.

Aunt Irene and her husband Heinz had also come to enjoy steamed carp – with white gravy and lots of parsley. Carp was the traditional Christmas dinner in Germany. I did not like the white gravy very much and still don't. We talked animatedly about the coming baby due in a month. They didn't have a name yet and our imaginations and suggestions ran wild. But Aunt Irene quietly insisted, "Once the baby is born it will name itself and then we'll let you know."

Granny offered to stay with them. Aunt Tutti was sad to lose her mother again after such a short time but Granny knew her family was going to move to Sassnitz because of Uncle Fritz having been transferred. Uncle Heinz was pleased and joked, "What fun to live with two women – maybe even three if we have a daughter."

The days between Christmas and the New Year were quiet. We slept into the New Year and every one of us had a BIG wish, not a resolution, on our minds. I know mine came true; Father's and Mother's did too. As it turned out it had been exactly the same: To have a place of our own, work for Dad and to live like a family again.

Irene's baby was born on January twenty-first. Uncle Heinz had his "third" woman – a little Ursula.

With a sheepish smile he revealed, "I had wanted a daughter! What a lucky man I am!"

It was a home birth with a midwife. It was a good thing that Granny was there because Aunt Irene was not well and had to be in bed for several weeks. Her bed was moved into the living room next to the big, ceramic-tile oven in the corner. It was heated every day so it was cozy and warm. For me, it was love at first sight. I became the "babysitter-big sister" for little "Uschi" like Lisa had been for me.

My fourteenth birthday was three days later.

To be fourteen and everybody talking to me about being grown up felt funny because in my mind I had been grown up already for several years. It was the beginning of an emotional problem I was not consciously aware of but it kept growing as time went by. Since I was eleven, I had been my mother's main support and confidante. Now she had Dad to talk to and I was supposed to be their child again. I simply felt not needed, put aside, redundant, was often sad, always close to tears. My relatives said it was "teenage hormones" but I knew better.

Confirmation on Palm Sunday

We had a real shock at one of the last few confirmation classes. A young man had turned up, several years older than we were. He asked if he could join us. He felt a great need to be with people reading and learning about the bible. He was the boy who had lived with his mother and two sisters in the now abandoned and nearly fallen down guesthouse where the Russian motor biker had been found in the well. We chatted about this and that when, all of a sudden, he took a deep breath and confessed, "I can't forget that Russian soldier. He was in the process of raping my fifteen-year-old sister close to the bushes where the well was. She screamed and we all came running. One of us (he did not reveal who) hit him with a piece of wood on the head and we pulled him off my sister and took his pistol away. A fight started between the four of us and we were able to knock him down. He hit his head on a rock and did not move anymore so we assumed he was dead. We put him into the old well and threw all the other stuff in to cover him. Then I pushed the motor bike down the cliff into the blackthorn bushes before we fled. It was self-defence and an accident but we were afraid to get shot if we reported it."

The rest is history and he was right. They had been living with relatives in a tiny fishing village far away from Altefähr. He felt strongly about becoming a pastor. He could not forget and wanted to serve the church in a time when religion was frowned upon. We were speechless.

He never came back to class but many years later, when I visited I asked and the pastor confirmed that he had become a very good pastor but far away from Altefähr.

I had received a coupon for a confirmation dress and silk stockings. The dress was dark green, very loosely woven and had a big white bow at the neck. The stockings were ladies stockings. One stocking was size nine and a half, the other size ten and a half with a fashionable seam in the back. I had long straps on either side of a children's vest to clip on the stockings. They were much too large, too wide and they curled around my thin legs. The seam that was supposed to be straight in the back was going any which way. When we walked to church from the pastor's house, always two girls, then two boys, the boys teased me about it. The mean Bubi Warsow, who had poked me with the geometry compass a few years ago, walked right behind me and repeatedly tried to trip me. He was the worst, "This kid has very shapely legs but she has no calves and look at that, for breasts she has a couple of peas on an ironing board...."

It was hard to "grin and bear it" and not to cry. When we proceeded to walk down the centre aisle in the church, my mother overheard a woman whisper to her companion, "What's that little one doing in there, she can't be old enough to be confirmed? She couldn't be much over ten...."

Yes, I was under-developed. I must have looked even smaller than I was because my school pal, Annemarie, was beside me and she was a whole head taller. She surely was a big girl. Even then, she looked more like a young woman than a teenager. She had beautiful large grey eyes and a lovely smile. She was destined to become my cousin because she and my cousin Siegfried got married a few years later. It was a match made in heaven. They never had children, but their love was clearly visible when they looked at each other.

The bible verse my parents had chosen for my baptism was 1.Corinthians, 13.13: "Now abide faith, hope and love but the greatest of these is love."

I was asked to choose a verse for my confirmation and decided there was no more suitable one than the one my parents had picked out for me fourteen years ago: "Faith, hope and love but the greatest is love." I have never told anyone that it had a lot to do with my cousin Siegfried – because I loved him dearly.

16: And Now What?

Dropping out of school

My teacher told me I could not go to High School in Bergen, about thirty or forty minutes by train, because my father had been a "capitaliste." It did not matter that we had been stripped of everything and evicted. It did not matter that Dad had been taken to a prison camp in Siberia for two years. It did not matter that we were very poor now. I was not very upset since I had not wanted to go anyway because I had no shoes or decent clothing. I had had to endure a lot of teasing in Altefähr and I figured in the city it would be even worse. When my teacher heard that, he was the one who was upset. He confided he had made inquiries and was confident he could get me registered because of my good standing. I refused. He talked to my parents, they talked to me, I cried, I just could not do it. So, my normal school days were over at the end of June 1948.

That summer saw me crawling across the fields again, thinning out turnips and doing farm work according to the growing season. Exactly the thing my mother did not want for me. But I needed to earn money for my English lessons which I still did not want to give up. After work, I had to take our goat, Lizzie, on a chain so she could eat her fill along the field paths. I would carry a big basket and cut grass and pull dandelions to feed the couple of dozen or more rabbits we now had. Very often, we had rabbit for Sunday dinner and leftovers during the week. I tried to make myself a hand muff or a hat out of the rabbit skins but I did not have the right salt to cure the pelts so they got very stiff.

On days when I did not go to a farm field, I had to take our four geese out to feed. This was not so bad because I could take a book along to a small pasture behind the gardens close to our home. Often I would be sitting in the grass against the fence, watching the geese and thinking of a way to kill myself. It should be a way that really hurt my parents. I wanted them to suffer because I was hurting and was so terribly unhappy. Sometimes I was wondering if I was in fact a stepchild. Oh, I knew well enough I was no stepchild. I had to help my parents more than my sisters did and still did not feel appreciated at home. When I asked, why me, why always me, I was told the same as when I was a child: you are the oldest.

We had been assigned one of the fenced gardens with even a cherry and a plum tree. Aunt Irene inspired me with her love of gardening and I tried to copy her. Cuttings of currant berries I had taken from the bushes growing through the fence rooted. I loved planting flowers. To be a gardener or landscaper would be nice if I could not be a seamstress.

Once or twice a week, I had a baby-sitting job looking after a toddler, only three houses away from ours. The nicest thing about it was that the couple had a whole bookcase full of books – all kinds of books, from history to novels. They allowed me to read when the girl was asleep. I found an anatomy book and devoured it because I did not know much about the human body.

Then the day came that changed my life. Aunt Tutti was visiting. She and my mother had the usual barley coffee and I overheard their conversation. They were talking about me so I kept quiet to hear what they would say instead of joining them. Aunt Tutti, my Godmother, was concerned about what would become of me. "Else, there are no apprentice places to become a seamstress or a flower gardener. That's what she told me she wants and she can't go to high school now that she officially dropped out. If things were still like before the war at least she could have become a house maid in one of those great houses of the estates."

Wow! That hurt! What? Me? – A maid? No way! I'll show you!

The anger that welled up in me awakened a drive that was almost too much and lasted my whole life. I could not take enough courses. I could not read enough books. I could not go to enough lectures and speeches, even political ones. Anything that was educational, I did.

I got very restless. Without telling anyone, I went to Stralsund to check with the Hansa High School but they were not allowed to enroll me since I lived on Rügen and the school had to be in my district. They suggested evening classes but since I had no way of getting back home after classes this was impossible. With my tail between my legs I went back to talk to my former teacher, Mr. Scheider. He could not help me anymore but suggested I work hard in the new compulsory agriculture class I would have to attend twice a week starting in the fall. It would be somewhat like High School but stressing the agricultural subjects. It could get me into university to take landscaping or garden design. Now at least I had some hope.

Maybe emotional stress caused it; I got a very bad sty on my left upper eyelid. When it healed up it came back on the right lower eyelid. When that was gone, it appeared on the left lower eyelid. I could count on it coming to my right upper eyelid. I just could not get rid of it and it hurt. My mother talked to many neighbours and several suggested a lady in Stralsund who was known for her psychic powers. They were convinced she was the only one who could help me. Mother was warned not to offer money but just leave a piece of bacon or meat or a sausage and never say "thank you" because that would jinx it and it would not work. I laughed and slyly pretended not to believe it but when we saw her, I prayed with all my heart that it would work. It did! When the present sty healed, I never, in my life, had another.

Mother had a conversation with her while I just sat there listening. She did not allow me to speak for two hours. Her neighbour was a master seamstress, who took several girls every winter for half a year to learn to sew "your own wardrobe." It cost thirty marks monthly but you did have to bring your own material and yarn. You would learn to make designs with paper on a dummy, cuttings, skirts, blouses, and a dress for yourself and clothing for children, as long as you had the needed material. My mother got the name and the address and the "witch" promised to put in a word for me.

That winter was a busy one. I was able to take the course but had to go to school twice a week. The nice seamstress allowed me to come on Saturdays with one of the other girls who had the same problem and therefore we got our hours in and our assigned work done. I never had new materials but begged for old clothing from our neighbours. One gave me a swastika flag. I took it apart and made a type of country dress out of it. The red became the body of the dress, the white from the circle was an insert around the neck and I cut the black from the swastika into strips and used it around the skirt and between the red and white in the top part. Finished off with a black belt it was a very beautiful fun dress. I do have a black and white photograph of me wearing it and found another of my third sister Ingrid wearing it years later. I always got enough old clothing to make something new for either my mother or my sisters or me. I thoroughly enjoyed doing it.

My first kiss

Our little piggy had grown up and one day it became pork. I do not want to go into the way it's done but the screams of the pig when it was taken out of its little sty reminded me of the screams I heard the night the Russians stood in line and raped Betty and Helen. It was weird but the pig seemed to know what was coming to it. The worst was that I had to stir the blood caught in a container in order for it not to set. Later, it was used to make a soup and blood and tongue sausage. I also had to help clean the intestines. These were used for sleeves for all the different types of sausages my mother, Granny, Aunt Irene and Aunt Tutti, who had come with her two oldest boys to help (and get a good food supply!) were making. They took ham and bacon to a neighbour who had a smokehouse.

In the late afternoon when the women had everything under control, they sent us into the children's bedroom. Furnished with four beds, it provided little room but there was a table and a few chairs. We played cards and board games. It became too boring and Manfred, twelve years old, started throwing pillows. Within minutes, we had a real pillow fight and a little feather was floating in the air. Siegfried, a year older than me, tried to catch it but I was faster. I kept it tightly in my hand while he tried to open it. I did not let go and all of a sudden he gave me a very quick kiss.

I was so surprised that my hand opened. My legs almost gave up on me and I was so weak I had to sit down. That tiny kiss overwhelmed me. It was just a brushing of lips but I thought it was wonderful and I hoped he would do it again. He held the feather high up in victory and laughed. I bet he did not even know what he did to me. I tried to get the feather back just to be close to him and give him a chance to repeat his action but he didn't. The pillow fight went on for a little while longer but Aunt Tutti came in and stopped it. When they left to go to Aunt Irene's house for the night, I went out with them. Siegfried stayed a bit behind and at the edge of our yard, I stopped and said "Good Night!" He put his hands on my shoulders and looked at me. I thought about him being a first cousin whom you can't marry because you won't get normal children but still hoped he would give me a kiss. He didn't. Did he wait for me to make a move? I didn't know and I was very shy. He told me years later that he had been waiting because he wasn't sure if I would have wanted it. My mother remarked, "Yaah, yaah, cousins are for practising."

I hated her for saying that. She insinuated something that in all honesty was not happening.

The experience left a big mark on me. We always had a deep connection but our lips never touched again.

Shorthand and typing on cardboard

My father had met an elderly couple who taught shorthand and typing. He suggested that I should take the three month-course and offered to pay for it. I jumped at the chance. It started first of June 1949. My sewing class was long finished and I had some reasonably nice clothing. We had also received three care packages from the USA with some used dresses in them but mainly milk powder, rice and other food items that would not go bad. Since the other three girls had dropped out, my English lessons were cancelled. By taking typing and steno, I wouldn't have to crawl over the fields again. I would make sure to be good at it and then try to find an office job.

We were eight students but there was only ONE typewriter! We had to bring a piece of cardboard and copy the keyboard onto it. On this, we had to learn the position of the letters and do the typing exercises so that our fingers would find the required letters. After the first week, we were not allowed to look at it anymore. Therefore, they hung a second piece of cardboard around our necks to hide what our fingers were doing. The teachers would dictate something and our fingers had to "type" the letters. It was surprising that they always saw when someone lifted the wrong finger. I "typed" on this cardboard for hours at home. My mother teased me but I was adamant to be "the best." Later we had turns on the real typewriter and that was great fun.

Shorthand was much easier. I found it intriguing to be able to make those little scribbles and read them. Amazing how fast one could write. I loved it! I asked Father to dictate or read to me and I would write it. He could not believe that I was able to read it back to him, even hours later or the next day. He was proud of me. He thought my next course should be bookkeeping and it was. They called it "double bookkeeping."

However, on weekends I worked as a waitress in a terraced-garden restaurant when the weather was good. I was super nice to my guests, smiled and talked to them and made them feel very good. I ran up and down those terraces all day. People complimented me and they always wanted to sit in my area when they came back a second time. They tipped extra well. After work, I had to turn all the money over to the owner. Mrs. P. would check my order vouchers and take the money owed to the restaurant. Almost daily, she would take more than I owed her and excused her actions with, "Nobody gives such high tips. You must have made a mistake and not turned in your order vouchers. I only allow six marks for tips."

I asked myself "for work all day?" She would keep what was rightly my money. The fact was I would not get ANY food out of the kitchen without the numbered voucher. After this happened a few times and I was accused of stealing, I was very upset and mentioned it to my father. He got very angry and told me sternly, "You tell her you quit."

Her husband was my father's tailor, a very nice man but Father also stopped going to him.

A deep German division

The standard of living in West Germany was incredibly high compared to East Germany. Many people still left East Germany, leaving everything behind for the chance to start a new life. A man called Konrad Adenauer, the former mayor of Cologne, was chosen to be the head of the "Christian Democratic Union" party, known as the CDU. He became the president of the Parliament Council and drew up a new constitution. In 1949, the Bundesrepublik of Germany, the BDR, was established and he became the Chancellor. The Eastern powers did not like it at all and their reaction was to establish the Deutsche Demokratic Republic, the DDR. They started to tighten up the borders and a shooting order for fleeing people was in place. The BDR introduced their own currency and the living conditions saw a further unprecedented upswing. The DDR followed suit and printed its own money as well. It was like Monopoly money and the coins were tiny and made out of aluminum. Every person received twenty Eastmark. Everybody was equal. Nobody had more than his neighbour. Our family of six started out with 120.00 Marks. The couple where I babysat had only one child so they had 60.00 Eastmarks. Single people were even worse off with only twenty Eastmarks. My parents had saved quite a bit of the previous money again because you could not really spend it. There was nothing to buy: no nails, no paint, no material of any kind. The old currency was worthless. They lost everything again.

Elections were held but there was no choice, there was only one party: The SED. You HAD to go and vote. It was compulsory and strictly controlled. All they did was to mark off your name when you came to the polling station, indicating you had voted.

I had written a letter to Aunt Erika and my friend Ingrid's address in Berlin and was very happy to receive an answer. They had found their dad alive. Their apartment was damaged but livable. They lived in the Western part of Berlin and life was quite enjoyable. They invited me to come and visit.

Shocking news for us

Father had closed his little garage shop. He had developed rheumatic and arthritic pain because he had always worked with the doors open in lieu of a window. His new job was with the old, but now restored, ships wharf in the engineering department. A regular pay cheque and much better working conditions suited him well. He took the train to Stralsund at 5:30 a.m. and came back with the one leaving at 5:15 p.m. We went together because I had to take the same train for my typing course. I was usually finished by 3:00 p.m. and had to wait two hours and on good weather days, I would just walk the eight kilometers home.

Over the winter of 1949/50, Christel had been weak and sick a lot. Finally, Mother took her to see a doctor in the hospital in Bergen where she had been when she had typhoid fever. He x-rayed her and announced that she had a shadow on her lung, not full-blown tuberculosis yet, but she would have to go into a children's clinic in Binz to be cured. We were devastated but we could do nothing about this predicament.

A narrow gauge train went from Altefähr directly to Binz. People joked because it was very slow and that "to pick flowers on the way is 'verboten'...." My parents took her to this beautiful resort town with a long sandy beach on the Baltic Sea and with gorgeous white villas in need of fresh paint. The Nazis had built several multi storey hotels within a pine tree forest along the sea. This resort, called "Kraft durch Freude" – "Strength through joy", was for deserving Party People who had been sent here for a two or three week holiday during the Hitler era. Now they converted it into a children's clinic for cases like my sister's.

My parents visited her several times. I was there once and could not believe all Christel did was eat what they gave her and lie still in a lounge chair in the shade. They covered her with a woollen blanket when the weather was fair or moved her under a roof when it was raining. She was always able to breathe the good clean sea air. She could have no sports, no running around, no play. Nobody could tell us if she had or would develop tuberculosis or how long it would take for her lung to heal or how long she would have to be there. She seemed quite content to just lie there and do nothing. It was a shock to see her like this. It was weird how shy I felt around her, as she would just be looking at me with her big blue eyes saying nothing. I could tell she was thinking something but she never put it into words. I hoped she would not die.

My first real job

I had done well in my shorthand/typing course and felt I was ready to start working in an office. Through my father, I had an interview at the ship wharf's inventory office. Trouble was I still looked like a kid with my braids wound around my head. Dad did not allow me to have my hair cut short and it was not common to wear it open as the girls do now. The ponytail was not invented yet or at least had not made it across the border from West to East. I begged to have it cut and get a perm but Dad thought then I would look like a floozy because I still had a kid's body. To my surprise, the interview went well. My typing was speedy and my shorthand was perfect. I was hired with a six-week probation period in November 1949.

I worked in a smelly, messy, dark, industrial office with another woman. This was not office work the way I had envisioned it. I did not like the job but had made up my mind that I needed experience and this was just a steppingstone as I was determined to work my way up. The first few days I had to count different types of nails, screws and nuts and mark down the few other things on the shelves. Products were scarce and often the men would sit around and do nothing because the items they needed were not available. They would sit, smoke, tell coarse jokes and laugh; they were paid anyway. It was not their fault they didn't have what they needed to do their jobs.

The office was in disarray and the other woman did not let me get it cleaned up or organized the way I thought it should be. She did what little letter typing there was. When she had nothing to do, she would read a book or file her nails. Once a month we got a form consisting of a number of pages, but every page and the back side, had rows of questions on it, an order form for supplies the workers needed. The pages were glued together at the top and the carbon paper had to be fitted perfectly. This was something the woman did not like to do and she handed the job to me. I had to type the numbers from my inventory paper onto this form, with a copy. I made a mistake with the carbon paper, put it the wrong way around between the second or third page and therefore the copy was on the backside of the previous page. The whole page was messed up and one could not mark what was actually to be listed on there.

All hell broke loose. It was the only form they would get and since it could not be used, they would not be able to order supplies until the next month. Short of being slapped on my head, I was verbally abused and subsequently fired. My job experience was three weeks. My father was very upset and exclaimed, "I'll never lift a finger and help you to find work again. This reflects on me and I don't like it. They hired you only because of me and now I have egg on my face. I hope there are no other consequences for me. I do want to keep my job."

For some reason I felt relieved but I was devastated for him. I just knew it was not the right thing for me but I would not have given up. The next day he apologized and expressed that it might have been the best thing that could have happened to me.

"I didn't like the environment and when I heard some comments made about you being a delectable little thing, I was sorry I even let you work there."

Ice cream anyone?

Time went by. Christmas passed without Christel and the New Year 1950 started. I sewed quite a few little dresses for other people's children. My father had "organized" an old Singer sewing machine for us. On most evenings I babysat or just pretended I had the job. I did a lot of reading about history, geography, literature, biology, anything that was in the bookcase of the couple where I babysat. Both had attended university. He was a professor at the Greifswald University and they liked me to come and spend time with them. They helped me a great deal; we discussed many topics and they answered my questions. It could be compared to home schooling.

Mother did not like me to spend time with them when they were at home and insinuated there was something else "going on." She could not trust anybody.

I went to Stralsund quite frequently to visit the little, second-hand bookstore. The woman who owned it and I laughed about my wrong-side-around-carbon-paper. I told her I needed a job so she let me check the ads in the newspaper. One day she pointed out that the famous Stralsund motorbike race was coming up again. The organizers were looking for young people to sell ice cream, beer, wieners and herring buns. I applied to the P.O. Box number and got an invitation for an interview. I was hired to work at an ice cream table at the racetrack for two days earning twenty marks a day. When the dairy who supplied the ice cream learned I lived in Altefähr, they asked me if I would be interested to take on a brand new ice cream kiosk on the beach in my village. The ice cream would come by ferry at nine a.m. in big milk churns. It was usually one during weekdays and two (with different flavours) on sunny weekends when the ferry was packed with lots of tourists who came over to spend the day at the beach.

Naturally, I took the job. On the race days, I was in Stralsund. I hated the noise the motor bikes made but liked the fact that I made lots of money with good tips. Nobody would go over to Altefähr during the race. I looked forward to eating ice cream every day but having it so readily available, I did not. But I was pleased I could treat my sisters Ingrid and Edith and they were hanging around all the time with a lot of other village children during the summer holidays. I had to make a certain amount of money out of one churn. When I made more money, I could keep it or I could give the ice cream away. Next morning, I would put the empty or partially empty churns on the ferry when I picked up the fresh ones. It got so busy that on some Sundays, they would send three or four churns over and I sold it all. I was always joyful and talkative with my customers and made them feel good. The kiosk closed when the beach season ended but my hard work had paid off.

Berlin here I come

Since I had earned enough money during the summer, I was finally able to accept the invitation to visit Aunt Erika and my dear friend Ingrid in Berlin. It was an exciting adventure. It was the first time I was on my own on a five-hour train ride. We had received ID cards, which we had to carry with us at all times. We joked and said "even to the outhouse." The DDR had also organized a new police force because enough young German men had grown up by now. They checked every passenger asking about why and where he or she was going. We were still allowed to visit friends in the west sector of Berlin.

I could not believe how many people were on the streets. How many shops there were – rows and rows of just shacks in front of the ruins but packed with merchandise: dresses, shoes, and sweaters, whatever your heart desired. I was amazed at how carefree the people acted. They were talking, laughing, and had fun. Such a life was unimaginable for me. At home, people were always suspicious and serious around each other, but never laughing! My first purchase was a box camera, a dream I had had for a long time. It was the start of my future hobby. I loved it!

Aunt Erika took me along shopping for produce. I stared at the bananas. I had never seen one, let alone eaten such a funny looking fruit. She laughed and bought me one but I did not know how to eat it. She opened it. The taste did not even appeal to me. It felt dry on my tongue and I couldn't understand what all the excitement about bananas was. Oranges were much more refreshing. Erika's husband told me to call him Uncle Gerhard. He invited us to come to his tennis club. It was a sunny Sunday afternoon. We walked about two kilometers through a landscaped park with trees placed strategically together with texture and color showing off their beauty and many flower beds with not a house in sight. The contrast between this park and the city streets with all the ruins and half-bombed out houses and people even living in them was a shock for me. I kept wondering and pondering. Compared to this life ours was grey and dull, even on sunny days. The atmosphere at the club was loud and noisy when the people were welcoming us, the women hugging and the men slapping each other's shoulders with cheery comments and all of them were drinking beer or lemon soda or something. I felt totally out of place with my braids around my head and my homemade, dull dress. It didn't take long before some young people surrounded my friend Ingrid. She introduced me; they started to tease me and called me "Gretchen" – but in a fun way that made me laugh, too.

The next day I wrote a postcard to home. I mentioned how nice everything was. I said that my braids were off as well and I thought I looked very nice. Mother wrote back about a week later that Father had only expressed his concern for me to take good care of my hair and not let it look cheap because of a fuzzy perm.

I jumped for joy! I had expected him to be mad. Now I could not wait to really do the deed and get them cut off! Ingrid accompanied me to a hairdresser she knew who had a shop on a street that was divided straight down the middle between East and West Berlin. The side we were on belonged to the West, the other side was part of the East sector. Looking carefully for a policeman and seeing none I ran across into the shop. The hairdresser was used to it. She cut my braids off and I took them home, wrapped in an old newspaper. She proceeded to give me a very nice perm and a flattering haircut. I could pay with my East Marks. I was in love with my looks. I could not believe how pretty I actually was. I looked into every store window to see myself, and when I met Ingrid in a cafeteria on the West side she hardly recognized me but for my East German clothing. Happy and excited, we went shopping and I bought myself a pretty, colorful dress, which I wore out of the store and enough material and thread to make myself another at home. The exchange rate was four-point-five East to one West mark. I also bought a pair of fashionable shoes. I noticed several young men giving me admiring glances. I wasn't used to that at all.

If there was such a thing as "cloud nine," I was surely on it!

Father had this funny little grin in the corners of his mouth when he saw me and just nodded. "Keep it that way," was his comment. Mother did not say much. Was she jealous? My sisters admired me and were thankful for the little gifts I had bought for them. I held my head higher. I walked with a new confidence. The school bullies turned around to look at me and a few weeks later wanted to have dates with me. Once I told four of them (separately!) to meet me at a certain spot (at the same time). I was not interested in any of them. I was hiding with one of my former English class friends and we watched for them. They came one after the other and started talking amongst themselves. When they found out why they were there, they got very mad and threatened to beat me up. I knew it had been nasty of me but it was "pay-back time." For weeks I was afraid to go anywhere by myself. It surely ruined my chances of finding a "boyfriend" in Altefähr. I didn't want one anyway. I wanted a job, a good job in Stralsund.

Once more, my second-hand bookstore lady was instrumental in pointing me in the right direction. The "District Sports Association" was looking for office help. Very confident because of my new looks, dress and shoes and the knowledge of my typing speed and shorthand, I made an impression and practically told them I was the best for the job. After an extensive test, I was hired. The office was in the beautiful old Gothic City Hall with some bomb damage. The work was very interesting. After a short training period, I was pretty much on my own. My two male bosses were hardly ever there because they had to visit large companies like the wharf and Co-ops to form sports clubs. The DDR wanted to involve young people in sports. Membership fees were mere pennies and if you had to travel for competitions, they paid for everything. I felt more and more at ease in my job and loved to work independently. I always did more than was required of me and never counted my hours. I did all the letter writing, first according to dictation and later I would compose them myself. I organized the filing system and answered all the phone inquiries. I had to co-ordinate the dates for soccer matches, volleyball or handball and athletic competitions. Once I had to take notes at a boxing match. I hated it. Boxing was a sport? It was brutal.

When everything ran smoothly they hired, and I had to train, another office girl. They sent me out into the country to attend meetings and aid villagers in forming sports clubs. It often was onerous because I could take the train to a certain village but then had to walk miles to another. My father built me a bike out of old rusty parts he found in the dump. That helped. Occasionally I even had to overnight in a small guest house/pub to go to another meeting in a different village the next day. At first, I liked the challenge but, in time, I grew tired of it. I would rather have been in the office again. In some villages, it was like "pulling teeth" to find a president, treasurer and so on. A few times, I even visited someone at home to talk him or her into volunteering. They wanted the club, mainly for soccer, but nobody wanted to be involved other than being a member. I certainly learned about the villages surrounding Stralsund.

The office of the Sports Minister in Berlin came up with the idea of introducing a "Sports Achievement Pin." You had to be a member of the

FDJ before you could take the tests. There was a red booklet outlining the three stages. The easiest was the number one pin in bronze, then number two in silver and number three in gold. All had the DDR flag as background, a male and a female runner painted on it with an oak wreath surrounding the lower part and the (translated) inscription:

"Ready to work and to defend the peace."

One had to do all the athletics from short to long distance running, broad and high jumps throwing discus, etc., swimming and a verbal test about the social political order of the DDR. The last was what people liked the least and most of them failed. I had to hold training classes outfitted with a stopwatch and a long measuring tape for athletics and also talk about the political questions. Personally, I only achieved the "bronze" pin since I had absolutely no athletic training and had never been very interested in sports.

I was in charge of organizing dates, times and places for people to come to do the athletic training and tests. They only had soccer fields in the country and very simple athletic installations for jumping or running. It was very tough to get folks to participate. Sometimes I let someone pass even if he or she was a few seconds or centimeters short but the pride with which he or she wore the pin got others to try again.

Aunt Tutti had a fourth son, Friedhelm. At Pentecost, 1950, he was baptised in Sassnitz and I became his Godmother and Siegfried, his eldest brother, his Godfather. My father was not jealous anymore that he did not have a son, "I am glad and thankful for my girls. First of all I have nothing to leave a son anymore and secondly, all boys will be cannon fodder in the next war."

Those were his words.

My job got easier in winter and I worked in the office again. In very early spring, 1951, I was "delegated" to attend a six-week course in the Sport School Hamberge. It was an accelerated course to prepare one to become a sports teacher. All subjects were taught with special attention to sport and after this course; I graduated with the title "Sport Instructor." We had to learn certain pre-choreographed movements/ gymnastics for the "World Festival of Youth and Students" in Berlin in August 1951 and I kept very busy teaching the selected youth in many high schools after I returned. I also had to train suitable girls to keep teaching these movements and get their class ready for the big day. For years, I remembered the sequences I had learned, practised and taught hundreds of times. For the trip to Berlin, my group received white shorts, shirt, socks, cotton runners and a dark sweat suit. The DDR put on this incredible two week Festival to impress the world with its supremacy in sports. Twenty-six thousand young people came from one hundred and four countries. We were told that West Germany had forbidden their youth to attend. Switzerland did the same. Many came illegally through Hungary and Austria. We were all on a "high," meeting and making friends with people from all over the world.

It was an incredible feeling to be part of thousands of white, red, yellow or black clad girls and boys performing the movements we had learned in a huge stadium in unison. It was amazing to see the "pictures" we formed while doing it – from the DDR flag to the Achievement Pin design, the Soviet star and, as a highlight, the Soviet flag with hammer and sickle. Thousands of people filled the seats and cheered. Everything was very uplifting. The speeches of the political officials were motivating to keep on training and try to become the best one could be to represent the DDR at future international sports competitions. It was reminiscent of the Nazis but with different colors of the flags.

It is well known that the DDR sport teams outperformed the BDR in almost all disciplines in the years to come and won more medals. At some world-class competitions or Olympic Games, teams from two German States were not allowed and East and West had to join forces. The East always outperformed the western members. It was not surprising. The East trained their people at special training camps for months; their jobs were safe, their salary paid and all expenses taken care of. In the West people had to work or study and train in their free time.

A new office and a great hobby

A re-organization had taken place and the former District Sports Association had been divided into a "Committee for Body Culture and Sports" for the city and one for the country. By this time, I had proved my worth and was head hunted by the lady who was in charge of the city committee. I got an upstairs office in the old boathouse where the rowers and the canoe club were housed. She belonged to the rowing club. My window looked out onto the warm-up training ground and the boat jetty leading down into the water. I seriously wished I could get involved in kayaking. One day the leader of the kayak racing team came in with the membership booklets for the canoe club to get the necessary permission stamp for participation in the provincial championship race in Rostock. We chatted and I asked many questions to find out about the canoe club. Politically we had to address each other with "Sport friend" or, if you were a member of the FDJ, "Youth friend." We did not need introductions or to know a name.

"Why don't you come downstairs one evening and watch the training? My friend Christa is the leader of the ladies' team and I am sure she wouldn't mind. Besides, we'd love to have more active members."

That is exactly what I did! I watched and a few days later I joined the training and Christa taught me to get in and out of the nutshell that was the single kayak. I learned to balance with my hips and paddle a few strokes. Then she asked me to get into a K II and paddle with her sitting behind me, giving commands on how to move. She showed me how to straighten my arms and lift them only to shoulder height, how to dip the paddle into the water, how not to pull it through the water but to push it with the other arm, and how to lift my elbows. In short, I could not have had a better introduction or coach. To make a long story short: Christa and I became a K II team. A year later, we won the provincial championship in Rostock over 500 meters as well as over the 3000 meters, the longest for ladies. What did not go over too well with her was when I won the 500 and 3000 meters in the K I, beating her in the process. When I came through the finish line after the 3000 meters, I fell out of the kayak, exhausted.

Alfred, her friend and leader of the kayak racing team, paddled me over to Altefähr after the evening training a few times. I saw him as a "sports friend" and appreciated this but had no idea that something had been going on between him and Christa. One evening she was sitting on the jetty waiting for him to return. Whatever it was that had kept them apart was resolved and they became engaged. After that, he talked another kayaker into paddling me across to Altefähr.

It was great having friends not necessarily in high places but at important places. Alfred was the manager of a grocery Konsum and often I got butter instead of margarine on my ration card and other good things you could not get anywhere. Christa's parents owned a bakery. Her brother, who was also a kayaker, was a baker and Christa was the sales girl in their shop sharing the task with her mother. She also attended a music school to earn her degree as a music teacher. To receive an extra couple of buns when picking up my ration of bread was incredible. Sometimes they had apple cake or in fall, I was even able to buy plum cake.

Alfred and Christa invited me to their wedding. I hoped to be able to buy a new dress at the "Wertheim Konsum," a shopping venue like a very small WalMart. They did not have any dresses but they had just received five sky blue men's bikes. I happened to be the first to see them – and yes, you guessed it, I bought one of them and ten minutes later they were all gone. I could not care less that they had a cross bar and were meant for men. I was as happy as if I had bought my first car.

At their wedding we all lined up with crossed paddles when they came out of the romantic, ivy covered little church. It was special and I felt very emotional and hoped I could marry like that!

Over the next few years, Christa and I won most of the races wherever we went to compete until she got pregnant and I had to paddle with another girl. I was disappointed when Inga D. and I only made third place in the K II in a big Dresden regatta. My K I race was still okay and I was by now considered one of the DDR class kayakers, received the top athlete silver pin (nothing to do with the achievement pin) and a light blue sweat suit indicating my athletic rank. That suit was the same color as my bike and, by gosh, was I ever proud to ride it!

On the third floor of the boathouse was a tiny little room and I inquired about renting it in order to avoid commuting each day. It used to be the storage room for the office in front of it. I got permission to bring a narrow bed, a chair and a small table. There was no room for more. My wardrobe was a few nails in a beam of the attic. I had lived in tighter, uglier attics with five other people – so I was in heaven. I was not allowed to cook, but I could warm up small meals in the boathouse club kitchen on the second floor or on my camping stove in front of the boathouse. I went home regularly when there was no training and Mother gave me prepared meals to take along when I left. But now, living in Stralsund, I was able to enroll in evening classes in the Hansa High School during the winter and spring. The classes were finished when the training season began in 1952. After an examination evaluation, I was placed in an accelerated learning class.

That summer Christel came home and she was so BIG from all the eating and doing nothing. At around fifteen, she looked like a young, but fat, woman. One of Mom's old dresses brought from Stresow just fit her. When I look at a family photograph I have from that day, she overshadowed us all with her size. Her lung had healed and now she had to catch up on a lot of schooling. She knew what she wanted to be in the future: a nurse.

My new love "Max"

Next to spending extra time on keeping my bike looking like new, I was almost obsessed with my new boat. I had bought "Max" from the Canoe Club President. He had built two the same: "Max" and "Moritz." He named them after the two nasty, sneaky boys in a famous children's story by Wilhelm Busch. He sold "Max" when he finished "Moritz" and I happened to be ready to become an owner. Both boats were clinker or lapstrake built, a method descended from the Vikings. It was not a kayak but a leisure paddleboat. The club provided our kayaks for the racing team.

The outside bottom of my boat was red up to the water line; the sides were white and the deck was natural, highly polished wood. The inside was light grey. It was five meters and twenty centimeters long and at least double the width of a racing kayak. It was a two-seater but very stable for a single paddler. It had a mast and a small five square meter sail. Nobody can imagine my excitement when I paddled or, with a good wind, sailed over to Altefähr where I enjoyed the bullies glowering at me with jealousy when I tied up the boat, and then went to get my sisters and parents to see it. A small two-wheel boat carrier came with the boat. I could pull it out of the water, place the front on the wagon, lift the back and roll it up from the beach to my parents' home. When I stayed overnight, I would park it in front of the two outhouses.

With many of the canoe club members, I paddled or sailed to wonderful beaches, bays or islands on weekends to camp. Most of the old timers, born in Stralsund had paddleboats and tents and shared them with everybody who needed a place. I always found someone to take my second seat and share the paddling. Most tents held four people. Some paddlers had guitars, several had mouth organs and Christa owned and always brought her accordion. We would sit around a campfire and sing through half the night. Once we were snowed in. It was the beginning of May and the first outing of the season. It was very cold with just a normal blanket for a ground cover, and about sixteen of us crowded into one of the bigger tents. One person sat between the legs of the one behind him and a bottle of rum made the rounds. We wore double layers of clothing. The first and the last person in the row had to change places occasionally because they got cold and were not as comfortable as we girls, who were in the middle of the row. Stories from other camping trips, songs, jokes and laughter kept us warm enough until the morning came, with the grey sky hanging low. We had to dig our tent and our boats out of the snow before we headed back home. I remember how my hands hurt with the cold and turned blue. You surely could not paddle wearing gloves since they would be wet in no time.

Father warned me, "You'll have to deal with rheumatism and kidney problems from always sitting in cold water, it's crazy! You'll be sorry...."

I did not have an apron cover for the boat opening. Some of the old-timers did and they remained dry underneath.

On my free, sunny days or late afternoons after work, I would just sit in my boat, hold the sail and let my thoughts drift just as my boat did. When I had to paddle, I used the racing style to pretend I was training. But this boat was surely not a kayak and it was too wide and much harder to get up to speed. Often I would take a book or some paperwork along but I was too distracted to achieve very much. But my boat, "Max," contributed to perhaps some of the happiest memories of my life. I never felt as carefree as when I was on the water either paddling, sailing, or drifting, rocked by or sometimes fighting the waves.

It was on the Altefähr beach that I met a group of four Berliners with their bikes. They had toured Rügen. I was not sitting far away from them and could overhear their conversation. Maybe they spoke extra loud so I could hear them. One of them, the tallest, with black curly-wavy hair and I thought him quite handsome, commented, "What are those green plants in the water along the beach? Did the Islanders plant green beans under water?"

It was spoken in the Berliner dialect! I burst out laughing. It was kelp – but the way the statement came out sounded so serious and really tickled my funny bone. Because of my laughter, they joined me. After a lot of happy banter, I invited them for a bite to eat at my parent's place and we had a fun evening. Especially my dad enjoyed the young men and asked many questions about life in the politically new Berlin. Heiner, the handsome guy, started writing to me and visited again a year later. My father found out that he was very involved in the leadership of the FDJ and made comments that caused me to stop a developing relationship before it really started. I did not want a Communist for a boyfriend. I kind of hid behind the phrase, Youth friend, and tried to keep it light and treated him like a comrade.

Sport Middle School

In the fall, I could not go back to Hansa evening classes. Instead, I was sent to "Sport Middle School" in Guestrow for three months. It was another steppingstone for my goal to get my Teachers Certificate. A married couple ran the school. The husband at thirty-one-years old was teaching academic subjects and his wife, Eva, twenty-eight, was a tyrant chasing us around the athletic field and working us to the bone in the gym. Another older teacher with a fantastic figure taught gymnastics.

I shared a room with five other girls. After the first day of testing our abilities, my whole body hurt. I was a speedy kayaker, yes, but surely not an athlete doing jumps, running, even and uneven bars and working on all the other gymnastic torture instruments. The next morning I could not move. I could not get out of bed. The others were gone already and Eva missed me, but not the way you miss a friend. She came and got me out of bed with a few harsh words, pulling my blanket away and grabbing my arm. The hardest thing was to go down the steep stairway; I had to hold on to the rail. I thought she was a Nazi witch. She looked exactly like Hitler had wanted German girls to look: Well built, blond, blue eyes, strong, proud and handsome with a beautiful facial bone structure. She reminded me of my cousin Erika who also had those same looks.

Did you know that Hitler had organized certain – dare I call them institutes? Selected young men and young women with these features were kept there to "breed" the totally Aryan people.

Eva did not drive us quite as hard on this second day but we had to repeat all the same disciplines. Over the next few days, with sports in the morning, theory from eleven to twelve- thirty and again from two to four, then sports again, we slowly got into a routine and actually learned a lot. She expected much of us having been chosen students with job security and our full salary paid at home.

Eva and her husband had a little two-year-old daughter who took to me and I loved her. I had offered to be her babysitter when her parents had to go to meetings. I got to know Eva a bit better and was surprised when she apologized one day about her rough treatment of me the second morning, "I had to do that, Gisela. If I had let you lie there in bed you would not have been able to move or walk for a week! You can only combat the pain after training by doing the same thing again, moving the blood and the lymph and getting the acidity out. You experienced yourself how it became easier, right?"

She was right. The more I learned about anatomy, physiology and sports psychology the better I understood. Actually, these three subjects intrigued me so much that another dream started to form, that I maybe could become a doctor, specializing in sports medicine. I never talked about it but Eva's husband warned me one evening when they were ready to go out and I was coming to babysit with my books under my arm to study when their daughter was asleep, "Sportfriend Gisela, you are driving yourself too hard. It's good to have ambition, but you are driven! You'll burn yourself out if you keep going like you do. You are young and all you do is study. You need to take time for some fun. You need to find balance."

We had heard through the grapevine that these two people had been very involved during the Hitler era, especially the husband, but we never could confirm any of it or find out what it was. Judging by his education, he must have been a teacher, professor or high officer. After the war, he must have joined the "right party" or maybe he had been one of the people who had conspired to get Hitler out of the way. Who knows! He was a serious kind of man and one could not help but have a healthy respect for him. It just did not seem right to call him by his first name or address him with "Sport Friend".

At the anniversary of the DDR in October, we marched through the city of Guestrow. It was not a big town but one without bomb damage. Three men and I were the only top-class athletes with our light blue sweat suits marching up front. I was the proud flag carrier. Someone took a photograph with my box camera. When my dad saw it, he had the same expression on his face that he had when he saw my Hitler post card on my night table. That expression always kept me from getting too involved politically.

At Christmas, I was at home again and back in the boathouse. Winter training for kayaking was sitting on a board placed over two chairs at either end, refining the paddle technique and co-ordination of hip, shoulder, arm and hand movements. Paddling in the air is harder than paddling in water! The rowers let us use their tank with a water circuit when they did not need it. To this day, I am not sure which acted as the greater penalty for failing to keep one's balance – tumbling onto a hard floor or falling into a tank of cold water. Both were great incentives for maintaining the correct posture.

Alfred was the coach and Christa and I were sharing the training taking place in one of the school gyms to exercise the whole body, since paddling was more or less only developing the upper body muscles. We also played table tennis. As always, I was very competitive, and in the following summer participated in the provincial championships and was surprised to win in singles. I received a thick book with the title: "The Wolga-Don Canal." It was my first ever- NEW book. It was interesting, maybe more for a man, but I did read it and it helped me later to impress my professor who was teaching "Social order and history of the Soviet Union." I learned more about the history of the Soviet Union than I had ever learned about the German history. To get ahead you just had to participate and get good marks, especially in this subject.

17: A Very Special Offer

A difficult decision

Usually this kind of "offer" would not be an "offer" but a delegation or request you could not deny. It was a great honor. I was offered a job at the Sports Ministry in Berlin. It would have been an incredible step up for me and "all my troubles with striving to get somewhere" would have been over. No more need to prove myself, not to Aunt Tutti or anybody that I had it in me to be more than a maid in one of the great houses of the past. I asked if I could think about it since my family lived here and I had my club and my boat and had never been so far away from home. I was only eighteen and 'of age' but still…

One "small" problem had to be solved though. I was not a party member and all I had to do was "sign here." I went to talk to my parents, especially Father. I knew his mindset but could not really blame him after his experiences in Siberia. Both were incredulous but got very upset when I tried to explain that my joining the SED would not change me. It was just something I had to do if I wanted to get ahead. Everybody did it. Also, what a chance this was for me to get involved in the sport organization at the highest level. I tried to "sell" them my view but they got very stubborn like mules putting down their feet. It came to the point when my mother with a cold voice uttered, "If you do that we will never give you a nice wedding. If you do that, you don't even have to come home anymore. We would not be able to trust you no matter what you say. Once the party has you in its grip you won't be able to remain who you are. You will have sold your soul to the devil and even unintentionally you will turn us in. You can do what you want but you know where we stand."

Therefore, that was that and I had to make my decision. The situation was bad and it hurt to hear my parents talk to me like that. I understood where they were coming from. I had experienced the horror of the last days of the war and the Soviet army which brought us the questionably glorified freedom, the freedom that "freed" us from our home and divided our family, the army that had killed and abused women and many children. Yes, I had seen and lived through it all. But that was the past and now was now. I needed to make a life, a new life in a new society for myself. Deep within me, I knew they were right but it was my future, not theirs we had been talking about.

Did I struggle to come to a decision? No. There was absolutely no question in my mind. I would find innocent reasons and an excuse to remain in Stralsund.

My boss was glad I stayed. She was going through a divorce and wanted to marry one of the rowers with whom she had carried on an affair. She confided she might quit her job since she had a better offer from one of the high schools to teach Physical Education. I knew she just had the same title as I did, Sport Instructor, but it did not matter because of a severe shortage of teachers. She hinted that maybe I could apply for her job when the time came, if I wanted it.

A movie star

Around the same time, I met Kurt, a member of the Stralsund swimming team. He was tall with the figure of a swimmer, incredible grey eyes, and medium blond hair and very handsome. My team was running along the seawall and so did his team. He kind of bumped into me. I knew I had developed a good running style and God knows why he singled me out. We talked a bit while running but his team, all men, was faster. But he knew how to find me! At the finish of my next water-training session, he stood at the boat jetty waiting for me. I was in my old training clothing, wet and with messy hair. He looked like he had stepped out of a model magazine. That bugged me and I was not very nice to him but he watched while I cleaned and dried my kayak and he tried to make pleasant conversation. He told me he was studying engineering and architecture. I found an excuse later to disappear. He did not give up. I rejected his frequent dinner and other invitations with the excuse that I had signed a "race training contract" and needed my rest.

After the race season was over, I gave in to go to a dance in the Union Club House. It was a beautiful former private villa three buildings from the boathouse. That villa had held some kind of attraction for me because of its architecture. I had enjoyed a lemonade now and then with my paddle friends in the summer restaurant set up on the seaside in the gorgeous park-like garden but I was dying to see the inside of the building. They held the dance in a very pretty hall. I took a tour to see the rest of the building. The rooms were very impressive with dark wood panelling. I stared at one room with a huge red flag with the hammer and sickle on one wall and a photograph of Josef Stalin on another. On the floor was the largest Persian rug I had ever seen and the biggest table with twenty-four chairs around it was in the middle of the room. It was the Union's executive meeting room. Barely ten years later I learned this villa had once belonged to my future husband's Grandfather, Richard von Kehler, the man who had a big hand in financing the Wright brothers' flight, the building of the Zeppelin Airship, and the development of the air industry in general. Was my attraction to this building – a premonition? I don't know. The family never got it back. It was confiscated for the people and belonged to "everybody." And everybody who worked, including me, was a member of the Union automatically. A membership fee was deducted from our salary, so I 'owned' part of it!

The City Theatre was open again and Kurt and I went to operettas, operas and some plays. This was a new world for me and I enjoyed it.

In October, when I had to give my parents a hand to harvest our potatoes, Kurt offered to come and help. I did not want him to but he did and my mother warned me after he had left on his bike, "Gila, he is way too good looking. You'll never have him to yourself. Other women will be after him like the devil and such men cannot be faithful."

Teaching sports full time

My boss called me into her office and explained that the Agricultural School in Stralsund was looking for a full time sports teacher. She strongly advised me to apply as she had heard through the grapevine that they might close our city committee and the organisation for country and city will be united once again. It was very unlikely that I would get a job there since several men were arguing already and wanted the jobs for themselves. She confided she had now given notice and would be starting work in the high school. She gave me a good reference and application papers. I dropped them off personally and met the principal. He knew of me because of the "sports achievement pin" sessions and grinned when he admitted I had been the one who had tested him. We had a nice chat and I was hired.

My students were between fourteen and eighteen years old and came from the villages surrounding Stralsund twice a week. Since I had attended the same type of school in Altefähr, I knew the routine. This school was much larger and employed six teachers when I was hired. The fourteen to sixteen year olds were in one class and the sixteen to eighteen in another. The latter was a bit of a problem. I wasn't much older than the older ones and one of the boys got into trouble at a gym session. One after the other did the exercise on the high bar. One young man just stood there, looked straight ahead and did not move. I called his name several times and nothing happened. I was about to walk up to him when another boy, standing next to him stated, "My goodness, Fräulein, don't you see that he is building tent and cannot move?"

I had not heard the expression before and did not know what he meant. The troubled boy was very embarrassed, had a dark red face and almost cried. I looked him up and down and then I saw his dilemma. Now I was embarrassed as well but casually said, "Okay Karl, you could have asked for a restroom break; you are excused."

I called up the next in line and we went on with the program. They were all much quieter than before. On the way back to school the one who had spoken up sidled up to me and expressed his thoughts, "Fräulein, you are just too young and too pretty to be our sports teacher.

A man would be better. If possible, could you at least wear a sweat suit instead of sports shorts?"

The school had an unused darkroom. Permission to use it was granted and I could now develop and print all my own photographs. I had taken a weekend course earlier. I spent lots of time in the dark room, which actually was not dark but lit with a red bulb. I formed a photo group and quite a few of my students joined during the winter. In spring and fall, they had to work on their farms and during the summer we all had holidays, more time for me to spend on the water.

When I quit my former job, I also had to move out of the little attic room. I was able to find a furnished room in the house of a former, now retired, teacher with the promise I would never have young men over or have any parties. Christa's parents knew this couple because they owned an empty lot next to their house where Christa and Alfred built a home. I was allowed to make little meals in the kitchen and in time, they got to like and trust me.

My nineteenth birthday 1953

This was the first birthday party I ever had! My parents had taken all the beds out of the children's room and left just the table and the chairs. I invited all my closer friends from the canoe club and we were twenty, plus my parents and sisters. It was potluck and we had many wonderful dishes. Naturally, Kurt was there as well and I got a single red rose from him, packaged in a white fancy box. As a group, they gave me a new fast-working butane camping stove and a frying pan. My mother mixed dough for making pancakes and each of us in turn had to make one and flip it in the air. With lots of laughter, we saw many pancakes fall only halfway into the pan or they hit the floor. I was proud to get it perfect after my second try. The trick was to flip and throw them higher! We had homemade wine. Christa had her accordion, which my father played and Jorgen brought his guitar. We danced and then I started to read "hands" and predicted the future to all who wanted to know their fate. It was all in good fun but many times I hit the proverbial nail on the head and they believed I had turned into some kind of a witch. My sister Ingrid was the last, she held out her hand, "Please read mine, too."

I took her hand, looked at her lifeline – and it was without thought that I told her, "Well, for a start you won't get very old…," and then I stopped. I had the weirdest feeling as if my hair stood on end and a cold shower ran down my back. I still had her hand in mine when she asked, "Will I marry before I die?"

After all, she was only fifteen! So I gave her a bit of reassurance but somehow my birthday came to an end with me feeling very uneasy. The paddlers and Kurt left on their bikes and I helped my parents with the cleanup and the refurbishing of the room.

Two years later Ingrid had her right arm amputated and her sports swimming career in breaststroke and diving came to an end. She died of a bone tumor only about five months after the diagnosis.

A revolution of patient people

All in all, my teaching career without having a teacher's certificate got off to a good start. My students got used to me and I accepted them the way they were. Most of them had no sports clothing and participated in skirts and blouses or whatever, playing volleyball or doing gymnastics and the boys wore their farm work clothing. The one thing I could never get them to do was learn to march and it was my duty to teach them that! We were supposed to "march" to the gym, which was in a different school and I got them into formation with great difficulty. As soon as I gave the command they walked all over the place, had fun doing it and made all kinds of political jokes to which I had to turn a deaf ear. They knew I would not report any of them.

Workers everywhere were under great pressure. They had to fulfill a five-year production plan but they had no materials to even attempt to do the required work – no screws or nuts, no nails, no paint, no nothing. The "Party Functionary" (a man representing the party) pushed with big political speeches and phrases because he himself was pushed from the next one above his station. But the DDR had absolutely no unemployment: Every able man or woman had a job. It did not matter if they sat around, smoked, talked or even played cards while waiting for supplies to get back to their work. As long as they turned up at the job site, they got paid. I had seen this already in 1949 but it did not get better. My father predicted, "The situation at the wharf is like a pressure cooker. I would not be surprised if one day it just exploded. The people are desperately unhappy."

That day came without anyone expecting it. Nobody could explain later what caused it but almost simultaneously all over the DDR people put their tools down, congregated and marched. At first, they were quiet. Father got caught up in it at the wharf, where thousands marched towards the big double doors at the exit and out into the street. Police jeeps drew up and loudspeakers demanded they break up the march and go back to their jobs or they would be sorry. The Soviets had been notified already. When the German police did not get a reaction from the quietly marching workers, shots were fired into the air and the "best friends of the workers" came in tanks and trucks using tear gas to herd them into the big sports field where I had held the training and tests for the achievement pin. Nobody died, but the tear gas made many people seriously ill. That was the end of the revolution of the oppressed workers of the German Democratic Republic.

With a new member of my canoe club, another Ingrid, who now worked at my old desk in the boathouse, I had taken off in my boat to the Isle of Hiddensee for the weekend. A steamship loaded with tourists and weekenders would bring more people to this island than lived there. Hiddensee was one of our favorite places, a small narrow island one could walk from one end to the other in a couple of hours. We often camped there and the people of Hiddensee, almost all fisher-men, knew and liked us paddlers. The diversity of the natural beauty was a big draw. The small isle had majestic cliffs and a lighthouse on the highest part on the narrow side facing Rügen and one had an incredible view over the Baltic Sea towards Sweden. It was not visible but we knew it was there. The Soviets had installed high-beam searchlights, which would start scanning back and forth over the water like long arms as soon as it was dark.

Walking down from the heights, we always enjoyed the little village of Kloster and visited the house of a much-loved poet, Gerhard Hauptmann. It was overgrown with roses and was now a museum. Our camping place was about one kilometer along the 'Sea and Bike Path" at a nice sandy beach. After another four kilometers or so the island would peter out into sandbanks.

Ingrid and I had several days to enjoy the island and I had a chance to show her what I loved so much. But thick dark clouds were gathering and we decided we had better pack up and head for Stralsund earlier than planned. A couple of fishermen saw us in the small harbor and warned us that for our 'little bathtub' the waves were too dangerous and we would be wiser to stay and wait out the storm. Ingrid was a beginner and had no strength in her arms and no paddle technique at all. We called people like that "Sunday paddlers" but I trusted my "Max" and myself to bring us the three or four hours across the open sea back home. It was impossible to sail, the wind had picked up, the waves got higher by the minute, but I did not want to turn back. I paddled like a mad woman, Ingrid helped very little and her paddles were often in the way of mine. We took on so much water the thought that this might be my last boat trip went through my mind. I kept looking out for a very low island, the Bird Island, closer to the Rügen coast. There was absolutely nothing on this flat straight patch of earth except seagulls. You could not even see it until you were almost upon it. I knew it from former visits on sunny days, when we had stopped and looked for seagull eggs and fried them on rocks hot from the sun.

After about four hours and with my last bit of strength we reached it. I jumped out of the boat totally wet and shivering. We pulled it up onto the narrow beach. Ingrid needed a hand to get out and jointly we dragged the waterlogged boat up onto the two-foot high bank. We unpacked the boat. Everything was soaking wet and some things had been floating around us. We turned the boat over to get the water out and left it upside down. With difficulty, we got the small tent erected. The wind helped to dry it but we had to doubly secure it in order not to have it fly away. Our sweat suits were in a big rubber bag and just moist but not wet. We changed and went in search of seagull eggs. We found several and they made our 'slurp' evening meal. They tasted very fishy but that's what seagulls lived on – fish.

Around five in the morning, the wind had abated and we hurried up to be able to reach Stralsund before we both had to report for work. A nice, not too strong wind was a great help. I could set sail and it was wonderful how "Max" sliced through the water.

It was close to eight a.m. when we reached the boat jetty. Two policemen were waiting for us.

"Where did you come from? Why were you out on the water at this hour? Don't you know a strict curfew is in place?"

We were dumbfounded and did not know what he was talking about. I tried to make a joke out of our arrival like "risen from the deep" because of the storm when they got crabby and told us in no uncertain terms to come to the police station with them. I apologized and asked very politely, "Tell us, sport friend, what is going on? We left Hiddensee yesterday, were stranded on Bird Island and left it with a good wind sailing at five this morning and we are glad to be alive! We both are expected at our jobs and have to hurry. And what does 'curfew' mean?"

They settled down, told us about the uprising the previous day, what we had to do and then let us bring in the boat. After changing very quickly, we hurried off to work. That day my students were NOT TO MARCH but walk at ease. Of course, they went into formation and marched smartly and I could do nothing about it. So I walked on the sidewalk and pretended I had nothing to do with them.

That happened on the 17th of June 1953. It is a National Holiday now in a United Germany in memory of the uprising.

Unexpected News

I received a letter telling me to come to Leipzig, register for my next accelerated course at the "Deutsche Hochschule fuer Koerperkultur and Sport", translated, "German College for Body Culture and Sports", part of the University. My boss had to sign my release papers and let me go with full job security and salary. Based on my previous achievements in the other preparatory courses, I expected now to finish the remainder of the normally three-year program during the next nine months. I would then be able to apply to write a thesis and a test to get my Physical Education Teacher's Certificate.

I did not want to lose my room at the nice house in Stralsund and I asked if my sister Christel could move in with me and then stay there on her own until I came back. It was not a problem. Christel was attending the Nursing School at the Stralsund Hospital and it was much easier for her not to commute from Altefähr. I started my studies in September 1954 and as usual put all my time into it. Only on one occasion did I join a group of students to go to the "Faustus Cellar", a famous student bar where they would hang out, smoke, drink and have fun. It did not appeal to me. I hated the noise and the smoky, stale air. I did not like beer and never went again. I shared a room with four girls and rather enjoyed the quiet when they had all gone and I could study. Because of my earlier training, I took all my notes in shorthand and consequently had much more to work with than the others. My papers always got high marks and it did not take long before the other students called me the "biker with golden handles and silver pedals," meaning that I was trying to impress the teachers.

My "aunt-babysitter-sister" Lisa had married Willy, a man in Jena, Thuringia. I visited with them quite often on weekends. Jena was just a couple of hours' train ride from Leipzig. Uncle Willy criticised me for the way I squished the toothpaste out of my tube and left the tube looking all weird and crooked. He showed me how to squeeze from the bottom up in order to leave the tube looking neat. I thought him presumptuous – but all my life I have followed his advice and I remember him often when I take my toothpaste into my hand. I also had to shake my washcloth to get the creases out when I visited and hang it neatly where it belonged. He was very orderly and Lisa said it had taken her a while to perform to his liking. Willy and I had a flirting, teasing relationship and he became one of my favorite uncles. Their only daughter Angela became my second Godchild.

One thing that was hard to get used to in Leipzig was the huge common shower for about thirty girls. They were all dancing around in the nude to catch the water coming down from the showerhead about two meters wide. Sometimes the water pressure was low and washing hair was a problem. A long row of twenty-four sinks was along one wall. I always tried to be the last to leave the bedroom until they figured out I was avoiding the nude "exhibition" and they teased me. So I learned to be just another nude body amongst them. It was tough because of my strict upbringing.

Just before Christmas 1954, my professor called me into his office and suggested I should change from physical education to sports medicine. He told me that I have the highest marks possible in all medicine related classes and he would be willing to become my mentor. The problem was that I would have to give "notice" to my school in Stralsund and lose the benefit of job security and salary. It would take about another eight years for me to become a fully-fledged doctor. I was incredulous that my secret dream could become a reality – but what about money? How would I pay for everything? Would my father help? I had to go home and talk to him about it.

I had neglected my friendship with Kurt, missed him and wanted to see him again. I started writing letters and told him about my life in Leipzig and the chance I had to go into medicine. Since I planned to come home at Christmas, would he pick me up at the station? Could he maybe get opera tickets for the second day of Christmas? His answer was a reluctant yes, but a yes nevertheless. We were like strangers and very careful with each other. We made plans to go to a New Year's Ball with his brother Eric and his girlfriend. At the ball, Kurt only danced with me once and I caught him looking repeatedly at a young lady who was sitting not far from us with her fiancé and her parents. She eyed him too and it did not take long until Kurt asked her to dance. He danced almost every dance with her and even the one at midnight, the dance into the New Year. I was very hurt, danced a few times with his brother but was mainly sitting by myself. I was afraid to leave and walk through the bombed out city on my own and there were no buses or taxies. You biked or you walked. So I sat there and waited and tried to make a happy face. "She" had to leave with her fiancé and her parents, and Kurt walked me home. In front of my steps, he started kissing me like crazy and begged me to let him come upstairs with me.

"What do you think you are doing? Taking me to a dance and then only dancing with another man's girl and letting me sit there like a wall-flower? If I hadn't been afraid to walk home alone through the dark city streets, I would have been long gone. No chance! You go and live your life as I will live mine. I'm glad I saw you again and really got to know you. My mother was right to warn me about you."

I opened my door and closed it in his face. In my room, I took out my diary and honestly wrote down all that had happened. I tried to be sad and cry but I could not. I tried to squeeze a few tears out to let them fall on my ink-writing for "memories later in my life." Even that did not work so I cheated and used a few drops of water. Somehow, I felt relieved. It was weird. The experience set me free but I never really fell in love again. It was more "I like you" but never love in the way of the first time. I protected my heart and always used my head in choosing male friends – but it always ended before it got serious. I must admit it always was my fault. I did or said something that angered or scared the boy away.

The girl Kurt had danced with broke off her engagement; they married and lived happily ever after. Years later, they had a community garden across from my sister Edith. I asked her to invite the couple to tea so I saw them again. I was visiting from Canada where I had become a big success story. I felt secure in talking and making jokes about our past. We had some good laughs about how "stupid" we had been, how innocent, how afraid to become intimate when we were in love that one summer and how well our lives had turned out. We remained friends.

The long talk with my father regarding going into medicine ended with, "You have a good profession. You are almost finished with your studies to become a Physical Education Teacher. You have a job that pays you well even during your absences, whether it is for your studies or your kayak competitions. I have three more daughters to help along. Sorry Gila, but I cannot help you."

My professor was disappointed and tried to get a scholarship for me. But after the first time I was to cut into a cadaver that was a dead person, I felt sick and I knew I couldn't do it. Thus ended my dream of becoming a doctor.

My teaching certificate

In June 1955, I proudly received my PhysEd Teacher's Certificate. Actually, nothing changed in my working life as I had been teaching for a few years by this time. The framed certificate was hanging in the lounge/meeting room with those of all the other teachers. At least I now felt "equal."

A real shock came when the math teacher did not show up for work. He had escaped to West Germany.

The principal played tennis every morning from seven to eight and one day asked me if I wanted to fill in since his partner was away. I jumped at the chance. I loved to play tennis but up to now never had good lessons. The cool morning air was invigorating and I was happy to prove I was not too bad a player.

With three other girls from my canoe club, I spent one week of the holidays on the Isle of Hiddensee. We camped and next to us were several tents with six young men from Saxony. They were wild-water kayakers and could do "the roll". They tried to teach us. We had a lot of fun with them building human pyramids because one of them was a gymnast. They loved sitting on the dune until late at night watching the searchlights of the police going over the sea. One even had a stopwatch. We didn't think anything of it, thought it was just fun for landlubbers! We made hula skirts out of sea grass for the ten of us. We used a lipstick to paint designs on the men and our faces and went to a dance as "Indians," making a lot of noise when entering the party and pretending to go ahead and "scalp" a few people. We won first prize (a bottle of Rum) for best costumes. We had suggested finishing it sitting on the dune that night. They were not in the mood for drinking but were excited about some shopping they did the previous day. They had bought expensive cameras with telescopic lenses and Zeiss binoculars and had not expected to find this kind of quality on the small island. We could not believe they would carry so much cash when camping. Credit Cards had not been "invented" yet.

The next morning they were gone. GONE! The tents were gone, their kayaks were gone, their belongings were gone. It was as if they never existed. We just stared at each other. Leaving without saying goodbye? After all the fun we had? Unbelievable!

In late September, I received a post card from Sweden. They had paddled in the dark, they knew when the search light would hit our area and simply did "the roll." They had escaped and paddled all the way to Sweden via Bornholm/Denmark.

During the rest of the summer of 1955, I participated in several regattas again and surprise-surprise, we were allowed to go to one in Hamburg! Hurray! That was something new and exciting – to go to West Germany and compete. One of our paddlers disappeared and did not come back with us. She simply remained in what we thought was paradise. I must admit the thought had gone through my mind as well. But just leave my boat "Max" and my family in the DDR? (Yes – in that order) My life had become pretty good. I had a well-paying, satisfying job and my canoe club. I had wonderful friends, my family and relatives, so why change it? I knew my teacher training would not have been recognized in the BDR and I had no idea how else I could earn my bread and butter. The regatta was also a disappointment. Being used to finishing either first or at least second in my races it was a blow to be fifth out of five! My lack of training while in Leipzig had come home to roost. I decided to call it quits and remain in the memory of the competitors as "oh, she was good" instead of "she had to quit because she got too old." The younger generation had caught up with us old-timers.

In mid-August, I had to go back to work to prepare for the new school year. The principal and I picked up the morning tennis sessions again and I enjoyed many single sailings with "Max" and just lived each day as it presented itself. My father had built a bee house and he and I would sit there for many an hour talking or just being comfortable in each other's company. He was very proud of me and of my achievements after the tough time dropping out of school in 1948. Actually, I owed it all to his sister, my Aunt Tutti, who got me going with her remark about just becoming a "maid," if times were different. I think my mother was envious of the close relationship Dad and I had and always stayed in the house. But she was also highly allergic to bee stings and once had almost died when she had helped Father to re-capture a swarm. Father could stick his hand into the hive. They would not even sting him.

Teaching was fun. I was a year older and my students were younger, it helped. During a meeting, the principal announced every teacher had to become a party member, "To shape and influence a young person's life a teacher must have the backing of the worker's party in order to impart the ideology and pride in the achievements of the DDR."

I had put the thought out of my mind since so far nobody had ever seriously pushed me to apply for a membership card. I knew in my guts that sooner or later I would have to face the music – but how to deal with my parents? I wondered if my principal knew of my reluctance. On the fourth day of October, he told me after tennis I would have to come to his house after school because there was something very serious he had to discuss with me and it demanded total privacy. I had an uneasy feeling but I trusted him and biked to the address he had given me. I expected to meet his wife but he said she was away. I did not like that at all; alarm bells went off in my head. I took the chair closest to the door and was ready to run. He proceeded to talk about the necessity of becoming a party member. He also admitted he knew of my reluctance because of my parents and he would be able to prevent me from doing so if I would agree to sleep with him. At that, I jumped to my feet, headed out the door, grabbed my bike and raced off as fast as I could. He did not try to stop me, just called out, "It's your only chance."

I biked across the bridge all the way to Altefähr, went straight to the bee house, sat there thinking, trying to calm down and waited for my dad. I knew he always went there after work. When he came, I immediately told him the whole story. He listened patiently but looked very pale when he said just three words to me, "Gisela, hau ab."

'Hau ab' means something like "get lost". These two words were known to express "flee to the West." He advised me not to let on or tell Mother since she was not able to lie to the police when certainly they would come to interrogate them. It was better for her if she did not know. It was a tense evening meal for me and Dad came along for a bit when I left and we talked about my boat. He would see my friend Alfred and ask him to sell it to a club member. There was a lot of interest. Dad hugged me hard fighting tears when he turned to go home and I biked off – not exactly into the sunset.

Escape to West Berlin

At 5:30 a.m. the next morning, I was on the train to Berlin with a small suitcase. It contained a set of bed sheets, a couple of towels, an evening gown and a change of underwear. No toiletries, not even a toothbrush. I wore my silver class sports pin on my lapel. When the police first came to check for travel documents, they wanted to know where I was going. I talked about a special course for top competitors. The young policeman kind of "lifted" my suitcase which was above me on the luggage shelf to check for weight. I prayed he would not open it because I had absolutely no sports clothing in it. I kept my eyes on his and turned towards him in such a way that he had to notice my silver pin. He must have seen my pride in my achievements displayed by this pin and reluctantly left. Somehow he must have had a bad feeling because he walked by my compartment several times with another policeman, always looking at me. Maybe they had never met a champion? I was sure they talked about me but I quietly held my book, gave him a little smile and nodded a greeting. Five hours later the train arrived in Bernau, a suburb of Berlin, and the end of the line for this train. Everybody had to get out, go down steep steps to an underpass and up again onto another platform. A table was set up with three policemen checking passports. All passengers stood in line. When the S-Bahn – city train – pulled in there were still seven people in front of me. I still cannot explain how, why or when I made the decision to run for it as soon as the conductor blew his whistle, lifted his paddle and called, "Careful at the train, doors close automatically."

I caught the last coach as the doors closed. Two Berliners realized what I was doing, held the doors open and pulled me in as the train rolled away. Two shots rang out but they just hit the pavement. They could easily have killed me. There were just a few meters between them and me. The men in the train took my coat off me and my suitcase and one of them hurried me through the train into another compartment. Somebody jumped up and the men pushed me onto the empty seat and handed me a newspaper to hide behind. I expected the train to be stopped, but it rolled along faster and faster and when it stopped again, it was at the station "Gesundbrunnen" and now I was in West Berlin. My rescuer had explained to me I would have to change to another train here in order not to go back into East Berlin again. I had also been advised how to get to a specific building to register as an escapee. On this day alone, over sixteen-thousand people escaped from East Germany, not just through Berlin but all the other places where it was still possible to cross the border although with much more difficulty. People were killed by stepping on mines or they were shot swimming across a lake or caught digging tunnels. Some even built a hot air balloon to drift over to the other side.

Thinking about it, East Germany lost so many young intellectuals and families that over the years the authorities just had to build a wall to keep them "in."

I was "processed" over the period of the following three weeks with many interviews by the Americans, the English and the French officials. After a week, I met my father at Aunt Erika's apartment as we had agreed upon on the evening before I left. He brought me the money for my boat and a few personal items. He was sad to go back the same day but there was no other way because nobody was supposed to "miss" him.

I was in a barrack with six bunk beds and reasonably well taken care of, considering the masses of people who were coming through. Most were put on direct trains to West Germany, trains that passed through East Germany but did not stop. For some reason they kept asking me questions I honestly could not answer about war installations on the Island of Rügen on the coast facing Sweden. They also wanted to know if I had ever seen or counted the tanks on trains across the Rügendam. Yes, I had seen them but it was part of everyday life. We didn't even think about it. No, I didn't know there were huge bunkers under the forest floor in the area of Binz where my sister Christel had spent time recovering from her lung problem. After three weeks hearing the same answers to their questions, they finally decided to fly me off to Hannover. The man assigned to my case explained that, because of my status in sports, my recent finishing University at the cost of the state, and the fact that I lived on Rügen and in Stralsund, it was wiser not to be on the train through East Germany which could be stopped at will. My first flight was a flight to freedom.

But what would happen now?

They placed me in a Catholic girl's home, even though I was not Catholic. We learned to make sauerkraut. We had to help with housework and had our simple duties. They told me that I was destined to go to Dortmund and the processing would take a while. After a week, I got restless. I liked Hannover. Just a few houses away from the home, I saw a "House of Sports." I stopped in and met a nice lady receptionist. I told her my story, told her about my kayaking career when she got very excited and exclaimed, "Wow! That is fantastic! The head of the Unemployment Commission is our Canoe Club president. I'll phone him right now!"

She did and I got an appointment to see him the next day. He gave me three cards with addresses to report to for jobs. The listed companies were looking for office help. Naturally, I had told him I had some office experience. I visited two of them but my typing was not fast enough since I never really had a typewriter and I had not practised it for years. My shorthand was okay but that alone was not enough. I had taken bookkeeping but never needed it. They did not want a raw beginner and especially someone who had so recently come from East Germany. There was a lot of discrimination to the point of them regarding me as a second-class citizen. I lost heart and did not even go to the third company but I still had to report to the Commission. The gentleman was not happy with me and said that the third one would have been the most likely one to hire me. It was the "Kneipp-Bund" (Kneipp Association) of Hannover, part of a worldwide health organisation. It was a bit farther afield. I was worn out and tired from all the emotional turmoil and had no money to take a streetcar. He gave me 50 pennies – one ride was 25, so I had enough to go there and back to my home.

I was interviewed and the Director was very interested in my whole story, not just in what I could do for them. After more than an hour he declared, "You are exactly what I had not even hoped to find. Your office skills may be limited but you'll gain experience. Your sports background comes in very handy for us and for you. We have an outdoor resort area where our members can play volleyball, fist ball, bocce, table tennis, socialize, do water treatments and we have been looking for someone to do exercises for women and children. Have you ever heard of Father Kneipp? No? Again, you'll learn. I think you will like the concept. We also offer exercise classes for women twice a week after work. You can earn a bit of extra money. Can you start work beginning of next week? Will the home where you live let you go? I'll have a word with Mr. X. at the Unemployment Commission, thank him for sending you. We will also help you find accommodation. I'll not let them send you to Dortmund, you stay in Hannover."

I was dazed. I walked all the way back to the home to process all this and saved the 25 pennies. I had agreed (what else would I do?) to the job and the pay and I was offered an advance to buy myself some things since I only had the one dress I was wearing. When I saw Mr. X. the next day, he behaved like an old friend. I wanted to give him the 25 pennies but he would not take them back.

"You keep that and take the street car to the Canoe Club. I told them you'd be coming. There is a young lady who needs a K II partner. She works for a butcher. She has also escaped from East Germany and she is not good in the K I."

I had visions of getting cheaper sausage through her. I also got the address of a lady who had a small furnished room for rent within walking distance from my new workplace. It had a single bed, a chest, a wardrobe, a small round table and one chair. In the corner was an iron stove for heating. I needed to buy wood or coal. I suffered the November cold since I had no money. Sometimes I put my coat on in bed. I was allowed to use the bathroom for a bath once a week; otherwise, I just used the sink. Mrs. O. did not want me to cook meals but I could heat up water for tea or heat a wiener in her kitchen. It was all good enough for me. For one Mark I could get a warm meal at the Youth Hostel every noon and, if I wanted to, in the evening as well. All were within walking distance. I was very glad to report to my parents my life seemed to be falling into place again and I hoped they were okay after I had "disappeared." I now know the police had made it hard for them and Father's advice not to tell Mother had been a blessing. Mother started to send me small packets of my clothing, one piece at a time.

On Christmas Eve, I had run out of money and food. I was too embarrassed to ask for another advance. I was in my bed dressed in all I owned to be warm. I was wondering what I would do when the front door bell rang and then my landlady knocked on my door, "It's for you, Fräulein."

I opened the door and a "Lutheran Sister" (somewhat comparable to a Catholic Nun) stood there with a covered basket on her arm. She smiled at me and introduced herself, "I am with the Evangelical Girls' Association. We just received your address from the Catholic home you stayed in when you first arrived in Hannover. We wanted to make sure you are all right."

I offered her the chair and I sat down on my bed. She looked around and noticed that my bed was not made, I had my coat on and the room was cold. She was so relaxed and friendly I told her that I had not received my salary yet, and I had no money to buy coal to heat the room. I said it wasn't so bad when I was at work because the office was warm and that I also had absolutely nothing to eat for the next few days since the Youth Hostel was closed for the holidays.

"Well, then I came at the right time! Here, take a look!"

She handed me the basket. A whole bread, butter, sausage, cheese, Christmas cookies and even chocolate were under the cover. My mouth watered and I started to cry. She gave me a warm hug and then invited me to come to the clubhouse for a social afternoon tea and Christmas dinner the next day. She truly was a Godsend. Or was she a Christmas Angel?

Several times in my life, I had already experienced that, when you are at the end of the proverbial rope, something happens to save you.

18: Father Sebastian Kneipp

I had never heard of him. Kneipp grew up a very poor boy, the son of a weaver in the 19th century. At five-years-old, he herded cows and watched as one which had hurt its foot limped into a small alpine stream and stood in the cold water, occasionally lifting the foot and then putting it back down. In the evening, the cow could walk again without limping. Sebastian Kneipp never forgot this experience.

During winters, he had to help with the weaving in his father's basement. As a ten-year-old kid, he started spitting blood. His father just said, "That's normal, my boy; all weavers spit blood."

On Sundays, the family attended church service in the exceptionally beautiful Basilica in Ottobeuren, Bavaria. Sebastian was impressed with the richness of its interior and the well-fed priests. He decided to become a priest and became passionate about it. Up to that time, a cobbler who acted as the village teacher had taught him. He searched for ways to improve his education. As a young teenager, he hired himself out as farm-help and attended school in the village away from home. The Danube River was close by and he jumped daily into the cold water, thinking of the cow he had observed as a little boy. As the years passed, he had many ups and downs in his health. He realized he had to learn Latin to be able to be accepted into a Priests' Seminary. His mother's cousin was a priest who reluctantly agreed to help Sebastian and to teach him Latin.

He found a farm job close to his uncle's home. He spent the days working, the evenings receiving lessons and the nights studying. His health declined and he picked up the water treatment again, jumping into the cold nearby river in his birthday suit. He did not own a towel so he would put on his clothing and run home, drying himself and raising his body heat by doing so. His immune system strengthened and eventually he cured himself of the tuberculosis which had given rise to him spitting blood.

At about thirty years of age, Kneipp was the oldest student ever accepted for study by the Priests' Seminary in Munich. With malnutrition and overwork, his TB came back. Studying in the Munich University Library, he happened to come across an old book written by two doctors, Father and Son Hahn, about the "Effect of water on the human body." He applied for a job helping in the University Gardens to get close to a water supply (hose and watering cans) and since he had nothing to lose but everything to gain, he started using the detailed methods given in the book. In secret, he "watered" himself, different parts of the body each time to re-invigorate his blood supply and thereby improve his circulatory system. He got well. Word spread and he "watered" other students.

To make a long, though very interesting, story short, Kneipp completed his studies and graduated as a priest at forty-two years of age. His initiation took place in the gorgeous Basilica in Ottobeuren where he had first received his calling. Placed by the Catholic Church at different churches, he not only did his duty as a priest, but also helped the poor people, who could not afford medical help, with his watering treatments. The doctors and apothecaries complained about Kneipp's interference with their business to the officials – and the church finally moved him to a small place called Wörishofen to shut him up with the stern warning to look after the souls of his parishioners and not their bodies. As might be expected, he could not help it and continued his activities. His "fame" spread. People came from farther and farther away. First there were the poor, then the Aristocrats who included the Emperor from Austria; even a Maharaja from India came with his whole Harem. Wörishofen became a busy construction site for guesthouses, hotels and eating-places. The Church officials threatened to ex-communicate him and finally called him to Rome to see the Pope. A wise man, dressed like a monk, called him one night and asked him about why he was so driven to help. Not recognizing the Pope, Kneipp explained he could not let people die and just give them absolution when he knew he could help them to live. In the end, this "Monk" asked for advice with his sleeping problem. A few days later Kneipp was officially received by the Pope, he got his blessing and the huge assembly of churchmen were told this message:

"We have found this man to be pure and honest. We would like to give him Our Blessing. And Monsignor Kneipp, I give you the order: Keep on Healing."

Kneipp, now in shock for having recognized the "Monk" and being addressed with "Monsignor" was dazed, apologized to the Holy Father who smiled, offered his hand for the ring to be kissed and whispered, "I slept well that night."

Kneipp came home to a jubilant Wörishofen. The village is now, nearly 200 years later, a world-famous health resort and a recognized "Bad-Spa" city with elegant boulevards, beautiful hotels (many of them 5-Star), guest houses, a thermal spa, 420 kilometers of groomed walking and biking paths through forests as well as wonderful homes, almost every one of them renting rooms and providing physician-prescribed water and massage treatments.

Sebastian Kneipp, the poor little boy struggling for many years to become a priest, became known worldwide as the "Waterdoctor". He never charged for his treatments but got donations from the rich. To keep the people from coming he wrote three books. These were translated into sixteen languages. With the earnings, he built three sanatoriums/cure homes:

1. The "Sebastianeum"

2. The Kneippianum

3. The Children's Hospital

The modern "Kneipp-Cure," based on his teachings and used in hospitals, is not an "alternative" but a "complementary" medicine. Research has proven people treated with both, conservative and complementary medicine get well much faster.

A complementary healing method

The Kneipp-System is based on five pillars:

1. Treatments with water in all its forms, i.e., cold, warm, hot, steam, ice. Full or partial bath, wrappings, rinses or ablutions
2. Herbs prepared as infusions, additions to bath or tea
3. Wholesome organic and simple food
4. Active exercise as well as inactive like massages and physiotherapy
5. Spiritual and mental stimulation and balance of body and soul

Kneipp was very concerned about his flock and always reminded them whenever he had the chance, "Don't forget your soul. If your soul is not well, the body can't be well either."

The medical profession has developed this system over the last hundred years. Kneipp died in 1897 and in his Will left his legacy to the medical profession with the words, "I want you to make my system available to all."

Learning about Father Kneipp had a great impact on me when I started working for the Kneipp-Association. At first my duties were simple, reorganizing the filing system and typing hundreds of the same letter asking for donations for a big fundraiser. When I asked why not copies, they told me every letter had to be an original. I knew that blessed letter in my sleep. My typing became very fast. I did not mind working a lot of overtime since my home was cold and in the office, it was warm. Doing the filing, I learned the Province of Hannover called Niedersachsen had a Kneipp Club in practically every town or village. It was all very similar to my work at the Sports Committee in Stralsund before I became a teacher. Two other employees went out to form more of these clubs and eventually I was involved in that activity as well. I knew all of the presidents' names and phone numbers by heart. When one of them phoned they often asked for me.

After three months, I got a raise. I went out, made a down payment on a bike and paid it off with 5.00 marks a month. In 1956, my boss gave me a Christmas bonus and advised me to go to a certain radio shop and pick up a small radio he personally had them put aside for me. It was a

Telefunken and it is now an oddity in my son's house. My boss, Mr. E. was always very nice to me, like an old friend. When I got some dictation, he would keep me in his office longer to tell me stories about his life as a teenager. He was involved in the Hitler Youth. Over the first couple of years, he revealed that I looked very similar to his first girlfriend and that even my demeanor was very much like hers. He laughed when he mentioned that it had been a big part in his decision to hire me but stressed that with my background I had just been the right one for this job. His wife had her desk in the front office where my small desk was. I sensed she was not happy when I was too long in his office.

In the New Year, another office help was hired. Mrs. D. was a Berliner, a widow and lived next to the Catholic home which had been my first billet in West Germany. She invited me for Sunday tea and Christmas since she lived alone. We told each other our experiences with the Russians. It was she who had seen her parents run burning with phosphor fire while she was not able to help and stood transfixed as she watched them die.

Our office organized the first of many week long "Health Convention and Exhibition Shows." My job was to write to all open-minded medical doctors to ask if they would give a lecture on their specialty. I still have a list with the topics: Leg problems, Heart and circulation, Insulin requirements for Diabetes, Physiotherapy or Chiropractic, Kneipp-Therapy at home, even Natural skin care and many more. Fifty-two M.D.'s were on my speakers list for the program and I met and spoke to them all. Mrs. D.'s job was to write to suitable companies to market exhibition space. I still have an adjustable ironing board I bought at that exhibition. I also bought my first juicer (wholesale price) and since my eye examination revealed I needed glasses, I juiced more than a hundred pounds of carrots over a year and had a big glass full every day! To activate the carotene, the precursor of vitamin A, which is important for the eyes, I had to add a few drops of oil. I looked as if I had a Florida tan but I did not need glasses until twenty years later.

In June 1956, I had my first official holiday. With my bike and a rucksack, I set off by train to Cologne and then cycled up beside the Rhine River to Mannheim. There I saw a sign to Heidelberg and visited the historic university town. On small roads with lots of grape vines growing on either side, I biked along the Neckar River and struggled (no gears!) uphill towards Stuttgart, well known because of the Mercedes Factory close by. Despite the lack of gears, I couldn't resist signs pointing me to the Alps: Kempten, Memmingen, Immenstadt. I managed the "The German Alpine Street" which started not far from "Schloss Neu-Schwanstein, which is the Disney image of Cinderella's castle. I biked from Reutlingen/Austria, just two kilometers from the castle, on top of the Alps all the way to Lindau at Lake Constance. I visited Switzerland for one day. Youth Hostels provided accommodation for one Mark a night and food was just as cheap compared to today's standards. In order to visit a girl I had shared a bunk bed with in Berlin (when we both had first escaped from East Germany), I turned my wheels to the Black Forest. She worked for a dentist and I spent the last short night of my two weeks there. At 4:30 a.m., I boarded a train and at 8:00 I sat at my desk in Hannover. My hands were very shaky from the biking, but I was happy and proud for having seen and accomplished so much. The sense of freedom riding alone most of the time and then to be able to stop whenever I wanted was a new experience.

But I would not allow any daughter of mine today to attempt that.

The "Health Week" had been a huge success and Mr. E. planned the next show for Cologne half a year later. Our Hannover office did all the organization, planning and writing with our existing staff. Two of the staff dealing with the set-up of the exhibition spaces left two weeks before the big date; my boss and I left five days before the opening in his Volkswagen beetle, Mrs. D. was to hold the fort and my boss' wife would join us a day before the Grand Opening. I was very impressed with the Cologne Cathedral. The beautiful, colored windowpanes had been replaced with glass during the bombing raids and therefore survived. One of the towers was still a ruin. It looked like a huge hollow tooth. The surroundings looked all very grey and sad.

The weekend before the Grand Opening my boss invited me for a drive along the Rhine River. We had dinner early in the evening in a historical building in the city of Goar. It was another new experience for me: a beautiful place, a fancy dinner and a glass of Rhine wine. It was around 8:30 p.m. when he said, "I have a surprise for you. I have booked rooms and we'll go back to Cologne tomorrow."

My alarm bell went off but he was very casual and I thought, "He said rooms, so I will have my own." When we finally went upstairs, he opened a door and let me go in. I noticed the king-size bed; I turned around and said one word, "NO."

He just laughed, "You can't walk back to Cologne, can you? You know I like you a lot and I won't hurt you. Just trust me. The bed is wide enough for both of us."

I sat down in a chair close to the window and contemplated my situation. There was no way out. I thought of my inexperience with this kind of thing and finally thought that it might be good to have "it" finally over with and know if I am a woman or not. I was nearly twenty-four years old and it was time to know what "it" was all about. A man like this would not risk making me pregnant. Maybe he would not even do anything.

The next morning he turned pale when he saw blood spots on the sheets.

"You were a virgin. Was this your first time? Oh my God, I will never get you out of my system now. I never had a virgin. My wife was older and she got pregnant when she seduced me and that ended my love story with my girl. I had to marry her for honor's sake. If we wouldn't have the two boys I would have divorced her years ago."

I just got up, went to the bathroom with my clothing, had a shower and came back out dressed. Somehow, I felt older, wiser, more grown up and somewhat relieved that I was "normal" and suggested, "Why don't you get ready too, have breakfast and go back to Cologne. There is lots of work waiting."

That is exactly what we did. I tried to put the episode out of my mind but I often saw him stealing glances, looking differently at me, softer and his voice changed towards me as well. Every chance he got he would put a hand on my shoulder but in a way that suggested nothing to others. I changed too, I think. I was much more confident knowing I was a real woman. It reflected on my work since I could now talk to men with more certainty. Maybe I also felt I had power over him and that I could ruin his life if I chose to. However, I know I did not think that way back then. I was much too afraid I would lose my job.

An unwanted affair

Back in Hannover, I had hoped things would just go back to where they were before, but they did not. He had the upper hand because he realized now I would not talk about it. I expressed the wish to take an "Esthetician Course" offered in the evening at the Rosa Graf School for Cosmetology. It took two years but I thought this might give me my independence later. I had attended the "Natural Skin Care" lecture at the Hannover Health Show and it had very much appealed to me. I had asked the speaker if there is a future in esthetics and she had been enthusiastic. Mr. E. supported this suggestion wholeheartedly and made sure I did not have too much overtime work on the three evenings a week I had to go to school. We did not tell anyone. I was ahead of the other students because of my semi-medical training from Leipzig and the practical work held its own attraction. I did not like manicuring – my hand was not steady enough for the polish application. All the other subjects were fun and intriguing. I read books on Acupuncture pressure and noticed during a facial massage, I could put people to sleep when using those points. I finished in one year.

I suffered from stress in the office. My boss took advantage of me whenever he had a chance. His wife was very cold and uncommunicative and the air was just thick, too thick to breathe. On Christmas Eve, I reached out my hand to his wife with pleading eyes to wish her Merry Christmas hoping I could enlist her help. She ignored me altogether. Later in the evening I said "Merry Christmas" to my landlady and sneaked out of my little home, ran to the station, bought a ticket and took a train to friends in a small village about fifty kilometers away. I felt light and free for the first time in a long time. We had a nice quiet family Christmas Eve with their daughter and nephew. I knew the nephew from Stralsund; he had been the math teacher at my school and had also escaped several months before me. We kind of "camped" with the nephew sleeping on the couch in the living room, the mother, her daughter and I in the master bedroom in the king-size bed and the father in the veranda on a foldout bed. The daughter and I slept in while "Aunt Lisbeth" was up to make breakfast on Christmas morning. She came to wake me about 9:00 a.m. and told me in a startled voice, "Gisela, you have to get up. You have a visitor. He insists and he wouldn't go when I asked him to leave."

I could have screamed. How did he ever find me? The next moment he came through the door, "Is this how you like to live? You get dressed immediately and you come with me."

When I declined, whispering, "Please let me be … I can't do this anymore," he became threatening. In the end, my new "Aunt and Uncle" were scared and urged me to go before something bad happened. A tiny spark between the nephew and me was extinguished; I could not even look at him. I left just saying to the aunt that the man was my boss, he was obsessed with me and I did not know how to get away. He was waiting for me in the car.

Without words, he drove along the country road. I did not say anything either. I could not even cry. I felt like a shell, was devastated, without any hope, despondent. In a small patch of forest, he stopped the car, got out, opened my door and pulled me out. He pushed me some way into the forest then turned me around, pointed a small silver pistol at me and declared, "I am of a mind to kill you. I cannot live without knowing where you are, without you in my life. I left my family on Christmas morning to find you. I will kill you and me if you ever pull something like this again."

He said and did some other things I do not want to repeat but eventually, after I promised (and I knew I lied) not to run away again, we got back into the car and drove back to Hannover. He delivered me to my place and he left for his home.

I had no one to talk to and cried a lot. I even recoiled from Mrs. D.'s inquiries and I blamed my behaviour on stress related to family problems. I remember the day when I rode my bike to the sports complex crying hard and almost caused a crash between a bus and a car. A policeman stopped me, threatened to give me a ticket but after my apology, sobbing hard while telling him why I was so upset. I had just received a letter informing me my sister Ingrid had been diagnosed with cancer. He was sympathetic and let me go with the order to walk my bike on the sidewalk instead of riding it on the street.

Subsequently Ingrid's right arm was amputated but the cancer had spread and after five months of suffering, she was gone.

I wrote a letter to my father's uncle, the Fritze who had been mad at Dad for taking my mother away from him when he was dancing with her. I got the address from Granny. He and his wife, Kate, lived in New York; they had no children. I told them of my escape to West Germany and I would really like to leave Germany and go to America and asked them for their help. I would be willing to work as a nannie or in a factory, anything to get a start. I did not get an answer and finally asked Granny if she had heard something. Through another sister of hers, Great Aunt Elisabeth, she had learned that Fritze had asked her, "Who is this Gisela? Who are her parents?"

When she mentioned Erich and Elsbeth in her next letter his answer was somewhat upsetting, "I'll have nothing to do with it."

However, I received a brief note from Aunt Kate saying they were not able to help. They had no connections; they lived a very quiet life and planned to leave New York soon to retire to Florida.

It was spring, the activities at the sports complex had picked up again and I had a "Kinderfest" organized. I met my friend Hilda there and she introduced me to her visiting brother. He studied law in Göttingen and I had never met him before. Instead of biking home, he pushed my bike and the two of them accompanied me. We had an animated conversation about universities, my experiences in East Germany, my ambition to become a doctor and how it all ended. It was nice to talk to people my age and not be obsessed about work and the rest of the way I biked home happily. Arriving I saw "his" Volkswagen.

"Oh no," I thought, "back to reality."

I leaned my bike against the fence and walked over to his open window.

"Get in," a rough brusque order.

Thinking of the gun I knew he had, I lightly answered, "Let me put the bike in the basement, I'll be right back."

"You better be...."

I was back. I pretended to be in a light happy mood and hoped I would be able to lighten his up as well. I chattered along about Hilda and her brother. He drove out of the city along a narrow road and stopped with my side very close to a fence with prickly bushes growing through it.

"Why did you come home so late? It does not take this long to bike from the "Edelhof" (the name of the complex). I left after you and waited over half an hour for you."

"My goodness, can't I have any freedom? I walked with Hilda and her brother before they turned back, I did not know you were expecting me. I really enjoyed the walk and the conversation with them."

"I don't want you to be with any young man. You could fall in love with one and I will not allow it. I'll endeavor to keep you away from all of them and I'll ruin every friendship you'll ever start. I mean it. Don't turn me into a murderer."

With that, he started hitting me. At first, I was stunned, then my anger was rising and I screamed and with both fists started to hit his face. After the first couple of blows, his glasses fell down. Apparently he felt helpless without them, screamed, "Stop! I cannot see." He bent down to retrieve them from the floor of the car and when he came up again, he put his head on the steering wheel and cried. I just sat there, could not get out, could not do anything, felt so terribly alone and hopeless, my tears were running down my cheeks as well. After a long time he uttered, "This can't go on. It kills me. We'll have to talk about it."

He blew his nose, put his glasses right and drove me home.

It kills him, yaah? What about me? It was killing me too. He was ruining my life.

An open talk

He took me to the elegant Maschsee Restaurant for dinner a few days later. It was the first time I ate lobster. I had been there once before after a kayak race on the Maschsee (lake) but our team had been in a more rustic room. The waiter put a finger bowl next to my plate. I did not know what it was for and proceeded to lift it to my mouth. It was lemon water. My boss grinned and stated I had a lot to learn, and he would introduce me to the finer things in life. As for this bowl, it was for dipping your fingers in the lemon water after using the nutcracker to open the lobster claws. I felt embarrassed when I met the eyes of the waiter – he gave me a tiny smile but otherwise was very polite when he cleared the dishes away. I remembered this episode when I saw the movie *Pretty Woman* with Julia Roberts and the first of the "snails" (the little buggers as she called them) flew away.

We talked. He wanted to ask his wife for a divorce. He had told his friend, a medical doctor I knew from the Health Show, about his attraction to me and apparently, this man had encouraged him. I was proud this doctor liked me enough but at the same time everything in me screamed "noooo." By now, I had finished my esthetician course and had my diploma. I had seen it as the road to independence and now this. I had also saved my money judiciously and had rented my own bachelor suite. I had bought furniture on a payment plan. However, I had over-looked the fact that now he could visit anytime. After he was finished talking he asked me what I thought. Would I marry him? Avoiding a direct answer I told him, "I would like to go to the Kneipp-Academy in Bad Wörishofen and become a Health teacher for the International Kneipp-Bund. I also think a divorce takes a long time and it would be good if I am away during the process."

I told him about the stress of working in the office with his wife and I would sooner or later have a total breakdown. No matter what, I would want to leave. He was incredulous and it took a while until he answered, "You got everything figured out! But it's a fantastic idea. I will inquire about getting you accepted. With your background, you are perfect for it. I'll find out if you would qualify for a small scholarship. But promise me to stay on until the next Health Show in Munich is over."

I did. I was much more at ease seeing what I thought was the "end of the tunnel." He had become very understanding and sent me to Munich six weeks before the opening of the show. I was experienced enough to run the office in the exhibition hall and work with the other colleagues responsible to sell exhibition space. Naturally, he kept tabs on us by phoning daily. Easter fell into this time and I booked a three-day bus tour to Venice. It was wonderful. In the famous St. Mark's Cathedral, I cried and looking up I saw an apparition of my dead sister. I thought I was losing my mind. I have been in Venice three more times in my life looking for her but I have never again experienced anything like it. On one occasion, the cathedral was in knee-deep water and a priest kindly let me in through a higher door towards the rear of the building. The last time I was there nobody could go in. Everyone had to walk by the open door on a high wooden kind of bridge. How long will it take this beautiful city to disappear?

After the show in Munich, work went on as usual in Hannover. He arranged that I would start my course at the Kneipp-Academy the following spring. In the meantime, we planned another Health Show in Münster Westphalia for the fall. I was very careful not to ask any question about the divorce proceedings. I did not even want to know if there were any. When I told him I was invited to see my Great Aunt and Uncle on the North Sea Island of Juist at Christmas, he was not upset and even drove me to the station. As a young kid, I had visited this Great Aunt and Uncle, admired their villa with a maid and met Gerhard, who was now their adopted and grown up son. He had married a rich, mine owner's daughter in the Saarland. He never went to America as he had dreamed as a young boy. My relatives had built a typical island red brick house and rented every room during the summer, including their own bedroom to holiday guests. The B & B with five rooms gave them a neat income. They slept in the basement and did all the work themselves. Just like my parents, they had lost everything.

We had not seen each other for approximately twenty years. During Christmas, they offered the opportunity for me to move in with them, share the work load and they would leave me the house when they died.

"What about Gerhard?"

"Gerhard does not need it. He is very well off now."

We talked about the pros and cons. I told them about my plans to become a Kneipp Health Teacher and I was registered to take a course for Kneipp therapists starting in a few weeks. They kept their offer open and I was to let them know before I left for Hannover again. I couldn't sleep. I thought long and hard; it was a wonderful way out but would I want to be stuck on this small island in the North Sea? Wouldn't I be something like a maid for many years to come? And what if they changed their mind about giving me the house some day? Oh, memories of Aunt Tutti!

I thanked them very much but I decided to go through with my plans and mentioned they had years to live. They could hire help and I would visit again in summer.

During January, I was totally exhausted and close to collapse. Coming home one evening, I wanted to make a cup of tea. I had a gas stove and I turned one knob. I did not understand why the flame did not come on before I saw that it was not turned on. So I turned it on. Unintentionally I had turned on the baking oven. It had filled up with gas and when I lit the top one the oven door flew open and a huge flame shot out, singed my hair, my eyebrows and my lashes. I jumped to the hallway; luckily, my clothing did not catch fire. The row of gas flames in the oven burned evenly and the top element was waiting for the kettle. I had less hair on the left side, my eye lashes curled, the left eyebrow gone. Not much of it grew back. I was very relieved when I was on the train to start a new chapter of my life – the train to Bad Wörishofen.

Water is an amazing element

I had a scholarship of 150.00 marks each month, bed and breakfast free. My bed was in the wide-open attic of the school. I had nails for a closet and I had a small bathroom. The course was more fun than I had ever imagined. A group of us went to a fair. I felt young and carefree. I loved riding the little bumper cars and tried to avoid bumping into anyone. I decided to take driving lessons, even if the dream of owning a car might be years away. I booked driver training and got obsessed with it. One night I dreamed I was sitting at the wheel and I got very tired. I wanted to lean back into the seat but there was none. I held on to the wheel but I just could not sit up anymore. I thought "what will the driving teacher think if I lie down" but I just let myself fall back. I hit my neck on the headboard of my bed. I had to see a doctor the next morning and he shook his head, "You were very, very lucky. You could have killed yourself by breaking your neck. Who would sit up in bed and do driver training?"

At the Kneipp course, I did not have as much to learn as the others. Once again, I had an advantage because of my semi-medical base from Leipzig. Anatomy, physiology and psychology were tough on some of the students, especially for a divorced, formerly-rich and now poor lady from Brazil. I agreed to give her extra help and became her private tutor. As a thank you, she held out a handful of semi-precious stones at the end of the course, "Here, pick any one you want. Without you I would never have graduated."

I was embarrassed but she insisted. I looked at an aquamarine but it was too pale for my skin color. I decided on a huge smoke topaz shaped like a coffin. I even had it made into a ring. It looked like a weapon and it became one!

After the course most of the people left for their hometowns or to wherever they found a job to work as Kneipp therapists. I stayed on to do my practicum. During this time, I took two more diploma courses: Sauna Therapy with a Finnish doctor and medical foot care, a step above pedicures. I participated in a series of seminars about wholesome nutrition and diet. The director of the International Association promised the Kneipp-Bund would hire me as a health teacher with an increase of my former salary by 200.00 Marks. When the time came the promise of the salary was not kept. I was very disappointed.

The Silver Wedding Anniversary

I dared to visit my parents for their Silver Wedding Anniversary in 1957, just two years after I had escaped but they had been granted a visa for me. All my friends and colleagues warned me I could be put in prison in East Germany for having "illegally left the DDR" and thirty years would be the verdict. I was homesick for my parents and knew they were worried about Ingrid who had been diagnosed with cancer so I took a chance. Their wedding date was April the 20th and it happened to be close to Easter. I left Hannover two days before Good Friday and I went to the police headquarters in Bergen to register my arrival on the Thursday. I also asked for my exit stamp for the Tuesday after Easter since the office would be closed on Easter Monday. On Easter Sunday, we had a celebration with all our Rügen relatives. After they left, I got very restless, had the weirdest premonition breaking out in a cold sweat and just knew I had to leave as well. Mother was not happy but Father supported me saying, "Follow your guts."

I left after dinner and went to stay overnight with my old kayaking friends, Christa and Alfred, in Stralsund. On Easter Monday (instead of Tuesday) at 6:30 a.m., I took the train to Hamburg. At the usual police control on the train, I explained my early departure with, "I have to work tomorrow." I was lucky; there was no phone or any communication between personnel on the train and their offices at the time. The offices, in any case, would likely have been closed or short staffed due to the holiday.

My father and I had worked out certain terms to use when writing to each other so our letters would sound innocent. In his next letter, he told me my "friends" had been visiting and spent several hours talking to them and were very disappointed they had missed me. They had so looked forward to learning all about life in West Germany. Those "friends" were obviously the local police. It was incredible, my premonitions had warned me and saved me from a fate that happened some years later to my brother-in-law's sister.

The Berlin Wall

In 1960, while still in Bad Wörishofen I had a very active mail exchange with my parents. My mother and even my father, who was never one for writing letters put pen to paper. My parents planned to leave the DDR as well, just as soon as my youngest sister Edith had finished her nurse's training. Mother had started to send one towel or one cup and saucer at a time in a small packet to my sister Christel, who had escaped in 1956 and lived not far from Hamburg. Almost all their "good stuff" was sent to Hamburg this way over a two-year period. I recall the summer of 1959 when I heard rumours suggesting that East Germany might be closed off permanently. I encouraged my parents in my letters in summer 1961 not to wait any longer and to leave as soon as they possibly could, "my house manager set a mousetrap under my bed and I am afraid the cute mouse will be in it in the morning."

Their answer was Edith is doing her finals and it is just a matter of days before they would take her on a little "holiday." Edith graduated at the beginning of August. They left the house on the 13th of August 1961, leaving behind an almost bare suite but hid the key in the little shack at the usual place. On the way to the station in Stralsund, my father had a severe kidney attack and was rushed to the hospital. My mother and Edith went back to Altefähr, picked up the key and the mousetrap had closed.

Without anyone knowing or even suspecting anything, a many kilometer long wall was built around East Berlin during one night and the borders between East and West Germany had death zones with mines, rolls of barbed wire and high fences all along them and towers with guards who had strict shooting orders. Many streets in Berlin had a wall in the middle of the road. People living in houses on the East side were "evacuated" and the windows closed with bricks. I was devastated since now I would probably never see my parents and my younger sister again.

19: A Change of Direction

A new job

How he did it, I do not know, but Mr. E. always knew what I did or what I was into, including outings with new friends. When he turned up one day, I gave him an earful and told him clearly I would leave the Kneipp Association and find another job. Through the Health Shows, I knew many good companies. My training as an esthetician and the other courses would qualify me as a lecturer at any of a number of these health-oriented companies. He talked me into staying on to join the team of five other health teachers and "get my feet wet"; the money would surely come later. He claimed I owed it to the Association for having underwritten my "free" Kneipp training. I gave in because he was right and I wanted to be fair.

He put me on the Kneipp-Bund speakers list and therefore I did not spend too much time in the office. Hannover remained my home base and I was mainly booked in the northern part of Germany. I enjoyed giving lectures and seminars. After my teacher training it came naturally to me. My topics ranged from *Skin Care from the inside out* to *Sauna, the hottest way to good Health*. Other topics were *Healing with Water through Kneipp Therapy, Healthy feet – healthy body, Eat yourself slim* and *Look younger as the years go by*. The Kneipp-Bund had no problem keeping me busy. I bought a used Volkswagen beetle and paid it off with the mileage money I received, driving to all the Kneipp Clubs for my lectures. I was happy with my work. However the "relationship" was continuing. He just did not give up. For honesty's sake, I must admit we also had some good times and I received a lot of good advice, guidance and introductions to important people from Mr E.

In an effort to be busy for too many meetings, I bought a Hohner accordion on a payment plan, took lessons on several evenings and played in a group on Saturdays. A few times, I met a nice man my age – but something always happened and it came to nought. When I had to overnight for my lectures, there were always flowers in my hotel room and a phone call to check if I was in bed by 11:00 p.m. It was very annoying but I had no control over this part of my life. When I caught on to what he was doing, I told the operator not to put any calls through because I needed my beauty sleep. The lectures were arranged by his office; therefore, he always knew where I was and if I had evening appointments.

I had often thought of reporting him but I knew the authorities would not have believed me because of his high social standing and involvement with the government, together with my East German origin. It would have been his word against mine and indeed, I would almost certainly have been in greater trouble. Today we call this stalking. As the victim, it was certainly very stressful and I felt not only afraid, but trapped. When I was easy-going he was very nice and brought me some nice gifts I could have done without. There was an onyx ring and a typical plain wedding band I had to wear whenever we went out to dinner or checked into a hotel. He even wanted me to wear it so other young men would see I was not free. That was what I longed for; I wanted to be free.

One day I just had enough. I told him I quit. Over a dinner, I quietly explained several health-oriented companies had approached me and I would like to get away from all the ongoing stress.

To my surprise, he agreed and helped to arrange an interview with the Grandel Company in Augsburg. They were looking for a Chief Esthetician to help develop and introduce a new line of high-quality, natural skin care products, based on wheat germ oil and wheat germ extract for the Health Food Stores. The extract was tested in a Hamburg hospital with incredible results. The company offered to advance me the money to buy a better car since a VW beetle was not representative enough for a company like Grandel. The mileage money I would be entitled to would pay off the interest-free loan. I would get a salary of 800.00 marks (I had 486.00 now) plus daily allowances of 20.00 marks for being away from home. The company paid hotels and food.

Wow! I was ecstatic and accepted with enthusiasm. I went back to Hannover to finish my present obligations and turned in my green VW beetle for 3.000.00 marks and bought a new white Opel Record for 8.000.00. The loan from the company was 5.000.00. I spent a couple of weeks in Augsburg in a beautiful small hotel tucked away in the old town centre and was trained by the head chemist. I added many ideas and we developed several new products I had suggested. They hired two more girls with just esthetician training and I had to train them for their new jobs by taking them along to my appointments. I could keep my Hannover apartment as my home base but I had to get a telephone installed. Not everybody had one but Grandel made it happen and I felt very privileged. After several weeks on the road, I would get several days off to go home.

Now all of West Germany was my playground! They always booked top hotels for me. Once I stayed in one of the five best hotels in Europe: The "Eisenhut" (Iron hat) in Rothenburg, which is one of the most beautiful cities (over a thousand years old) along the world-renowned Romantic Road. Usually I would drive to the appointed city, check into the arranged hotel and then phone or visit the president of whatever Kneipp Club or the head of a "Reformhaus" (Health Food Store) who had arranged my lecture or seminar for the evening. Sometimes I had slides but most of the time it was just a talk. I had my personal unique style and always made people laugh at the beginning. At the end were many questions and I did not mind staying on and answering them all. The following day, my duty was usually to be in a Reformhaus for consultations. The line-ups of the people waiting surprised me. The sales of the Grandel food and supplement products and the new skin-care line made me shiver. What if someone were allergic to the product? Often the shelves were empty and the owners expressed concern, "How could we have known the sales would be this good? Next time we'll order more."

I did not feel like a "second class" citizen anymore. I was accepted, respected and well trained. With my good income and the representation of one of the best Health Food companies in Germany, I was well-groomed. I wore elegant suits for the lectures, chic shoes and had my hair done regularly. One thing I could not understand: when having dinner in my, or any, hotel restaurant, they always placed me at a little table in a corner. They seemed to do that to single women. It started to annoy me and in time, I quietly requested a different one. Once, a gentleman who also sat at one of these small corner tables approached me and asked if I would mind company. At first, I wasn't sure but I just pointed to the chair. We had an animated conversation during which we discovered we had both booked theatre seats the same evening. We met again at the intermission and walked together in the beautiful park surrounding the theatre. I declined his invitation to meet later for a drink. He gave me his phone number but I was busy. As I was in a different city every two days, I intentionally lost his card. Other men tried to get to know me but my gypsy life prevented me from ever forming a relationship. However, the main reason was that I was afraid. Every time I came into a hotel, a huge bouquet of flowers with a card was waiting for me.

I asked the secretary in the company office, "Who gets the schedule for my program, the dates and list of hotels I am staying in?"

She claimed only her office had this information, nobody else. How did Mr. E. always know where I was? How could he turn up at my suite when I came home to Hannover after a week or even two of my travels? I started to suspect he had hired a private investigator.

Pneumonia

Because of my East German origins, the company flew me to West Berlin for two weeks for a series of lectures in different parts of the city. It was November and miserably cold weather. I caught the flu and all the speaking caused a very bad laryngitis. It got to the point I had to see a doctor in Berlin. He warned me I could lose my voice permanently if I did not stop using it. I had no choice but to phone the company and fly home to Hannover. My friend Hilda looked in on me. She lived with her parents within walking/biking distance. One day she brought me some home-baked buns and a small glass with goose fat her mother had prepared for me. She watched me to make sure I ate it. After a couple of days, it was finished. She grinned at me and asked, "Do you have any idea what you ate?"

"Well, buns with goose fat. My mother used to love it."

"Oh, no," she said, "it was goose fat mixed with dog fat. It's supposed to cure or prevent pneumonia. Would you have eaten it if you knew?"

"Don't know. It tasted good with a bit of herbal salt on it. But where did your mother get dog fat? She didn't kill one, did she? I never know what is in medicines either. How did she get it?"

"Apothecaries used to sell it but my mother got the last of it."

I believed I was getting better but I was still very sick. I hated the visits of Mr. E who always brought something: fruit, juice, vitamins, chocolates, flowers. I could not get better and I developed pneumonia so I was admitted to a hospital. The doctors treated me with intravenous medicine but my fever just would not go away. After a week, I wanted to go home but they did not let me.

"You have to be free of fever for several days before we let you go."

Two weeks later Dr. Grandel himself called, "We need you. I've talked to the hospital doctors. They will let you go but you have to sign a release form and take the responsibility. I will personally take that responsibility. I have booked a four-week Kneipp cure in one of the best sanatoriums here in Bavaria; the owner is a friend of mine, a very good doctor and he'll look after you. Please phone the train station and arrange a first-class sleeping car from Hannover to Augsburg and my driver will take you to the sanatorium. Just let us know your arrival time. My company will pay for everything; we'll re-reimburse you for the train ticket."

Two days later, I was released though wobbly on my feet. Mr. E. drove me home from the hospital. An express letter from the company gave me details about the sanatorium with address, names and phone numbers. Mr. E. offered to drive me to the station the next day. However, as soon as he left I packed my suitcase and placed it in my car. Quite early the next morning I drove off watching a glorious sunrise. I was not even a hundred miles out of town when I felt totally healthy. I took it easy and enjoyed the drive, stopped every two hours for refreshment and a little rest, booked into a small hotel in the evening and slept peacefully without expecting or receiving any phone calls. Nobody knew where I was. It took another full day of driving and I arrived in the afternoon of the third day in the sanatorium. Mrs. Krautheim, the doctor's wife received me and could not believe I had come by car and was not the sick person they had expected. I phoned Dr. Grandel right away and he was not happy I had not followed his instructions with respect to the sleeping car. I had some explaining to do. When I entered my room, there was the usual big bouquet of flowers and a card, "When I went to your house I saw your car gone. I do not appreciate that but hope you arrived well and look forward to welcoming you back. I'll phone you. All my love."

He gave me "hell" during the later phone call and made me feel very upset. The next bouquet was so big it did not fit in my room. I asked that it remain in the lobby and at dinner, all the guests teased me about my admirer. They had asked the waitress about the gorgeous flowers and she told them they were mine. I had confided in Dr. Krautheim during his first examination that "my admirer" was a man I could not shake off and his frequent phone calls were annoying to me. I would appreciate a room without a telephone. His wife arranged it. She also made sure I would not be called to the phone because I had a treatment, a massage or was in bed with a big wrapping and that the doctor had ordered complete undisturbed rest for me. Mrs. Krautheim became my friend and confidante; but because of Mr. E.'s high standing in the Kneipp community, I could not tell her who this man was. I regained my health and was released to go to Augsburg after four weeks to spend another week in Dr. Grandel's country home under the supervision and care of a feisty neighbour woman. She spoiled me with fresh eggs, trout out of Dr. Grandel's converted swimming pool, homegrown organic produce and wonderful meals. I walked in a forest in which Dr. Grandel himself had planted every tree forty years earlier. Never in my life have I felt so at ease, balanced, relaxed and good.

After another two nights in the five-star "Drei Mohren" Hotel in Augsburg, for briefing and meetings with the chemist about new products, they sent me to a fashion boutique with the order to pick out three dresses: the invoice would be billed to the company's account. They had arranged a lecture tour on my way back to Hannover and I surely had not taken appropriate clothing for that to the sanatorium. I had readily agreed to another four weeks, I did not want to go home. In the beautiful old city of Kulmbach, I saw a very unusual floor lamp in a shop window when driving by. Taking the next parking space, I returned to the shop, learned the base of the lamp was ceramic and hand-painted silk was applied to the tall truncated cone-shaped shade. It was so beautiful I could not help but buy it. They took it apart and I had it in my trunk for almost four weeks. I still own it after more than fifty years despite living halfway around the globe from that store. It is always a conversation starter and I have been asked many times if I would sell it.

The long separation with hardly any contact (he had sent letters and insisted I write to him via the Post Office) must have had an effect on Mr. E. and somehow our relationship changed. I think I had changed too. He mentioned his family life had improved and I congratulated him on it. We still had an occasional dinner but no intimacy at all. He begged me to remain his friend while he would give me all the time in the world to realize nobody would ever love me as much as he did. He declared, "I know that one day we'll be together. I'll not give up and you can count on it. My feelings towards you will never change."

Confrontation with a Rapist

I was scheduled to lecture on the North Sea island of Sylt. Arriving in the late afternoon by ferry, I checked into my hotel. I put on slacks, a big sweater and flat open sandals. I briefly stopped at the Health Food Store to make sure everything was in order for the next day. They advised me to enjoy this evening and go down to the beach to have a long walk and be amazed by their incredible sunsets. The weather was glorious and I felt as if I was on holiday. Sylt was an elegant holiday destination. It was very different from Juist where I had visited my relatives. I walked close to the water on the hard sand, listened to the sound of the waves almost lapping onto my feet and watched the sun go down over the sea. A tiny voice whispered it may be time to turn around but it was so wonderful to walk along the long stretch of beach with seeing no one in front of me, just the sun slipping into the water on the horizon. I passed the part that was marked "Nude Beach" with dozens of those typically German beach chairs and promised myself to turn as soon as the sun was gone. I stopped, watched it disappear and only now noticed I was not alone. A man had caught up with me. He stopped and started talking to me. He was younger than I, well dressed, slim and friendly. I was suspecting nothing bad. I was polite and listened to him talk about the beauty of the evening. When I turned to leave, he coerced me up the dune just to sit, enjoy the view and have a nice conversation. He said there is a path up there back to the city, shorter and easier to walk than in the sand. Once up there, he grabbed me and tried to force me down. I used both fists and punched him in the face. My big smoke topaz ring was on my finger and I happened to hit him with it in one eye. He fell over and was out cold. I stood there transfixed, thought I had killed him and froze. Was I a murderer? I did not know what to do. I thought I could not run away and leave him there. He groaned after a bit, then turned around and mumbled, "Run away, I am like that. I'm on probation... RUN!"

I tumbled down the dune. I tried to go as fast as the deep sand allowed heading to the water were the sand was packed. I cried, hyper-ventilated and ran as fast as I could, prayed aloud "Please God, please help me, please, send someone along, please, please..."

A few times, I fell but got up and kept running. Then I heard light footsteps behind me. I turned to look. It was nobody sent by God. He called for me to stop but I didn't. He soon caught up with me. He had recovered and was talking quite normally. He told me he was a taxi driver from Hamburg. He had raped two of his passengers, the last one had reported him and he had been in prison for it for a year. Now he was on parole and could not afford to do it again. He apologized and begged me not to ruin his life by going to the police. Since we were still the only people on that long beach, I was afraid he would murder me so I pretended to be compassionate and understanding. All the while, I was looking out for someone. When we came to the "Nude Beach," he wanted us to sit in one of those beach chairs. I knew that it would be the worst I could do. I tried to talk to him about all kinds of things. I tried to keep him walking and I tried to take his mind towards something else. I asked him questions about how long he was on the island already, and what one could do here for entertainment. I felt like *Scheherazade of the stories of Thousand-and-one-Nights* and it got darker by the minute.

He got aggressive again. I lifted my fists but he was prepared, grabbed me by my long hair and pulled my head backwards. It hurt and I could not move. He started kissing me. I begged him to let me be for today, "I am not like that. I need to know you better, let's meet tomorrow after my job."

He laughed, "You'll never turn up."

He did not let go of my hair but my face was towards the dune. After maybe an hour, I could see five figures up there, playing with a flashlight, switching it on and off apparently simulating a light house.

"Please let me go – or shall I call for help?" I made sure he faced the ocean while I faced the dunes.

"Call for help? Are you crazy? There is nobody around, just you, me, the ocean and the sand. Nobody can hear you. But try anyway!"

I tried, I could just croak and the figures up there could not hear me. He had fun. He laughed heartily, "My goodness, you can't even call for help. Here, try again."

He held my head back less tightly and I cried out with all my might, "H-E-L-P!"

A second of hesitation, the light up there went dark but I could see the figures tumble down the dune. They called out to each other and my attacker heard them. He gave a strong tug to my hair before he let go, "You bitch."

I said, "Run, I'll meet you tomorrow night at eight at the little bridge."

The next moment my knees gave up, I was exhausted and cried my heart out. The figures changed into five young boys, "What's the matter? Is that your boyfriend?"

"No, he is a rapist. I resisted."

Two of them stayed with me, three went after him. When they came back they proudly announced, "Well, we really gave it to him. He would not feel like raping anyone now. What do you want to do now? Do you want to go to the police? We'll go with you!"

They helped me up the steep sand dune and we walked on the path up there after we stopped at their camp where they reported to their leader. He gave them permission to accompany me. At 12.30 a.m. we arrived at the police station. After giving my statement, the young boys, fifteen-year-olds, were driven back to their camp by the police. I was ordered to go to the little bridge the next day and two policemen in plain clothing would be watching me. They hoped to catch the guy.

The next morning I had to go to a hairdresser. They were incredulous that I had a whole bunch of hair missing on the back of my head. I told them the story and enlisted them as witnesses for an eventual trial. They agreed. I was a guest on a radio talk show and then spent all day in the Health Food Store for consultations. In the evening, I had to appear at the police station. My two protectors advised me how to act. If I saw the guy, I was to lift my right hand and stroke over my hair. They would watch me. I waited at the little bridge for a long time. He did not turn up. One of the policemen walked by me and ordered, "Go to the plaza where the music plays. Lean against the sea wall and just watch the people walk past. Stroke your hair should you see him. We'll not be far from you."

I did see him. He wore huge dark glasses. The police told me later he had good reasons to be wearing them. Between my rescuers and I, we had given him quite a shiner.

About six weeks later, I had programs in Bayreuth, the Wagner Festival city in southern Germany. A registered letter waited for me in my hotel. Three days later I was to appear in Emden, the gateway to the North Sea islands for my court case. I immediately phoned the number listed in the letter. I explained my situation and asked if they could postpone the trial. An absolute "No" was the answer unless I let go of my accusations. I did not want to do that. If I did not turn up at the trial, the man would go free. I phoned my company and told them of this legal matter. Dr. Grandel was very upset but in the end allowed me to go. I drove day and night to get to Hannover first, slept there and had the shock of my life in the morning. My bell rang, I opened the little window in my door and my attacker stood in front of me. I slapped the window closed, expected him to punch his arm through, reach in to open the door or maybe shoot me. I slid down against the door. I did not know what to do. Then he started talking. He begged me to give up on the trial, he would have to go back to prison and I would ruin his life. My address was on the invitation to the trial and his lawyer had advised him to see me. I had a chance to do a good deed. I never acknowledged hearing any of this. When he was quiet, I crawled towards my balcony, looked around the corner and called my neighbour, Fräulein Zwanzig. She helped me to climb over to her balcony. She offered to go out into the hallway and pretend to bring her garbage down. She came back and said he was gone.

I drove to Emden and was there in time for the trial. The small courtroom was packed. A rape case was something exiting for the people of a small city. I had no lawyer and had to state my case. My attacker had someone with him but was ordered to tell his story. The judge asked him, "I don't understand you. If a lady punched me in the face I wouldn't keep trying to get her to change her mind. Why did you not give up?"

Oh, the gall of this guy, "I liked her. And looking at her I must say I still like her."

It took minutes until the laughter in the courtroom died down. He had the laughers on his side. I stood there with a red face. His sentence was to pay 200.00 marks and he would be home free because he had not actually raped me. I bet that hardly any girl would have had the nerves to withstand him for so many hours. A girl cannot win.

Was it fate?

I was fed up. I was fed up with men. I had seen often enough now married men had affairs, even ones I would never have suspected had made advances. I was fed up with my "gypsy" life. I was fed up with the fact that at twenty-nine years old I had nobody in my life with whom I wanted to start a family. I had so much love to give and was longing to have and be part of a family again. I could not go "home" to my parents, not even for a respite. Why were there no men around who were more like my father, or all the other men I knew from my childhood, kind, loving and protective? What was this crazy obsession with their sex drive? Were girls merely "instruments" they could play at will? I was really, really upset and disgusted with the outcome of the trial. I could have saved myself a lot of time and heartache if I had not reported the attack. Is that why so many women shut up about their abuse or rape and do not talk about it?

However, life continued and 1963 had started. Time was just flying by. I was scheduled for several programs in and around Bremen. When I arrived at the beautiful hotel in a park-like setting, the receptionist told me, "Sorry, we have no reservation for you. We cannot even give you a room; we are fully booked. I can try to phone several other hotels."

She did but everyone was booked because of a big convention. Distraught I sat down in a lobby chair to think. I got up again to buy *Constance*, a women's magazine, in the little snack shop. A supervisor approached me and offered a small room in a building about two hundred feet from the Park Hotel. The main floor was a pub and the second floor had some servants' rooms with a single bed, a sink and a telephone. Toilets were in the hallway. The man was very apologetic looking at my elegant outfit. I had no choice and accepted graciously. The bellboy carried my suitcase up the narrow stairway, I followed him. It was around five o'clock and the pub was packed with men drinking beer. One called out, "Look what the wind blew in. Hey lady, come back down and have a drink with us!"

Several whistled and I heard other similar remarks. I locked myself in my room and lay down on my bed with feet up against the wall to prevent the swelling of my legs after a long drive. I had one green Granny Smith apple in my bag; it became my supper. I never left the room that evening. I read the *Constance* from cover to cover. Finally, all I had left was to peruse the classified ads. One caught my eye: "Divorced man looking for love and little Isabelle needs a new mommy. Own building lot and car in beautiful Vancouver B.C. Canada. Please write to *Constance* at # …"

I read all the other ads as well. The little girl got to me. I don't know how it could be possible that she seemed to be reaching out to me over the ocean that lay between us. I could not stop thinking of her. Why did she need a new mommy if the old one was alive? Even if divorced? Why did she live with the father and not the mother? Usually the courts placed children with the mother and the father had them only on certain weekends. I did not even consider the father. Finally, I decided to write but I had no paper. A small note pad was next to the telephone. I wrote three pages about myself and apologized for the fact that I had no stationery. I found a very small photograph in my purse. It was taken with my box camera in Grönenbach standing on my balcony. On that day I had been wearing a two-piece Bavarian dress, a black skirt with little pink roses, a pink top and a green apron. The next morning I asked for an envelope at the hotel desk and mailed it. My heart was beating fast when I put it in the mailbox. I never really expected an answer.

That little girl accompanied me from now on in my thoughts when I was driving along the autobahn. After several weeks, I came home to Hannover. To my surprise, I found a very large envelope with beautiful stamps on it from Canada on my hallway floor. It had been pushed through my mail slot. I had to sit down. I held it in my hands for a long time and just stared at it. I was afraid to open it. I had a premonition my life was about to take a huge turn. It was March 1963.

Three magazines entitled *Beautiful British Columbia*, a letter, lots of photographs of Vancouver and several of father and daughter, taken by a photo studio, were on my lap. The father was not really "my type" but the girl, oh my God, what a cutie. A face like a porcelain doll with slightly curled very blond hair, huge sad-looking blue eyes with mile-long black lashes. Finally, I read the letter. I liked the handwriting. I liked the way it was written. No grammatical mistakes. He was a former German man living in Canada for seven years; now, after a nasty divorce, in room and board with a nice Canadian family who looked after the girl when he was at work. Isabelle was four years old and she had picked out my picture from about three-hundred replies and declared, "I want her to be my new Mommy."

Included was a drawing that she had made for me: A (stick) man and a woman holding a little girl's hands and a huge sun in one corner.

I sat paralyzed in my chair for a long time. I stared at the beautiful pictures of Vancouver. I stared at the photos of the two people: Father and Daughter. Would they become the most important people in my life? What was it that finally brought me to this point? Why had I always felt in my younger years it was important to learn English? Was this in my cards all along? Thinking back it seemed to me I was always led to the people or places to which I needed to go. First, there was the little used-book shop in Stralsund that led to my sports career. Next was the escape to West Germany and my employment by the Kneipp-Association where my East German training was the base for a new career in complementary medicine. Now the mishap with the hotel reservation which caused me to read, and even respond to, one of the classified ads I would not normally have read. I felt as if I was in a boat on a fast river. The current takes hold of you and all you can do is to try to avoid the rocks and stay afloat – but you cannot change the direction.

What would happen next? I felt apprehensive but knew in my guts that I could not change what would happen next.

The song "Let's buy a little house in Canada...hunt for wild horses because there are so many...tell our friends good bye and asked them to visit..." went through my mind repeatedly. I had listened to the vinyl record of it and now I could not get the melody out of my head.

How do you answer a letter from a total stranger and, if things work out, wants to marry you? Join him in Beautiful British Columbia, one of the ten provinces of Canada? Not only that, - can you imagine fulfilling a little girl's wish to be her "new mommy"? Can you handle it and just leave a very busy, interesting and exciting professional life with financial independence behind to become a housewife? Imagine sitting on a bench in a playground watching your new four year old little daughter playing in the sandbox? Push the swing for her? Rely on a man you honestly don't know?

My reverie was suddenly interrupted by the ring of the telephone. Back to reality, Gisela! The voice at the other end was not one I knew. "This is Dr. Ludwig Bader. I practise law in Wiesbaden and it is my son who wrote to you from Canada. I thought it would be nice for you to know he is not a 'fly-by-night' and naturally, my wife and I want to know a bit more about you as well."

I was totally taken by surprise. Checking up on me already? He made it easy. We had a very nice and open conversation. I told him about my apprehensions and the thoughts which had just gone through my mind. He had an answer for everything. When he learned I would be in the Mannheim-Heidelberg area in a couple of weeks he invited me to visit for a weekend. He encouraged me to write the answering letter because his son, also named Ludwig but called 'Louis' in Canada and little Isabelle were waiting. They had phoned him earlier. Before we rang off, Dr. Bader gave me his telephone number and promised to always be available for me to ask questions or even just have a chat. I had told him my parents lived in East Germany and except for my sister in Hamburg I was pretty much on my own. "A good reason to give my son a chance and, heaven knows you may like having an instant family."

An active letter exchange started. The mail took a week to get from Canada to Germany. After the first few we just wrote to each other without waiting for one and questions asked in the one on the way were already answered before they arrived.

"Is it alright to visit you next Sunday?" They were very welcoming but warned me the autobahns would be packed because of a soccer game. "If you leave Mannheim early enough you will be here around eleven and be in time for dinner at noon. We look forward to meeting you very much", Dr. Bader said and actually, I did too. I bought a nice bouquet of flowers as is common to hand to the hostess. A black Mercedes in front of their house impressed me. I felt pretty much at ease when Dr. Bader shook my hand but, while taking the wrapping paper off the flowers before handing them to the lady, I committed a faux pas. I was a modern young woman and she was one of the old guard. I addressed her with 'Mrs. Bader' and she told me later, when the conversation flowed easily, I should have called her 'Frau Doctor'. "But you are not a Doctor", I countered. My second faux pas! She tried to teach me manners while I felt like a "second class citizen" again, put into the role of the "Ossy", the former East German person. I was aware an effort was being made, not so much through words but behaviour, to show me I was not part of their 'upper class'.

As the evening approached I wanted to leave. Dr. Bader switched the radio on. The autobahns were packed with endless traffic jams. He decided: "You stay here. It is not safe for you to drive, you can leave early tomorrow". I tried to reason with him, "But Dr. Bader, I don't even have my toothbrush." "That doesn't matter, you can use a finger." It caused a good laugh and I had no choice but to stay.

There was a big guestroom on the lower level of the house. A thick curtain divided it into a sitting area and a bedroom with two beds. Their young boy, Dietmar, who had been out with his Scout Group until the late afternoon, had a room downstairs as well. He came to chat with me until his mother turned up and admonished him to go to bed. I wondered how the son in Canada could be thirty-six and Dietmar only eleven years old. "Frau Doctor, you don't seem old enough to have a son who is thirty-six!" The comment brought a blush to her cheeks and she explained she was a second and younger wife. They had tried for twenty years to have a child and then just gave up. When she started to gain weight in her mid-forties she went to a health resort to lose it and was amazed when the doctor there told her, "Nothing is wrong with your weight. You are pregnant."

Indeed, it was, perhaps, a nice family to belong to. A week later I spent the whole weekend with them. I was on my way home to Hanover for a few days off. By now "Frau Doctor" allowed me to just call her 'Frau Bader'. Dr. Bader told me about an outing with his secretary to buy her a birthday gift of her choosing. "I saw the most beautiful antique vase and wished I would have a daughter-in-law I could buy things for," he told me. Was he testing the waters? I did not comment.

He cooked the Sunday meal and I helped him in the small kitchen. Frau Bader set the table in the living room, dressed as if on the way out for a visit. Later I helped her to load the dishwasher. It was a very small one, placed on the counter. She told me of her aristocratic Grandparents, of volunteering to be a nurse during the war and meeting Dr. Bader, who had been a high ranking officer in the German Navy. She briefly mentioned his first wife who was now in an old age home. They had a friendly relationship because of the three grown up children, of which Louis in Canada was the youngest. He had two sisters, Barbara and Marion, both living in the United States. Their oldest boy was killed at nineteen in a U-boat in Russia. Since it was a sunny spring day we spent the afternoon sitting at a large table on the patio looking at photo albums. Dietmar and I made fast friends, I really liked him. He was keen to show me childhood pictures of his half siblings as well as lots of his own. His mother mentioned they had recently had the talk about "the birds and the bees..." Dietmar had listened attentively and then had commented: "So Dad did it four times with his first wife and only once with you."

A conference call

Coming home I found a letter from my parents. My father had written, not my mother as she usually had done. He was very concerned about my newest 'adventure' as he called it; going to Canada to marry a stranger, a divorced man with a child was unthinkable. "Are you out of your mind? Aren't you old enough to think this through? How do you know it is all honest and above board? You can't just judge this man by his handwriting, his nice way of writing and by the beautiful pictures. For all you know he might be a talented con-man. Gisela, I am very worried about you." And so he went on. I had just started to answer his letter to tell him about the Canadian man's parents, the Bader family in Wiesbaden when my phone rang. Another voice I did not know but this time asking for a person who was not me. The voice explained something about a conference call regarding some business deal. I made a joke and suggested "maybe I should be involved" when another male voice cut in and yet another. The first one was from Hamburg, the next from Hanover where I lived and the third, who did not say much, from another place. It was fun to quip with no one knowing who I was. Finally it was decided they had dialed the wrong number but I would not reveal mine. "Too bad" the first voice said, "I would have loved to talk to you again. You are fun! I'll just have to try all kinds of combinations of the number I misdialed to get you again." He had an incredible laugh, a nice laugh such as I had never heard from a man before. It was contagious and it surely put a smile on my face. Just a day later he phoned again: "Hi, there you are. I had just switched the last two digits," he laughed, "it wasn't hard at all to find you again. Do you mind us having a chat?"

Puzzled and uncertain

A few weeks later I met Hannes, the telephone man. How come, for years I never met anybody I liked enough and now I felt already obligated to the Baders and guilty about liking Hannes. What was I to do? I knew what my dad would say. Why did "fate" put these choices in front of me: My dream to go to Canada and be part of a family, or to stay in Germany in familiar surroundings? After a few meetings Hannes had made it quite clear that he was serious about me. Naturally I had told him of my "pen friend" in Canada.